JOHN CLARKE • JANET NEWMAN • NICK SMITH
• ELIZABETH VIDLER • LOUISE WESTMARLAND

CONSUMERS

CREATING

CITIZEN-
CONSUMERS

Changing Publics & Changing Public Survices

Los Angeles | London | New Delhi
Singapore | Washington DC

SAGE Publications Ltd
1 Oliver's Yard
55 City Road
London EC1Y 1SP

SAGE Publications Inc.
2455 Teller Road
Thousand Oaks, California 91320

SAGE Publications India Pvt Ltd
B 1/I 1 Mohan Cooperative Industrial Area
Mathura Road
New Delhi 110 044

SAGE Publications Asia-Pacific Pte Ltd
33 Pekin Street #02-01
Far East Square
Singapore 048763

British Library Cataloguing in Publication data

A catalogue record for this book is available
from the British Library

ISBN 978-1-4129-2133-6
ISBN 978-1-4129-2134-3 (pbk)

Library of Congress Control Number: 2006904850

Typeset by C&M Digitals (P) Ltd., Chennai, India
Printed and bound in Great Britain by CPI Antony Rowe, Chippenham, Wiltshire
Printed on paper from sustainable resources

Mixed Sources
Product group from well-managed
forests and other controlled sources
www.fsc.org Cert no. SGS-COC-2953
© 1996 Forest Stewardship Council

FSC

Contents

Preface

When we began the research project on which this book is based we had no idea how much political and public attention would focus on our subject matter – the introduction of a more consumerist, choice-oriented approach to the delivery of public services. The research project – *Creating Citizen-Consumers: Changing Identifications and Relationships* – was funded by the Cultures of Consumption research programme, a joint initiative of the Economic and Social Research Council and the Arts and Humanities Research Council (grant no: RES-143-25-0008) and ran from April 2003 to May 2005. It was based in the Department of Social Policy at the Open University, and the research team comprised all five authors of this book.

In the process of conducting this research and developing this book we have incurred numerous debts. Frank Trentmann, the Director of the Programme, has been a consistent source of support, encouragement and opportunities – particularly creating a variety of public events at which we have talked about the research and its implications. The programme itself has been an unusually engaging collaborative process, given the intellectual diversity of the projects it contained. We have learned much from our colleagues in the programme, both within the 'public' cluster and beyond it. The programme has also been a pleasure to be part of because of the way it has been administered by Stef Nixon.

We could not have done any of this without the support and collaboration of people associated with the three services in the two urban settings where the research took place (Newtown and Oldtown). The generosity of spirit with which people opened their offices, places of work, homes and thoughts to us was remarkable – and confirmed for us the importance of public discussions of public services, their reform and the difficult and demanding relationships between changing publics and changing public services. As we hope the book makes clear, we have learnt a lot from the experience.

Our colleagues at the Open University, within Social Policy and beyond, have provided diverse forms of intellectual and organisational support – from the transcription of audio tapes to listening to the first workings out of position papers. We can think of no audience with whom we would rather take such first tentative steps and we hope they can see the effects of their comments, suggestions and advice in what has now emerged. Particular people made us think about specific things: Eugene McLaughlin got us thinking about the police as part of this research in the first place; Clive Barnett engaged us in important reflections on both consuming and a dialogic public; and Margie Wetherell tried to help us think about discourse. During the project we had enormous support from our advisory group: Nick Ellison, Sharon Gewirtz, Caroline Glendinning, Mary Macleod and Sandra Walklate. Our limitations are our own responsibility.

We have benefited enormously from the academic networks that have allowed us to present some of our work in a variety of conferences, seminars and workshops. It is always rewarding to find people taking our local obsessions seriously – and we have been generously supported and stretched by such conversations over the last three years. The people involved are too numerous to name, but we are pretty sure that we could not have got to where we have without the following: Dottie Holland, Fabian Kassl, Wendy Larner, Greg Marston, Catherine Needham, Catherine Neveu, Tine Rostgaard, Holger Ziegler.

And last, but not least ... thanks to the Labour governments of 1997–2006 (the date of writing) for the policy developments that ensured that our work was always guaranteed a high level of interest from, and engagement by, public, professional and academic audiences.

Introduction

'... the rise of the demanding, sceptical citizen-consumer...'
(Secretary of State and Minister for Welfare Reform, 1998: 16)

This book is about this strange figure – the demanding and sceptical citizen-consumer. We explore how s/he was discovered and interpreted and – most importantly – how s/he came to play a central role in the continuing remaking of British public services. It is important to spend a little time thinking about the strangeness of this figure of the citizen-consumer – and why s/he became the focus of considerable political and policy controversy at the beginning of the twenty-first century. Academic, political and popular debates have swirled around the notion of citizen as a consumer of public services who expects to exercise choice in the provision of public services, just as s/he exercises choice in the 'consumer society'. As the Prime Minister announced in 2004:

> In reality, I believe people do want choice, in public services as in other services. But anyway, choice isn't an end in itself. It is one important mechanism to ensure that citizens can indeed secure good schools and health services in their communities.
> Choice puts the levers in the hands of parents and patients so that they as citizens and consumers can be a driving force for improvement in their public services. We are proposing to put an entirely different dynamic in place to drive our public services; one where the service will be driven not by the government or by the manager but by the user – the patient, the parent, the pupil and the law-abiding citizen. (T. Blair, quoted in the *Guardian*, 24 June 2004: 1)

As we shall see, not everyone accepted this view of the citizen, nor did the co-ordination of public services through choice prove to be a universally popular proposal. Despite that, by 2006 the principle of choice was being extended across a range of public provision – from parental choice in education to the fields of health and social care (though in very different forms). This book explores the construction of the citizen-consumer and the connections to ideas and practices of choice in public services. We begin though with the figure itself – this peculiar hybridised and hyphenated combination of citizen and consumer. They are not words that are readily associated, so their hyphenation already marks something distinctive. Taken on their own, each term is usually taken to identify a particular field of relationships, identities and practices (Hughes, 1998). These fields differ from one another in almost every respect. The citizen is an egalitarian figure, lodged in a republican imaginary of liberty, equality and solidarity. The horizontal relationships of citizenship are ones that stress egalitarian principles (one person, one vote; everyone is equal before the law, and so on). The vertical relationships in which citizenship is produced and practised are typically those between citizens and the state. These evoke bonds of mutual obligation – the duties each owes to the other. But they are also mutually productive. It is the consent of the citizen that empowers the state; while the state provides and secures the conditions that enable citizens to lead their lives. In these very abstract terms, the citizen is a *political construct*: a key figure in the liberal social imaginary of Western capitalist democracies (on social imaginaries, see Taylor, 2004).

In contrast, the consumer is located in economic relationships. S/he is engaged in economic transactions in the marketplace, exchanging money for commodified goods and services. These, too, can be understood as relationships of liberty and equality – though in rather different ways. The freedom here derives from what Macpherson (1962) called 'possessive individualism' – the capacity to dispose of one's own property as one wishes. The individual is self-directing, capable of choosing how their own well-being may best be served. There is a version of equality here, too. All individuals (subject to certain legal restrictions) are equally endowed with the capacity to be self-directing: all are 'free to choose'. At the same time, the relative anonymity of market exchange underpins a different sort of equality: all money is equal. The market responds to 'price signals' rather than personal characteristics. The market – through its 'hidden hand' – reconciles the wants of many producers and consumers (subject to available resources). In these abstract terms, the consumer is an *economic construct*: a key figure in the liberal social imaginary of Western capitalist democracies. Indeed, it is important to understand that both figures – the citizen and the consumer – are critical elements in the liberal social imaginary: they co-exist in more or less uncomfortable combinations with one another. But they do co-exist. Indeed, they may be seen as the defining figures of the liberal social imaginary: the framing conceptions of how people and societies are, and of how they should be.

The citizen is embodied in public identifications and practices; where the consumer is usually thought of as a private figure. The citizen is associated with the rise of a 'public realm' in which both citizens and public institutions are more or less insulated from private interests and passions (du Gay, 2005). In the public realm, people as citizens fulfil their obligations to one another, engage in mutual deliberation and exercise thought and choice in the definition and pursuit of the 'public interest'. By contrast, the consumer is a figure motivated by personal desires, pursuing their own interests through anonymous transactions in which relationships between buyer and seller are characterised by mutual indifference.

These two figures dominate the liberal political imaginary and embody its conceptions of liberty, freedom, individualism and equality. They exist in a degree of strain with one another, but are also co-constitutive of each other: the 'public' figure of the citizen forms the other face of the 'private' figure of the consumer. For most of this book, we will need to keep these two issues in view: the tensions between the citizen and the consumer and their interconnectedness. It is generally easier to see the differences and antagonisms between them. They appear to embody essentially different relationships, practices and principles of social co-ordination. Not least, they have come to stand for the two principles of co-ordination – the market and the state – which dominated the twentieth century. The citizen embodies what Esping-Andersen (1990) called the 'de-commodification' of public rights, goods and relationships – their removal from the market-generated or market-related patterns of wealth and income inequality.

In socialist and social-democratic thought, then, the state and citizenship have been bulwarks and buttresses against the vagaries and vicissitudes of markets. Such a conception allowed for uneven and contradictory consequences. The state never fully displaced the market (even in state socialist societies) – the inequalities generated by markets could be mitigated but not removed (though the range of 'acceptable' inequality differed substantially between societies) and the state might effectively function as a support for the reproduction of capitalist societies by mitigating their worst effects. For liberals – and more recently, neo-liberals - precisely the reverse has been true: states interfere with the proper functioning of markets (or, at least, states that go beyond their basic business of securing the conditions for doing business). Markets co-ordinate society more efficiently and effectively than states (or 'command and control' co-ordination) can ever hope to because they are dynamic and responsive.

In these general terms, the citizen and the consumer embody a series of binary distinctions:

CITIZEN	CONSUMER
State	Market
Public	Private
Political	Economic
Collective	Individual
De-commodification	Commodification
Rights	Exchange

Now, these are simplified distinctions. We need to attend to different sorts of complications associated with them. The first is a reminder that these different figures co-exist within the liberal political imaginary – citizens and consumers occupy different areas or domains of social life (Taylor, 2004). But the alignment of, and balance between, political and economic spaces is variable – both between societies and over time. For much of the twentieth century, capitalist societies of the West were marked by movements and struggles that sought to confine and diminish the scope of the market, while broadening the de-commodified public realm. Enlarging political democracy and constructing public arrangements of welfare were two of the widespread dynamics, culminating in what has been called the 'golden age' of the welfare state, and of the nation-state (Huber and Stephens, 2001; Leibfried and Zürn, 2005). From the late twentieth century, we have seen constant efforts to revise that balance between public and private, between state and market.

In particular, efforts have been focused on liberating the market from its state-imposed inhibitions (forms of regulation, direction and constraint). Such trends have been discussed as freeing capital, the market, the entrepreneurial spirit and even enabling labour to be more 'flexible' (Harvey, 2005). But they have also been represented as freeing 'individual choice' for consumers in almost all areas of life from food to travel to entertainment. As we will hear in more detail later, there are claims that the defining characteristic of modern Western societies is that they have become 'consumer cultures'. Such consumer cultures are dominated by the 'cash nexus': the exchange of money for desired goods and services. (It should be noted that, although the sociological term is the 'cash nexus', the most advanced consumer cultures – in the UK and USA, for example – have been fuelled as much by credit/debt as by cash.) It is in this context that the hybrid figure of the citizen-consumer begins to appear, indicating the potential spread of market-based experiences, expectations, practices and relationships to the public realm.

Before pursuing that development, we need to note two more complications about the figures of the citizen and the consumer. The first is that they are less substantial or solid than their representation in the liberal social imaginary suggests. In that imaginary, the citizen strides forward, the bold embodiment of the republican tradition. S/he self-confidently articulates political views, engages productively in public dialogue, and makes demands on the state as of right. Equally, the consumer forms judgements and makes choices, assertively pursuing self-interest and bursting free of social and political constraints. In practice, both of these figures have proved more contingent. Citizenship, as Ruth Lister has argued, is an 'essentially contested concept' (2003: 14, see also Isin, 2002). Much of this contestation has been about the enlargement of who is entitled to count as a citizen – against limitations by property relations (including slavery), gender, race, age and a variety of criteria of 'competence' and 'belonging' that have structured patterns of exclusion from citizenship (Lewis, 1998). Citizenship's substance – the content of rights and entitlements – has also been the focus of extensive conflict, aimed at enlarging (or diminishing) the areas of life that are 'de-commodified', or made subject to social or political, rather than economic, calculation.

More recently, we have seen efforts to 'roll back' such arrangements or to reform them in ways more compatible with the flexibilities and freedoms demanded as the price of participating in the new global marketplaces. In the process, some have argued that citizenship had become overblown, exceeding the proper limits of the political sphere and extending social and political calculation into places where it had no business being. We might distinguish three interwoven arguments here. The first centres around questions of intrusion and interference: there are domains of life in which the state has no proper place. The realms of the market and the family are the two most frequently claimed spaces of 'natural freedom' and the state should be restrained from 'interfering' in them. Here we can see a connection to the second set of arguments which work on the distinction between the public and the private. Again, the market and the family are treated as essentially private domains in which public interest and public powers represent an intrusion. Finally, there are arguments that centre on distinctions between individualised and collective domains of life where citizenship threatens to transform areas of individual concern and practice into inappropriately collectivised ones (often dismissed in terms such as 'social engineering' or the failings of 'mass' provision). Later, we will see how these types of arguments have come to bear on the provision of public services and voiced the need to reform them in more consumerist directions.

But the consumer has also been a more complex figure. Historically, there have been different types and images of the consumer (Maclachlan and Trentmann, 2004; Trentmann, 2006b). At times, the consumer has been looked upon with scorn and criticism reflecting an anxiety about consuming as a practice that 'uses up' scarce or valued resources. Such concerns persist, of course, in environmental and ethical politics around the excesses of contemporary consumerism (Malpass et al., 2006). Consumers have also been the focus of collective mobilisations – a pattern somewhat at odds with the current valorisation of the consumer as the highest point of individualism. As Trentmann (2001) details, the consumer interest was collectively organised around food (such as bread and milk) in nineteenth and twentieth century Britain. More recently there have been consumer mobilisations around such diverse issues as automobile safety, corporate politics, 'McDonaldisation' and economic globalisation (Hilton, 2003 and 2006). Despite the dominant rhetoric of consumer sovereignty, imbalances between the collective power of producers and individualised consumers have provided a fertile ground for such mobilisations.

In parallel with Lister's observation about citizenship, Gabriel and Lang's examination of different conceptions of the consumer emphasises their contested and complex character. They argue that '... by stirring various traditions together we are seeking to reclaim some theoretical recalcitrance for the concepts of consumption and the consumer. We introduce the concept of the "unmanageable consumer" to express this recalcitrance...' (1995: 4). We will return to Gabriel and Lang's concern with the recalcitrant and unmanageable consumer at various points in this book. Here, though, we want to stress the multiple views of the consumer that they explore. Their book offers nine variants: the consumer as chooser, communicator, explorer, identity-seeker, hedonist, victim, rebel, activist and citizen. The image of the consumer that has dominated political and policy debate in recent years is the first of these – the consumer as chooser. This imagery is derived from economic discourse, or perhaps, more accurately, what Thomas Frank (2001) calls 'market populism'. As we will see, critical challenges to the consumerist turn in public policy have tended to rest on a mirror image of the consumer as chooser – the consumer as victim. In such debates, consumers are either the sovereign heroes of their own lives (independent, confident, judgement-forming and choice-exercising agents) or are the cultural dupes preyed upon by forces beyond their control (and often beyond their knowledge). This heroes/dupes split has been a recurrent one in arguments over popular culture (Clarke, 1990).

The contemporary world is marked by a drive to universalise the consumer as chooser – to spread the relationships, experiences and practices of (market-mediated) consuming to new places and new populations. It is one of the core dynamics of corporate globalisation. The freedom to 'spend one's own money' is one of the defining elements of the combination of freedom and democracy that characterises the 'new world order'. In the process, the consumer has been constructed – and celebrated – as a universal identity. In this book, we talk about this as a process of spreading or installing 'consumerism' and use related terms like consumerist imperative or orientation to describe its place in policy formulations. This draws on what Matthew Hilton (2006) has called a 'pejorative' meaning of consumerism, but here we mean it to identify the tendency to treat the consumer as an organising figure for policies, processes and practices. As with citizenship, however, the would-be universalism of the consumer proves subject to some social (and spatial) limitations. Most obviously, access to 'one's own money' is profoundly unequally distributed. Consuming (in its market-mediated form) requires money or its proxies. Consuming thus has implications for the organisation of lives such that increasing attention needs to be given to the acquisition of money or its functional substitutes (mainly credit or theft).

There are, of course, 'magical' representations of consuming as a practice detached from its conditions of existence. These circulate widely, both in advertising and in wider political-cultural discourse, and they hold out the prospect of consuming as an ungrounded activity, in which the self can be produced. This contemporary imagery of consumption is a fundamentally aspirational formation – one driven by the promise of future fulfilment. This psychic structure works both for individuals and whole societies (think of the relation between the promise of consumption and the break up of the Soviet bloc, for example). As we will argue later, 'choice' is the focus of a variety of aspirations and anxieties and – in its consumerist form – rests on a promise that the problems or dissatisfactions of the present can be remedied by more or different choices in the future (Clarke and Newman, 2006; Clarke et al., 2006; Vidler and Clarke, 2005).

So, both the citizen and the consumer are more contingent, contested and contradictory figures than their conventional depiction might allow. What matters for us, though, are the consequences of that complexity for the process in which they become hyphenated. This book explores the conditions and consequences of the particular hyphenation articulated by New Labour as the basis for modernising public services in the UK between 1997 and 2006. What happens if citizens are addressed and treated as consumers of public services? And what are the consequences of practices and identities of consuming if they are displaced into the realm of citizenship?

The book is based on a research project that investigated the elaboration of discourses of consumerism and choice by the New Labour governments in the UK, examining how public service organisations responded to these new policy discourses, and their impact on relationships between public services and their publics. The project set out to explore changing relationships and identifications in three services (health, policing and social care) in two UK sites ('Oldtown' and 'Newtown'). Further details about the project are set out in the **Appendix** and can also be found at www.open.ac.uk/socialsciences/citizenconsumers. This book presents the results of the project, together with an assessment of their significance for understanding the political-cultural formation of New Labour.

Chapter 1, *Changing Times: Perspectives on the Citizen-Consumer*, considers the turmoil that has surrounded public institutions since the 1980s. For almost three decades, public services, ideas of the public interest and the composition of 'the public' as a collective entity have been challenged and contested. We address the problems of analysing such turbulent times and the transformations that they have brought into being. In particular, we situate our analysis in this book between three major perspectives on these topics – a Giddensian view of modernity; a political economy approach to global capitalism and its alter-ego neo-liberalism; and a Foucauldian approach to changing forms of governmentality.

Chapter 2, *Public Service Reform: the Rise of the Citizen-Consumer*, explores the conditions of New Labour's adoption of the 'citizen-consumer' as the emblem of public service reform. We trace some of the different political and cultural currents that made this hyphenated figure both possible and plausible. In doing so, we consider some of the contradictory and unstable features of New Labour's programme of reform.

Chapter 3, *Delivery Problems? Consumerism and Institutional Variation*, shifts the focus of attention to the impact of New Labour's consumerist orientation on three different public services – health care, policing and social care. The institutional formations and policy trajectories of the three services are different in a number of important ways and highlight some problems about thinking of the process of change as simply involving a shift from citizen-centred services to consumer-centred ones.

Chapter 4, *Unstable Encounters: Users, Staff and Services*, looks at some of the reactions of staff and users in these three services to the consumerist orientation. Drawing on key concerns about consumerism developed in Chapter 1, we consider how users and staff view Challenge (the relation between professional/organisational authority and lay responses), Choice (as a means to improving services), Inequality (as a possible effect of increasing choice in public services) and Responsibility (in the transfer of responsibility from state to citizen for well-being, independence and social order).

Chapter 5, *Managing Consumerism: from Policy to Practice,* considers the reactions of managers in the three services to the consumerist orientation. Again, these vary across the three services, revealing different institutional formations and policy trajectories. The chapter also explores how managers – and the organisations they direct – have received, interpreted, inflected and adapted the consumerist imperative in the light of existing organisational orientations and other governmental pressures. Each of the services discussed here was already caught up in the difficult process of thinking about how to reconstruct its relationships with a changing and turbulent public. New Labour's consumerism engaged with these concerns and tried to shape them in a particular way.

Chapter 6, *Sites of Strain: Consumerism and Public Services,* examines some of the dilemmas arising from consumerism in public services. More specifically, we look at how this consumerist orientation has intensified and exacerbated a series of persistent troubles in the organisation and provision of public services. The focal points are the tensions between choice and equity; the problems of reconciling needs, wants, rights and resources; and the challenges to professional authority wrapped up in the tangles of the 'knowledge/power knot'. The chapter concludes by examining the idealised – and problematic – figure of the 'responsible consumer'.

Chapter 7, *What's in a Name? In Search of the Citizen-Consumer,* explores the problem of 'naming' the people who use public services. Both providers and users of services seemed uncomfortable with the imagery of consumer and customer. However, this was not a simple rejection of the consumer image in favour of the citizen. We suggest that the dominant binary distinction between citizen and consumer failed to capture how people think of themselves in relation to public services. Other conceptions conveyed a more active and collective sense of the publicness of public services. In this context, 'choice' appears as a focus of ambivalent and ambiguous personal and political reactions. The relationship between the public and public services, we suggest, remains a turbulent issue – not resolved by New Labour's turn to consumerism and choice.

Chapter 8, *Beyond the Citizen-Consumer,* offers conclusions about some of the issues brought to light in the book. Three things stand out for us. The first was raised by the ways in which people addressed their relationships to public services – offering complex, mobile and relational reflections. We suggest that social scientists may need to take such 'reasoning subjects' seriously, rather than seeing them as subordinated or subjected by dominant ideologies or discourses. Secondly, we consider New Labour's discovery or invention of the citizen-consumer as part of a political and governmental project, and the problems of analysing such formations. Finally, we contemplate the prospect of the decline or disappearance of the citizen-consumer in the continuing ferment about the future of public services and their relationship to changing publics.

1

Changing Times: Perspectives on the Citizen-Consumer

From some perspectives the rise of the citizen-consumer is viewed as 'empowering', a means of challenging the paternalistic power of the professions and of ensuring that citizens might benefit from more flexible and responsive public service provision. For other commentators, it marks a shift towards a more marketised and privatised form of service delivery, driven by commercial rather than public service values. In this chapter:

- we explore three different perspectives on the citizen-consumer: the sociology of modernity, the political economy of neo-liberalism and Foucauldian conceptions of governmentality;
- we highlight how each understands the place of consumerism in modern times, and draw out some of the analytical and political implications of each.

We begin by noting the slipperiness of the boundary between academic analysis and the perspectives that inform policy and politics. The policy documents or political speeches we make use of during this book all reveal how their authors draw on implicit – and sometimes explicit – theories about how the world has changed, how citizenship is being remade, how economic and social forces imply the need for yet another cycle of reform or modernisation. Similarly those analysing – and often critiquing – the consequences of reform do so from a particular theoretical standpoint, with implicit political implications and evaluations.

'The world has changed': the sociology of modernity

One important area of sociological theorising – work that treats contemporary society as modernity, or as a particular phase or development of modernity – has immediate and compelling relevance for thinking about the citizen-consumer. As Edwards (2000) has argued, consumer culture seems to be intimately bound up with the character of late, reflexive or even post-modernity. Although these different versions of modernity vary in their accounts and assessments of consumer culture, all of them identify it as a core component of modern societies.

Despite such variations, we will refer primarily to the work of Anthony Giddens and Ulrich Beck in this context, partly because they have constructed analyses of modernity in which dynamics of individualisation and reflexivity provide the conditions for 'life politics' as projects in which individuals come to define themselves, both individually and collectively. The rise of a consumer culture provides one site through which individuals can define and project their identities. The underlying dynamics that produce this phase of 'reflexive modernity' are, in Giddens' account, a combination of globalisation, de-traditionalisation and social reflexivity. For Giddens, reflexive modernity is a 'post-traditional social order' (1994: 5) in which 'tradition changes its status. Traditions have to explain themselves, to become open to interrogation or discourse' (1994: 5; see also Giddens et al., 1994). The rise of reflexivity dislocates varieties of 'taken for granted' or institutionalised social arrangements:

> The development of social reflexivity is the key influence on a diversity of changes that otherwise seem to have little in common. Thus the emergence of 'post-Fordism' in industrial enterprises is usually analysed in terms of technological change – particularly the influence of information technology. But the underlying reason for the growth of 'flexible production' and 'bottom-up decision-making' is that a universe of high reflexivity leads to greater autonomy of action, which the enterprise must recognise and draw on.
>
> The same applies to bureaucracy and to the sphere of politics. Bureaucratic authority, as Max Weber made clear, used to be a condition for organizational effectiveness. In a more reflexively ordered society, operating in the context of manufactured uncertainty, this is no longer the case. The old bureaucratic systems start to disappear, the dinosaurs of the post-traditional age. In the domain of politics, states can no longer so readily treat their citizens as 'subjects'. (1994: 7)

De-traditionalisation also implies that societies have moved away from cultural formations of deference that supported forms of hierarchical authority and social order. This view of traditional authority in decline links Giddens' concern with the democratising impact of reflexivity to conceptions of post-modernity (e.g., Lyotard's view of the loss of belief in 'grand narratives', 1984), and the dissolution of class/status formations (Bauman, 1998). We might also see connections between the rise of consumer culture and the decline of deference and 'respect' for traditional order or traditional authority. Consumer culture features a populist and quasi-egalitarian impulse, asserting that everyone is entitled to consume and to consume what they want. It disrupts conventions and hierarchies of taste and access. Alternatively, it might be that the decline of deference has made possible the populist sensibility of mass consumerism. The collapse of the Soviet bloc and its aftermath suggests that the dislocation of established authority and the rise of a consumerist (as well as political) conception of individualised freedom are closely associated.

Public services were intimately bound up with established or 'traditional' models of authority as governing the relationships between state, services and public. The Policeman (and the implied connection between masculinity and authority is significant) and the Doctor have served as particular embodiments of professional and social authority. It is not just 'bureaucratic' forms of organising authority that have been affected by the decline of deference. Forms of embodied occupational or professional authority have also become vulnerable.

Giddens argues that reflexive modernisation involves a shift towards democratisation – linking more democratic forms of personal relationship, the rise of social movements, the dynamics of organisational decentralisation and the dialogic potentials of an emergent global order (1994: 117–24). Our own view would be somewhat different, suggesting that the decline of deference involves a *populist* shift in politics and culture that does not necessarily translate into democratic or progressive political forms. On the contrary, one effect is the rise of a 'demotic populism' that celebrates the people/the popular. Such developments are not intrinsically democratic, even though they may appropriate some of the mechanisms and trappings of institutional democracy (opinion polling, voting by phone/e-mail, etc.). But they are demotic because they claim to speak in the voice of the people. Demotic populism rests on claims that the voice of the people is typically excluded or repressed by the dominant institutional forms of politics and social life. Forms of demotic populism are often framed in an anti-elitist discourse that challenges concentrations of privilege and power in the name of people. As we shall see, this model of populism has strong connections to New Labour's conception of citizen-consumers.

In several ways, consumer culture embodies this late or reflexive modernity. It is associated with both economic and cultural dynamics of globalisation that create the conditions for the proliferation of commodities and their increasingly aestheticised – or signifying – character (Edwards, 2000). It promotes de-traditionalisation, unlocking taken-for-granted associations of taste, style and social position (developments that are discussed in Featherstone, 1991; Lury, 1996 and Tomlinson, 1990, for example). Finally, consumer culture is associated with reflexivity and some versions of life politics, in which identities are constructed through the signifying practices of consumption choices. As Giddens argued: 'Life politics is a politics of identity as well as of choice' (1994: 91). There are, of course, substantial arguments about whether consumer culture is a site of politics (even individuated 'life politics') or is a displacement or subordination of politics (e.g., Bauman, 1998).

But we need to step back a little from this general view of the emergence of consumer culture as a core element of late or reflexive modernity to discuss some of the problems with this as an analytic framing for the rise of the citizen-consumer. Almost all aspects of this sociology of modernity have proved controversial, from the view of globalisation to the conception of individuated and reflexive subjects – and some of these are taken up in the following two sections of this chapter. Here, though we concentrate on questions of the time and space of reflexive modernity. A foregrounding of globalisation is often linked to a diminution of spatial differentiation (Massey, 1999). Although Giddens (and Beck) do not treat globalisation solely as a homogenising force, they do see its mix of economic, cultural and political dynamics as generalising a 'cosmopolitan' reflexivity across national boundaries – weakening traditional institutions and authorities wherever they are encountered. The spread of such cosmopolitanism looks more spatially uneven than this, with forms of corporate, religious, military and authoritarian political power being reconvened alongside pressures for democratisation.

This view of modernity and its different phases (early/late; simple/reflexive) tends to collapse spatial difference into time, producing one modernity to which societies approximate in terms of being more or less advanced. Geographers have critiqued this displacement of space by time (Massey, 2005). Others – especially those deriving from post-colonial studies – have challenged the conception of a singular modernity, arguing that the Euro-American model of modernity co-exists uncomfortably with others (even if its economic, political and cultural dominance often obscures their presence, see, for example, Chakrabarty, 2000). There are also questions about the timing of the rise of the consumer culture and the figure of the consumer (see, *inter alia*, Brewer, 2003; Maclachlan and Trentmann, 2004; Trentmann, 2006a). The threads of consumer culture – commodified consumption, conspicuous consumption and consumption as a site of collective mobilisation and social regulation – have long histories predating the rise of Fordist industrial production and the associated growth of mass consumption usually taken to be the economic and social preconditions for consumer culture (see Edwards, 2000). But more significantly for our work here, Trentmann has argued that both historical studies and contemporary sociology have neglected the 'subjectivities of the consumer' (2006a: 2). He suggests that:

> The expanding literature on consumption has enriched our understanding of the central role of material culture in the reproduction of social relationships and status, everyday routines and selfhood, but has offered surprisingly little in the way of explaining the evolution of the consumer as a master category of collective and individual identity. Put simply, all societies have been engaged in consumption and have purchased, exchanged, gifted or used objects and services, but it has only been in specific contexts in the nineteenth and twentieth centuries that some (not all) practices of consumption have been connected to a sense of being a 'consumer' as an identity, audience or category of analysis. (2006a: 2)

Our study contributes in some ways to redressing this lack of attention to the consumer as a social category, identity and identification. Rather than assuming that 'consumers' exist, our inquiry explores how they are summoned in one field of social practice (the use of public services) and how people experience themselves – and what identifications they deploy – in relation to those practices.

Before leaving the sociology of modernity to explore other perspectives, it is worth noting the ways in which sociological analysis has connected with the more situated politics of New Labour's citizen-consumer. There are strong links between this sociology of modernity and the politics of public service reform in the UK. As we will see in more detail in the following chapter, New Labour's approach to public service reform has been constructed around the imperatives of modernity and modernisation – drawing on sociological accounts of social changes, including globalisation and more reflexively demanding, less deferential individuals. More particularly, there was the critical role of Tony Giddens in theorising the relationships between late or reflexive modernity and the rise of (and need for) 'Third Way' politics (1994, 1998). We can trace ways in which New Labour's version of the Third Way incorporated and adapted – selectively, and in very specific ways – the Giddensian view of modernity. The familiar narrative – 'the world has changed, people have changed' – was used as a device to underpin a third element: the imperative that 'public services have to change' (see, for example, Blair, 1998). The idea of reflexive individuals has been used to legitimate the need for the public – as consumers – to have access to new sources of information in order for them to make more informed choices. And the individuation thesis is linked to calls for more personalised services tailored to the needs of individuals. Themes from the sociology of modernity are selectively appropriated in order to create a new normative framework of policy development.

Not all sociologists of modernity share the relatively optimistic reading of social and political developments offered by Giddens and others. For example, Zygmunt Bauman's writings on the rise of consumption associated with what he terms 'liquid modernity' and its implications for welfare states (and their subjects) presents a much bleaker set of analyses. In Bauman's work, consumption has displaced production as the site of moral worth and value – and (individualised) choice has become a master value. Those excluded from the realm of consumption – primarily because they lack the economic capacity to make and realise choice in the marketplace – are now multiply excluded: from the activities of consumption, from the exercise of choice and from the moral realm of the worthy. 'It is the fault of the excluded that they did nothing, or not enough, to escape exclusion; perhaps they even invited their fate, making the exclusion into a foregone conclusion' (1998: 85).

Bauman explores the ways in which social divisions and inequalities are reconstituted and recoded through the rise of (commodified) consumption. He is also concerned by the de-politicising effects of the transition from a 'work ethic' to an 'aesthetic of consumption' as the dominant principle of social organisation:

> Contemporary society engages its members primarily as consumers; only secondarily, and partly, does it engage them as producers. To meet the social norm, to be a fully fledged member of society, one needs to respond promptly and efficiently to the temptations of the consumer market; one needs to contribute to the 'supply-clearing demand' and in case of economic trouble be part of the 'consumer-led recovery'. All this the poor, lacking decent income, credit cards and the prospect of a better time, are not fit to do. Accordingly, the norm which is broken by the poor of today, the norm the breaking of which makes them 'abnormal', is the norm of consumer competence or aptitude, not that of employment. First and foremost, the poor of today are 'non-consumers', not 'unemployed': they are defined in the first place through being flawed consumers… In the book-balancing of a consumer society, the poor are unequivocally a liability, and by no stretch of imagination can they be recorded on the side of present or future assets. (1998: 90–1)

Accordingly, the complex social and political ties that had connected the poor-as-unemployed to the politics of a society governed by the work ethic have been undone. The mixture of fear, concern and solidarity that underpinned welfarist politics has no place in the consumer society:

> And so, for the first time in recorded history the poor are now purely and simply a worry and a nuisance. They have no merits which could relieve, let alone counterbalance, their vices. They have nothing to offer in exchange for the taxpayer's outlays. They are a bad investment, unlikely ever to be repaid, let alone bring profit; a black hole sucking in whatever comes near and spitting back nothing, except, perhaps, trouble. Decent and normal members of society – the consumers – want nothing from them and expect nothing. (1998: 91)

These are concerns that are shared in some ways by writers from our second main theoretical perspective: the political economy of neo-liberalism, albeit from rather different intellectual starting points.

States versus markets: the view from political economy

Many of the criticisms of Giddensian conceptions of modernity have been raised by authors writing from the standpoint of critical political economy or varieties of Marxism (e.g., Benton, 2000; Ferguson et al., 2002). In some cases, critics point to the underestimation of continuities in capitalist social formations – particularly the persistence of class as relations of production, as a form of (deepening) inequalities and as a mode of political organising and conflict. For others, it is the persistence of a capitalist mode of production on an international and global scale that is missing from the model of modernity. As Edwards (2000) has suggested, in relation to conceptions of consumer culture and consumer society, there are also significant distinctions to be drawn between analysts who focus primarily on the symbolic domain (stressing the sign value of commodities or treating consumption itself as a privileged site of signifying practice) and those who emphasise the more 'materialist' analysis of production and consumption practices. In this later view, consumer culture is marked primarily by the extension or deepening of commodification: 'in contemporary society, almost no human need or activity avoids commodification, and consumer society, despite its internal contradictions, is increasingly all-encompassing' (Edwards, 2000: 5). From the standpoint of critical political economy, such changes mark the extension of the power and reach of capital into new sites – both spatially through its globalising ambition and socially through the subjection of new areas of human activity to the logics of commodification and market exchange.

In this view, the shift from citizen to consumer marks a new phase in western capitalism, predominantly theorised as the moment of neo-liberalism (Harvey, 2005). This has something in common with earlier political-economic discussions of globalisation because of the centrality of the spatial universalisation of the rule of neo-liberalism. But it differs in identifying a particular political and ideological formation that represents itself as a new 'logic of capital' and seeks to liberate capital from the shackles of earlier political compromises – not least the impositions of national governments (in the form of taxation and regulation).

> Neoliberalism is in the first instance a theory of political economic practices that proposes that human well-being can best be advanced by liberating individual entrepreneurial freedom and skills within a framework characterized by strong private property rights, free markets and free trade... There has everywhere been an emphatic turn towards neoliberalism in political-economic practices and thinking since the 1970s. Deregulation, privatization, and withdrawal of the state from many areas of social provision have been all too common... Neoliberalism has, in short, become hegemonic as a mode of discourse. It has pervasive effects on ways of thought to the point where it has become incorporated into the common-sense way many of us interpret, live in and understand the world.
>
> The process of neoliberalization has, however, entailed much 'creative destruction', not only of prior institutional frameworks and powers (even challenging traditional forms of state sovereignty) but also of divisions of labour, social relations, welfare provisions, technological mixes, ways of life and thought, reproductive activities, attachments to the land and habits of the heart. (Harvey, 2005: 2–3)

As Harvey indicates, one specific institutional framework that neo-liberalism has sought to revise has been the welfare state. Welfare states represented a bargain extracted by European working classes (and their political parties) as part of the construction of a Fordist phase of capitalism (see, *inter alia*, Huber and Stephens, 2001; Jessop, 2002). Since the 1970s, welfare states have been subject to pressures of retrenchment, reform and reduction, becoming (in some accounts) worlds of 'post-welfarist' capitalism (Clarke, forthcoming c).

In this view of neo-liberalism, such social democratic incursions into capitalism have been 'rolled back'. With social defences reduced or in disarray, we have seen the intensified subjugation of everyday life to the logics and processes of capitalism. Exemplified in Esping-Andersen's view of welfare states as the site of 'decommodification' (1990), political economy understands social formations as dominated by the *economy* (alternatively conceived as the market, systems of capital accumulation and social relations of production) and *politics* (or class struggle, or the capitalist state). For Regulationist approaches, the move from citizen to consumer is an aspect of the move from Fordism to post-Fordism (see Jessop, 2000, 2002). In part this is a shift in scale, with previously national arrangements being remade in the context of global dynamics. Indeed, this shift is understood as part of the extended scope, scale and power of capital in its 'global' phase in which more and more spaces and relationships are subjected to the logic of the market. It is a process of extended commodification or re-commodification.

In the context of British society, these changes are viewed as having been carried and implemented by neo-liberal political and ideological movements, first in the form of the 'Thatcherite' Conservative party (governing with and without Thatcher between 1979 and 1997) and subsequently in the Blairite 'New Labour' governments of 1997 onwards. The changes wrought by these governments on social institutions and political culture are seen as marking the shift from social democratic politics to neo-liberalism: the market is elevated over the public realm. Marquand, for example, points to the centrality of marketization and privatisation as central strands in the remaking of public and private realms:

> New Labour has pushed marketisation and privatisation forward, at least as zealously as the Conservatives did, narrowing the frontiers of the public domain in the process... Ministerial rhetoric is saturated with the language of consumerism. The public services are to be 'customer focused'; schools and colleges are to ensure that 'what is on offer responds to the needs of consumers'; the 'progressive project' is to be subjected to 'rebranding'. (2004: 118)

More significantly, the transformation of citizens into consumers is understood as diminishing the collective ethos and practices of the public domain (embodied in the figure of the citizen) and both privatises and individualises them (in the figure of the consumer). For Needham, this corrodes the public domain as the site of both collective solidarity and political choice and mobilisation. The shift from citizen to consumer individualises relationships to collective services and depoliticises 'choice' by subjecting the public domain to the logics of markets and management that constitute 'choice' in the private/market domain.

> This process has profound implications for the relationship between government and citizen. It restricts citizens to a passive consumption of politics,

excluding them from playing a creative and productive role in civic life. An individualised and commodified form of citizenship is taking hold in which communal and discursive elements are lost.

    … . there is a more fundamental question to be asked about the extent to which people do in fact expect government and public services to relate to them in the same way as private sector businesses. The danger is that by encouraging this read-across, government may itself be eliding a crucial distinction between the public and private domains without which public engagement with democratic processes, and support for public provision, is ultimately bound to be undermined. (Needham, 2003: 8, 28)

The consumer thus embodies the private (rather than the public), the market (rather than the state) and the individual (rather than the collective). Neo-liberalism has been a critical reference point for assessing and explaining these changes – and New Labour's role in articulating them. It is a convenient term, since it bridges or fuses the political and economic elements of political economy. As a concept, neo-liberalism promises to resolve analytical doubts and difficulties about the relative autonomy of politics and ideology from economic relations. Instead, it can be demonstrated how economic, ideological and political power have become fused in a new class project on the part of capital (Harvey, 2005). It describes the subjugation of the public to the private, the state to the market, and the social to the economic.

At the core of this perspective is a foundational distinction between state and market (or politics and economy). This distinction residualises other fields or domains of social formations – and, in the process, residualises forms of social relation other than class. The resulting binaries (state/market; public/private; capital/labour) produce thin abstractions of social relations and social formations (see Clarke, 2006a, and Newman, 2004). In particular, political economy operates with a residual or 'thin' conception of the social: those domains of life that are 'extra-economic' and thus subsidiary or secondary to the dynamics of economic forces and their political conflicts. But the substance of the social tends to be a shadow of the 'real' or 'material' forces. Social relations, divisions and identities tend to be reduced to class relations, or to their functionality for forms of capital accumulation (the gendering of social reproduction or convenient 'divisions in the working class', for example). One particular consequence of this concerns the 'consumer' identity. The consumer is treated as if s/he is the incarnation of neo-classical economics; as if, indeed, people behave in the ways they are imagined in economic theory. This is a serious analytic and political problem since the complex potency and reach of 'consuming passions' (Williamson, 1986) outruns the limited representations of consumers as sovereigns or dupes. As Gabriel and Lang (1995) have argued, consumers do not necessarily behave in the ways prescribed by the concept – in practice, they may prove unpredictable and 'unmanageable'. The consumer identity, in the view from

political economy, is not 'social' but merely the bearer of economic relationships and dynamics (commodification combined with commodity
fetishism). Trentmann suggests that there are problems about forcing the
consumer identity into the binary of citizen versus consumer:

> A simple linear transfer model from citizenship to commerce and from other-
> regarding to self-regarding actions, altogether ignores the diverse 'collective'
> forms that an interest in the consumer has taken in the past – from totalitarian
> policies to liberal radicalism, progressivism to socialism. It also distracts from
> the ongoing contestation of the 'citizen consumer' in different local, national and
> supranational arenas of public policy, commercial business and knowledge.
> (2006a: 13)

We might insist on a similar complexity surrounding citizenship – it has
been the site of extensive struggle and contestation, and not just by class
forces. On the contrary, social movements based in gender and racialised divisions have been significant in both demonstrating the partial, selective and
uneven embodiment of citizenship, and trying to redress those inequalities.
As much scholarship has shown, both citizenship and the European conception of a public sphere have been profoundly structured by assumptions
about gender and race (Fraser, 1997; Lewis, 2000; Lister, 2003; Pateman, 1988).
And such divisions continue within neo-liberalism's reworking of those
domains (Kingfisher, 2002). Citizens – like consumers – have been differently
imagined and harnessed to very different political formations and projects.
    We do not mean that political and economic processes, forces and pro-
jects are unimportant. Rather they might need to be viewed as more
uneven, differentiated and unfinished. Other forces contend the world
alongside and in relation to neo-liberalism – and neo-liberalism (as a
political-economic project) has to negotiate complex formations of people,
places and politics, even as it tries to dominate them. Catherine
Kingfisher's analysis (2002), exploring the varying reform strategies and
politics of neo-liberalism as it seeks to rework the relations between
gender, welfare and the state in different places, exemplifies a more differentiated – and more thoroughly 'social' – treatment of neo-liberalism.
She argues that 'the story of neoliberalism's globalization' is in practice 'a
series of stories characterized by disjointed, disjunctured articulations'
(2002: 50). At this point, it is possible to see sites of potential intersection
and overlap between this expanded view of neo-liberalism and our third
perspective, based on Foucault's interest in 'governmentality'.

The governmentalised citizen-consumer

Foucault's development of the concept of governmentality as a way
of thinking about the forms in which societies are ordered has been influ-
ential in shaping innovative work in very diverse fields – from social
policy to projects of globalising governance (see, for example, Larner

and Walters, 2004; McDonald and Marston, 2006; Petersen et al., 1999;). Governmentality was used by Foucault to denote the conjunction of forms of governing and the mentalities (forms of thinking) that informed and directed them (Dean, 1999). The object of these inquiries has been the varieties of liberalism – liberalism as a mode of governing at a distance, rather than Liberalism as a specific political philosophy or ideology. Where modernity provides the organising concept for the sociology with which we began this chapter, and capitalism performs the same organising role in critical political economy, liberalism forms the central concept – and has the same epochal reach – within studies of governmentality. Not surprisingly, some Foucauldian scholarship has taken an interest in the relationship between liberal governmentalities and neo-liberalism:

> In ordinary parlance, neoliberalism refers to the repudiation of Keynesian wel-
> fare state economics and the ascendance of the Chicago School of political
> economy – von Hayek, Friedman, and others. In popular usage, neoliberalism
> is equated with a radically free market: maximized competition and free trade
> achieved through economic deregulation, elimination of tariffs, and a range of
> monetary and social policies favorable to business and indifferent towards
> poverty, social deracination, cultural decimation, long term resource depletion,
> and environmental destruction. …
> While these referents capture important effects of neoliberalism, they also
> reduce neoliberalism to a bundle of economic policies with inadvertent political
> and social consequences: they fail to address the *political rationality* that both
> organises these policies and reaches beyond the market. (Brown, 2006: 37–8)

For Wendy Brown, the challenge of thinking about neo-liberalism as a distinctive political rationality is to 'consider the way that this rationality is emerging as governmentality – as a mode of governance encompassing but not limited to the state, and one that produces subjects, forms of citizenship and behavior, and a new organization of the social' (2006: 37). This takes neo-liberalism beyond political economy, both as a political project and as a set of policies, practices and ways of governing. Within studies of governmentality, there are some disagreements about whether this phase of liberal governmentality is better addressed as neo-liberalism or 'advanced liberalism' (see the discussion in Rose, 2000). But a new phase – and a new governing mentality – is one that most post-Foucauldian scholars emphasise, distinguishing it from the earlier phases of 'classical liberalism' and 'expanded liberalism', associated with the discovery and regulation of the social through a variety of apparatuses and agencies (see, for example, Dean, 1999; Petersen et al., 1999).

Here we consider some of the arguments developed by Nikolas Rose whose explorations of advanced liberal governmentality have provided starting points for much recent work. For Rose (1999) and others, the 'social' is a field of investigation, knowledge and regulation produced by the shift towards 'government from the social point of view' during the twentieth century:

It is not, then, a case of whether or to what extent various countries developed 'the welfare state'. Rather, it is more useful to understand this as government from the social point of view. Organized attempts to govern conduct, in particular but not exclusively the conduct of the poor, proliferated in Britain, Europe and the United States around a variety of different problems, but underpinned by the same socializing rationale... (1999: 130–1)

It is this 'social' – a field that was both the object and the effect of 'expansive liberal governmentality' – that is currently in retreat or decline, being displaced by the conceptions and practices of 'advanced liberalism'. Rose argues that 'society' is in the process of being re-imagined, most obviously as a 'community of communities' in a field of self-regulating, self-governing and self-regarding relations. In this shift, the citizen mutates into a consumer, both as a subject engaged in practices of 'consuming' and as a citizen whose relationship to government is being transformed by the extension of the idea of 'consuming' to new fields of relationship. Rose proposes that the 'entrepreneurial' self who is the central subject of advanced liberalism is also being constituted in the changing relations between citizen and government. In a suggestive argument about how relationships between the citizen and the state are being reworked, Rose suggests that they are being subjected to a 'politics of the contract':

In this new field, the citizen is to become a consumer, and his or her activity is to be understood in terms of the activation of the rights of the consumer in the marketplace. Consider, for example, the transformations in the relations of experts and clients. Whilst social rule was characterized by discretionary authority, advanced liberal rule is characterized by the politics of the contract, in which the subject of the contract is not a patient or a case but a customer or consumer... Of course, these contracts are of many different types. Few are like the contracts between buyer and seller in the market. But, in their different ways, they shift the power relations inscribed in relations of expertise. This is especially so when they are accompanied by new methods of regulation and control such as audit and evaluation. ... The politics of the contract becomes central to contests between political strategies concerning the 'reform of welfare', and to strategies of user demand and user resistance to professional powers. (1999: 164–5)

The account of the transformation of the citizen into the consumer as a governmental subject makes visible several dynamics that are different to those scrutinised in the sociology of modernity and the political economy of neo-liberalism. For us, it also raises several problems. It may overestimate the decline or displacement of citizenship, neglecting the multiplying varieties of citizenship visible in New Labour's policy initiatives: citizenship is being both fragmented and proliferated (Clarke, 2005a). At the same time, we think it underestimates the difficulty of articulating this 'consumer' version of citizenship with other versions: active citizens, activated citizens as the products of workfare, local/communal citizens, national and transnational citizens and so on. Finally, we suspect that

Rose's analysis may overstate the 'contractual' form of this reconfiguration, taking the contract/charter as the new mode of relationship. In our study, there are substantial empirical variations in the forms of relationships between services and their users (discussed more extensively in Chapters 3 and 4). Certainly expertise and 'producer power' have been challenged – but their re-working through the citizen-consumer remains an uneven and contested locus (Clarke, 2006a). As we shall see in the following chapters, policing, health care and social care are marked by very different adaptations of the 'consumerist' imperative, shaped by very different institutional logics and trajectories. The quasi-contractual form is not a dominant feature, though it appears alongside varieties of individuation, personalisation and communalisation of services (see also the discussion of varieties of personalisation in Leadbeater, 2004; and the critique by Cutler et al., forthcoming). Institutional forms of choice and contract are also interwoven with forms of involvement that range from the consumerist forms of expressed want/need or surveys of perceived satisfaction through to more participatory forms of consultation about services and service design (from citizens juries to user panels). Empirically, then, the transition from the 'welfarist' citizen of expanded liberalism is both more complex and less uni-directional than this view of advanced liberal governmentality might suggest (Larner, 2000).

There is one other significant issue that is raised by the concern of governmentality studies with the constitutions of new 'subjects': in this case the construction of consumers where once there were citizens (Clarke, 1997, 1998; Larner, 1997). The question of constructing such subjects is important for our analysis because of the implication that people come to think and act as consumers in their encounters and engagements with public services. Subjection – the process of producing subjects – is too often treated as a presumed effect in many of these analyses, rather than being treated more problematically as an ambition which may or may not be achieved in practice (Clarke, 2004a). For our study, a critical question was: do citizens (itself a problematic, incomplete and contested subjection) now perceive and experience themselves as consumers? Mitchell Dean's overview of governmentality formulates this process of subjection as a general issue:

> Regimes of government do not determine forms of subjectivity. They elicit, promote, facilitate, foster and attribute various capacities, qualities and statuses to particular agents. They are successful to the extent that these agents come to experience themselves through such capacities (e.g., of rational decision-making), qualities (e.g., as having a sexuality) and statuses (e.g., as being an active citizen). (1999: 32)

However, the empirical investigation of the 'success' of subjection has not been a central feature of many governmentality studies. Rather the *categories* of subject have been the predominant focus of attention. Governmental texts and practices have been examined for the types of subject that they aim to produce: the 'job seeker' rather than unemployed person; the actuarial self, taking responsibility for his/her welfare futures; or the consumer of public services. Exploring such discursive formations is important – and in the following chapter we go on to explore some of the characteristic forms of New Labour's discourse of the citizen-consumer. But it is also important not to 'read off' social consequences from such ambitions. As we shall see, it might matter whether people see themselves as consumers or citizens – or even other types of subject – in their relationships to public services.

Different perspectives, different visibilities

Do the different dynamics of how citizenship is being transformed, sketched in the preceding account, simply reflect different theoretical and political points of view? Each of these perspectives has something to contribute to the analysis of the turn to consumerism in public policy. A Giddensian view of modernity – and of New Labour as a modernising project – foregrounds the social dynamics of reflexivity and diversity and the political/policy concerns with activation and empowerment. We would also see the dislocation of traditional institutions as a central dynamic, with a decline in deference enabling a greater challenge to established forms of authority. A more complex view of expertise and a more contested view of knowledge would also be part of the field of relationships between individuals and institutions in reflexive modernity. From such a standpoint, the reworking of the relationships between the state and the citizen towards a more autonomous and individuated form of citizenship is both necessary and desirable (Giddens, 1994, 1998). Such an analysis blurs the distinction between the sociological model of reflexive modernity in general and New Labour's own conception of the process of 'governing in the modern world' (Miliband, 2000; see also Clarke and Newman, 2004).

In contrast, Foucauldian work on governmentality takes a more pessimistic view of the dynamics of activation and empowerment (Cruikshank, 1999). Rather than liberation, they represent new modes of subjection that have their location in the transition from expansive to advanced liberalism (or from welfarism to neo-liberalism). For Foucauldian scholars, the shift away from expansive or welfarist liberalism can be traced through the knowledges, apparatuses and practices of governing the social (e.g., Petersen et al., 1999). A key difference from more conventional sociology is the Foucauldian concern with how particular sorts of subject are constituted in the knowledges and practices of governance: the job-seeker, the hard-working family, the socially excluded, the rationally calculating investor, the carefully choosing welfare consumer and so on.

Finally, political economy focuses on the realignments of power, interest and politics in a different way – treating citizenship as a condition achieved by struggle, political mobilisation and (class) compromise. Nevertheless, there is – especially in what might be called the social democratic variant – a strong tendency towards nostalgia and a sense of loss about the retreat from the 'golden age' of the welfare state (Huber and Stephens, 2001; see also Leibfried and Zürn, 2005). In the UK context, David Marquand has advanced such an analysis of the 'decline of the public' (2004). There are some problems with this view of citizenship and the public realm – not least the ways in which other patterns of exclusion, marginalisation and subordination have led to both citizenship and the public being intensely contested concepts (both analytically and politically; e.g., Isin, 2002; Lister, 2003; Warner, 2002). Missing from this political economy view of citizenship and the public are those difficult questions about the gendered dynamics of the constitution of the public and the private/personal. The family/household/domestic still tends to be squeezed out by analyses that centre on the binary distinction between the state and the market. Questions of the nation and its racialised formation have tended to be neglected by all three perspectives, despite both the long history and growing salience of struggles over defining national membership and national culture as both the nation and the nation-state become profoundly unsettled (e.g., Clarke, 2005b; Gilroy, 2005; Lewis, 2000).

However each of these three perspectives – the sociology of modernity, governmentality studies and political economy – reveals something about the dynamics of citizenship under New Labour's rule. We want to argue rather pragmatically for the value of keeping multiple dynamics in view, rather than assuming the analytical or political superiority of one standpoint and its conception of what has happened to citizenship. In part this is a way of trying to keep the heterogeneity of the present visible rather than subsuming it into a singular narrative (Barnett, 2005; Larner, 2000; see also Clarke, 2005a and 2006b). The sociology of modernity recognises something of the complexity of contemporary political and cultural formations. It highlights the multiplicity of groups, identities and claims, however ineptly these are captured by the traditional-modern distinction so central to this form of sociology. Governing the (modern) social involves the problem of how to manage diverse, differentiated and mobile populations. These populations are also 'reflexive' and becoming detached from previous forms of authority, identity, identification and attachment. One result with particular consequences for New Labour is that governing public services has become problematic because of the unstable and unpredictable combinations of popular doubt and desire (Clarke, 2005c). Substantial majorities continue to want public services and expect to see them improved, suggesting some limitations to the hegemonic claims of neo-liberalism. But, at the same time, the public is increasingly cynical and/or sceptical about party politics and the claims made by government (including those about the improvement of public services).

In contrast, Foucauldian studies of governmentality have tended to be more sceptical about the claims of modernity (and about optimistic readings of it). There is no going back on the importance of the Foucauldian view of subjects and their constitution through multiple apparatuses, practices and discourses. Governmental analyses also have much to offer in making sense of New Labour as a political and governmental project. They are particularly productive in drawing attention to the diverse forms of citizen being invoked by New Labour policies and practices. Finally, political economy draws attention to the persistent and recomposed social relations of capitalism in its shifting forms (in particular the retreat from or retrenchment of welfare capitalism).

Each of these positions has flaws and they certainly do not sit comfortably together. But each reveals specific dynamics that we should not neglect. In constructing our empirical study of New Labour's citizen-consumers, we drew on each to fill out what a consumerist imperative for the reform of public services might look like. What sorts of aspects or dimensions of the 'consumer' might we expect to find? Combining these three perspectives – and adding them to the dominant 'rational choice' model of the consumer – we were able to construct four key dimensions of public service consumerism to explore. These were Challenge, Responsibility, Choice and Inequality.

Challenge is a way of registering the supposed decline, or greater vulnerability, of forms of traditional or conventional authority (including that embodied in state institutions). Our study explored how ready people were to challenge public service providers in health, policing and social care, and how willing staff in such agencies were to be challenged. In some ways, **Responsibility** might be seen as the (Foucauldian) obverse of challenge. Where the sociology of modernity sees more active and more empowered citizens engaging reflexively with public institutions and sources of knowledge, the Foucauldian view of advanced liberalism sees subjects being recruited to responsibilised positions – being made responsible for their own well-being, security and welfare. So we were interested in the extent to which staff and people using services saw responsibility shifting to the individual.

Choice – as a focus of our attention – derives both from the neo-classical economic model of the consumer and the way it has been inscribed in the New Labour conception of public service reform (see also Clarke et al., 2006). Choice, it has been claimed, is both what people want and the driver of service improvement. We discuss this more in the following chapter. But in our study, we were interested to discover whether staff and those using services saw choice as a means of bringing about improvements in services. Finally, **Inequality** is one of the themes to be derived from critical political economy, in which it is argued that market dynamics tend to produce, reproduce and deepen social inequalities within and between nations. For many critics of New Labour's approach to public service reform, the commitment to a mix of user choice, marketisation and privatisation were likely to produce intensified social inequalities. Consequently, we were interested in whether people using services, and the staff working in them, perceived increased choice and voice for users as likely to produce inequality.

These four dimensions of public service consumerism are derived fairly directly from the perspectives discussed above. They capture and make visible different aspects of the consumerist imperative in public service reform. But a second major concern of our study emerged around the wider question of the transition from the citizen to the consumer. We wanted to know whether people using the three public services perceived themselves as consumers, or as citizens, or as other types of subject. To the extent that people do not identify themselves as consumers or customers of public services, New Labour's narrative of social change and public service reform might be rendered problematic. At the same time, some of the analytical frameworks in which the citizen/consumer binary plays a central role may also look awry. We take these issues up in both Chapter 2 where we explore New Labour's construction of the citizen-consumer and in Chapter 7 where we examine the sorts of identifications and relationships that people using public services valued.

These different perspectives also inform – both positively and negatively – a further dimension of our inquiry into New Labour's citizen-consumers and public service reform. In each of the perspectives, we have traced links between the general theorising about contemporary societies and the phases that they are going through (reflexive modernity; neo-liberalism; advanced liberal governmentality) and the specifics of New Labour reforms. In most accounts, New Labour functions primarily as an exemplar of the general dynamics: as a reflexive Third Way ('Beyond Left and Right' in Giddens' terms, 1994); as a neo-liberal politics; or as a governmental practice of advanced liberalism. While these three perspectives certainly highlight different aspects of New Labour (and provide different political evaluations of its politics and policies), we are troubled by the way that the move between the general and the particular seems to over-simplify, reduce or essentialise the particular. New Labour turns out to be an example of the general trends, rather than something distinctively shaped by a particular conjuncture of time and place.

Our own interest is rather more focused on exploring New Labour as a distinctive political and governmental project both shaped by, and trying to direct, the particular conjuncture of the United Kingdom in the transition from the twentieth to the twenty-first century. We take this up further in the following chapter, but this orientation raises important questions about the relation between the particular and the general in theorising about social transitions and transformations. It may be that a study like ours simply adds detail and complexity to the larger scale theorisations of the present as advanced in our three perspectives. Such detail might provide interesting examples or complex illustrations but the complexities revealed are *analytically* inconsequential. The particular is, in the end, merely particular. Not surprisingly, our view differs from this – we think that the complications and complexities that our study reveals are analytically (and politically) consequential. We think they evoke the need for some 'rethinking' of reflexivity and modernity; of neo-liberalism and of advanced liberal governmentality. In particular, we see this study as restating the case for careful analytic attention to the condensed combinations of forces, movements, tendencies and possibilities that constitute conjunctures as the sites (and objects) of political and governmental projects. These concerns will recur throughout the book – and will be addressed again explicitly in the conclusion.

2

Public Service Reform: the Rise of the Citizen-Consumer

The citizen-consumer has formed a central figure in political discourse about the reform and modernisation of public services in the UK and beyond. In this chapter:

- we examine the rise of the citizen-consumer in political and policy discourse;
- we explore how this figure has both displaced and subordinated other terms in discourse about public services and their reform;

In doing so we draw on Raymond Williams' approach to 'keywords' in cultural analysis (1976; see also Bennett et al., 2005). Williams was interested in how particular words were adapted, changed and deployed in the debates about relationships between culture and society. For him, this meant avoiding the preoccupation with uncovering the proper or correct meaning of words, and engaging instead in an inquiry into 'historical and contemporary semantics' through which one might trace:

> ... a history and complexity of meanings, conscious changes, or consciously different uses; innovation, obsolescence, specialization, extension, overlap, transfer; or changes which are masked by a nominal continuity so that words which seem to have been there for centuries, with continuous general meanings, have in fact come to express radically different or radically variable, yet sometimes hardly noticed, meanings and implications of meaning. (1976: 17)

Writing in the first half of the 1970s, Williams was already drawing attention to how the 'dominance of the capitalist model' meant the 'extension or attempted extension' of the word consumers to 'such fields as politics, education and health' (1976: 70). In this chapter, we focus on how the citizen and consumer have become hyphenated in more recent political discourse, and what the consequences might be for the relationships between publics and public services.

However we want to make two points that frame the analysis in important ways. First, as we argued in Chapter 1, such studies need to be attentive to particular configurations of time and space: a focus that has been described as conjunctural analysis (see, for example, Grossberg, 2006; Hall, 1996; and Williams' discussion of 'authentic historical analysis', 1977: 121–3). More specifically, the process of constituting 'citizen-consumers' takes place in the context of specific national cultural formations, rather than in some universal or global form. By insisting on the specificity of national cultural formations, we do not mean to imply that such formations are spatially closed. Our conception of the nation refers to a relationally constituted political and cultural space, formed in and through varieties of transnational conditions and connections (Clarke, 2005b; Clarke and Fink, forthcoming; Sharma and Gupta, 2006). But nations in this sense are particular places and remain one of the privileged sites of political and cultural conflict. Frank Trentmann, writing about the emergence of notions of consumerism in the nineteenth and twentieth-centuries, argues that:

> Before there could be a popular notion of consumer sovereignty, the consumer had to be cultivated. The consumer as a project took different shape in different traditions – in national economics in Imperial Germany the consumer was appropriated for the project of building a strong community and economy, whereas in Britain it fused into a language of liberal self and citizenship. (2006a: 9)

As we argue below, the figure of the public service consumer in the UK was framed by this liberal tradition, especially in the radical conservatism of the Thatcher years. However our main focus is on the ways in which the citizen-consumer – an uneasy, hyphenated figure – emerged in the context of struggles to create new political settlements in the late twentieth and early twenty-first centuries. Our focus is on the New Labour governments in the UK, but their attempts to introduce modernising reforms are located in a context in which, it was widely argued, the European 'social model' or social democratic welfare states were becoming unsustainable. The New Labour project has important resonances (as well as institutional connections) with other European governments of the centre and centre left, and with the compound neo-liberal/neo-conservative formations that dominated US politics and policy in the same period.

Secondly we need to highlight the limitations of focusing exclusively on governmental strategies and discourses. The citizen-consumer did not spring ready made from the pens of government speech-writers or policy drafters, but was constructed in relation to other social, cultural and political movements, tendencies and discourses. The consumer might, as Trentmann argues, be 'cultivated' by governments and other powerful actors, but:

> Whether the consumer 'took off' as a social identity... was ultimately not determined by academic traditions [of different nation states] but by the ability of political languages to provide a synapse between these new analytical categories and social movements and popular politics. (2006a: 9)

We are, then, interested in the ways in which governmental discourses on consumerism attempt to create 'synapses' with such movements and popular sensibilities, drawing on, amplifying, transforming and institutionalising the challenges presented by such movements and orientations. In doing so, governmental discourses may also transform – or even residualise – the politics that shaped their development (on such 'transformism', see Steinberg and Johnson, 2004a and Hall, 2003). In what follows we begin by tracing some of the precursors to New Labour's 'citizen-consumers' in the Conservative governments of the 1980s and 1990s. We then turn to a more detailed examination of the place and significance of the citizen-consumer in New Labour's approach to modernising and reforming public services. Here we explore New Labour's account of the centrality of a 'consumer culture' to the emergence of a 'modern' society; and subsequently explore New Labour's discursive negotiation of the multiple political and cultural conditions to construct a synaptic connection between the public and public service reform through the figure of the citizen-consumer. Finally we step back a little to consider the problems of making sense of New Labour as a political and governmental project.

Discovering the consumer within: Conservative approaches to public services

As we suggested in the Introduction, one critical condition for the rise of the citizen-consumer was the elaboration of a neo-liberal view of the world – one that emphasises the antagonism between the state and the market as forms of social coordination, and that produces an imperative to dissolve that antagonism by enlarging the reach of the market. In the UK, this view was promulgated by the Thatcherite Conservative Party that came to power in 1979 and was itself part of a transatlantic New Right. Although there had been other views of 'consuming' public services before then, the trajectory of the contemporary figure of the citizen-consumer takes off from this political-cultural moment (and is paralleled in other Anglophone states, see, for example, Larner, 1997).

Choice – and its capacity to articulate the contrast between the active consumer and the passive citizen – was a key element of Thatcherite anti-statism and anti-welfarism. Although often combined rhetorically and in specific policies, anti-statism and anti-welfarism were never exactly the same thing. Anti-statism sought to rework the boundaries between public and private in both its meanings: as the distinction between market and state; and as the division between public institutions of the market and the state, and the private sphere of the household/family. Anti-welfarism sought to rework state power and its relation to the 'social' (including the private/ familial sphere). It combined the neo-liberal and conservative tendencies of the New Right in its claims to liberate the 'entrepreneurial spirit' and create independence in place of the demoralising 'dependency culture' created by state benefits (Clarke, 1991: Chapter 6). The transatlantic

New Right consistently emphasised the difference between the virtues of the Market in contrast to the oppressive, inefficient and monopolistic State.

A key element in the articulation of the citizen-consumer was provided by the rise of public choice theory (e.g., Dunleavy, 1991; Niskanen, 1971) which offered an 'economic' critique of public bureaucracies and provided one of the intellectual cornerstones for the 'New Public Management' (Clarke and Newman, 1997). Pointing to the perverse combination of absent market disciplines and the potency of incentives to 'empire building', careerism, and an inwards focusing of organisational attention, public choice theory challenged claims that such bureaucracies were led or guided by a public service ethos (du Gay, 2000, 2005). On the contrary, the approach suggested that public servants were just as self-interested and venal as everyone else – but were not inhibited in the pursuit of such self-interest by the challenges and controls of market dynamics. In the elaboration of this view, public choice theory distinguished between Producer interests and Consumer interests, with bureaucratic monopolies being driven by Producer interest at the expense of the Consumer.

> The movement towards a free and more competitive economy necessitates a sceptical attitude towards the state. The market theorist doubts that officials, elected or appointed, are motivated to act for the public good. He assumes they are no less immune to self-interest than familiar market transactors. Elected politicians are likely to provide policies favourable to politically significant interest groups while officials are motivated by non-pecuniary forms of aggrandisement, such as expansions of the size of their bureaux. (Barry, 1991: 233)

The binary split between consumer and producer interests was elaborated in relation to other figures in the New Right imaginary. In the UK, Thatcherism drew distinctions between the tax-payer, the consumer and the scrounger (Clarke, 1997). The tax-payer was defined as a fiscal subject, having an interest in the efficient and economical provision of public services: driving down costs could drive down the 'tax burden' (Cooper, 1998: 83). In contrast, the 'scrounger' fraudulently or unreasonably exploited public services (especially income maintenance systems) and, in doing so, added to the excessive burden on the tax-payer. The 'consumer' was the non-exploitative, non-fraudulent user of public services who had an interest in service quality, responsiveness and 'value for money'.

The consumer/choice link was a potent feature of Thatcherism's remaking of the welfare state and public services in the UK during the 1980s. Most notable were the decision to sell council houses to tenants in the Housing Act of 1980 and the creation of a quasi-market to enable school 'choice' in the Education Reform Act of 1988 (see, for example, Fergusson, 1998; Forrest and Murie, 1991; Gewirtz et al., 1995; Pryke, 1998). Choice was identified as the defining characteristic of the consumer's relation to public services and had a complex relationship to marketising processes (see, *inter alia*, Bartlett et al., 1998; Johnson, 1995). The 'right to buy' in housing dissolved (partially) the distinction between the public and private sector, and shifted public resources (at a subsidised price) into private ownership. Choice in schooling gave parents (as the proxy consumers of education) the non-cash mediated right to choose schools for their children. More precisely, it gave them the right to *express* a choice of school since not all parents ever achieved their school of choice. As a result, parents attempted to choose schools – and schools got to choose children (and their parents). Elsewhere, a commitment to 'market stimulation' involved spending public money on creating markets of competing providers (for example, in the field of domiciliary and residential care following the 1990 National Health Service and Community Care Act). Competition between providers (whether in an 'internal' or an 'open' market) was expected to drive down costs, improve efficiency and deliver better results to the users or consumers of services (Cutler and Waine, 1997: Chapter 3).

The development of the citizen-consumer was to take a further turn in the post-Thatcherite landscape of British politics. The Conservative party in the 1990s turned to the 'consumer' interest as a way of realigning the relationship between the public, government and public services. Thatcherism had been profoundly antithetical to conceptions of the public and 'society', inclining towards privatisation either to the market or to the household. While continuing the trend towards markets, however, the Major governments adopted a stance of improving the quality of public services. This commitment was embodied in The Citizen's Charter (launched in 1991) and the subsequent proliferation of further 'Charters' for a range of other public services. The Citizen's Charter (and its offspring) articulated a particular fusion of consumerism and managerialism in public service provision (Clarke, 1997; Pollitt, 1994). Six principles of public service were identified:

- Setting, monitoring and publication of explicit standards
- Information for, and openness to, the service user
- Choice where practicable, plus regular and systematic consultation with users
- Courtesy and helpfulness
- Well-publicised and easy-to-use complaints procedures
- Value for money (Prime Minister, 1992, cited in Pollitt, 1994: 9)

This new articulation of the citizen and consumer involved a particular positioning of government as mediator in the relationship between the public and public services. Increasingly, the reform of public service provision had placed service providers at 'arm's length' from government. Marketisation, devolution, decentralisation and the construction of Agencies responsible for delivery (as opposed to policy-making or strategy) were distinctive features in the emergent new governance of public services (Clarke and Newman, 1997; Flynn, 1997). This new mode of governance enabled the government to position itself as the 'People's

Champion' – acting on behalf of users/consumers against recalcitrant, inflexible or incompetent service providers. The move away from direct provision to a model of government as funder, strategist, regulator and evaluator created the discursive space – the 'arm's length' – in which this new identity could be elaborated. The government would challenge service providers to perform on our behalf. And armed with the shield of the Citizen's Charter, we could imagine ourselves as citizen-consumers, since what the Charters established were not the *substantive* rights of citizens but the *process* rights of consumers. Despite such efforts, one of the critical conditions for the electoral success of New Labour in 1997 was their celebration of the importance of public services – and the commitment to modernise them.

From a rationing culture to a consumer culture: narrating public service reform

New Labour came to power in the UK in 1997 committed to a programme of public service reform and modernisation. This commitment reflected a typically confusing mixture of continuity with, and change from, the preceding period of Conservative governments. Public services had already experienced 18 years of reform under those governments, in which they had been subjected to diverse principles and mechanisms – fiscal retrenchment, privatisation, decentralisation, marketisation and quasi-marketisation – whose variety was stitched together by the connective thread of managerialism (Clarke and Newman, 1997). In this sense, the reforming zeal with which New Labour addressed public services had some strong continuities with the experience of 'permanent revolution' in the Conservative era. New Labour's original commitment to maintain Conservative public spending limits deepened this sense of continuity. At the same time, though, New Labour spoke of public service values and public purposes. They stressed processes of collaboration, partnership and 'joined-up' government as alternatives to the fragmented and competitive world of services created by Conservative reforms (Newman, 2001). This positive disposition to public values and public service seemed like a sharp break with 18 years of Conservative degradation.

In New Labour's eyes, public services were in need of reform and modernisation to bring them into line with defining characteristics of the modern world. This conception of modernity was a powerful organising theme in New Labour discourse: defining a sense of time, constructing New Labour's 'newness', disarming criticism ('old thinking') and linking questions of the nation's future to its place in a modern world. There are potent links to the sociology of modernity that we discussed in Chapter 1, not least for how the definition of the modern necessitated the emergence of a political Third Way (see Finlayson, 2003a). The modern world differed from the old world in which public services were created – the moment of post-war social democracy – in a number of critical ways (Clarke and Newman, 1998, 2004). Talking about the need for welfare reform in 1998, the Prime Minister argued that:

> Reform is a vital part of rediscovering a true national purpose, part of a bigger picture in which our country is a model of a 21st century developed nation: with sound, stable economic management; dynamism and enterprise in business; the best educated and creative nation in the world; and a welfare state that promotes our aims and achievements.
>
> But we should not forget why reform is right, and why, whatever the concerns over individual benefits, most people **know** it is right. Above all, the system must change because the world has changed, beyond the recognition of Beveridge's generation. The world of work has altered – people no longer expect a job for life; traditional industries have declined; new technologies have taken their place. There is a premium on skills and re-skilling through life. The role of women has been transformed. Family structures are different. We live longer, but work for fewer years. And the expectations of disabled people have changed out of all recognition, from half a century ago. We need a system designed not for yesterday, but for today. (Prime Minister, Foreword to Secretary of State for Social Security and Minister for Welfare Reform, 1998, iii–iv)

In this discourse of modernity, globalisation had changed the economy and the forms and habits of work that were valued in it. Gender roles and patterns of family or household formation had altered, and, most importantly for public services, Britain had become a 'consumer society' or a 'consumer culture' in which a proliferation of goods and services enabled a wide variety of wants and needs to be satisfied. Such a dazzling array of choice, it was felt, highlighted the mean austerity of public services, whose 'one size fits all' model of provision was shaped by the experience of wartime and post-war rationing:

> Many of our public services were established in the years just after the Second World War. Victory had required strong centralised institutions, and not surprisingly it was through centralised state direction that the immediate post-war Government chose to win the peace. This developed a strong sense of the value of public services in building a fair and prosperous society. The structures created in the 1940s may now require change, but the values of equity and opportunity for all will be sustained. The challenges and demands on today's public services are very different from those post-war years. The rationing culture which survived after the war, in treating everyone the same, often overlooked individuals' different needs and aspirations… Rising living standards, a more diverse society and a steadily stronger consumer culture have… brought expectations of greater choice, responsiveness, accessibility and flexibility. (Office of Public Services Reform, 2002: 8)

The rise of a consumer culture is much debated in academic circles. The conditions, characteristics and consequences of such a society – and its consuming subjects – remain the focus of considerable controversy (see, *inter alia*, Edwards, 2000; Gabriel and Lang, 1995; Hilton, 2006; Lury, 1996; Miller, 1998; Mort, 1996; Trentmann, 2006b). Such debates have little direct connection to New Labour's narrative, though they surely shape its sensibility about the 'modern', especially in the links between consumption and identity. Steinberg and Johnson suggest that this conception of the consumer culture is central to New Labour's conception of citizens:

> The Blairite citizen is invited, rather than exhorted, to affirm, to assimilate, to include him/herself in the (neo)modernising project of state allied to market. This is the consumer citizen, who harnesses his/her own active agency in the exercise of market choices and branded identities; proletarianises his/her own labour; inserts him/herself into the marketised collectivity. This is the worldly, globalising citizen, of an intellectually muscular, arbitrating and moral nation, who does not hanker back to former glory in empire, but forward to a world of nations, a world community of markets and assimilationist values. (2004a: 31–2)

If these conditions defined the 'modern world', they also constituted the reference points against which public services should be judged as well as indicating the mechanisms and direction of 'reform'. The narrative of modernity as consumer culture was a recurrent and compelling one in New Labour approaches to public services. Almost every policy document and many of the major speeches grounded themselves in this conception of the tradition to modernity symbolised by the figure of the consumer. It was a narrative that used social change as the imperative for public service reform:

> People grow up today in a consumer society. Services – whether they are private or public – succeed or fail according to their ability to respond to modern expectations… People today exercise more choices in their lives than at any point in history. Many can afford to walk away from public services which do not command their confidence. (Milburn, 2002c)

In this approach to public service reform, choice came to play an increasingly central role. Whereas early formulations of public service reform tended to stress responsiveness and accessibility to users, by 2004–5 choice was signalled as the crucial element of reform in health care, education and social care. We will discuss this further in later chapters, but it is worth underscoring here how choice emerged as both the defining feature of the consumer experience and the 'lever' for reforming sluggish or recalcitrant public services. Indeed, choice was multi-talented and multi-purpose for New Labour. In a submission to the 2004–5 Public Administration Select Committee on Choice and Voice in Public Services, Ministers of State argued that choice must be central to public services reform because:

- It's what users want;
- It provides incentives for driving up quality, responsiveness and efficiency;

- It promotes equity;
- It facilitates personalisation. (Ministers of State, 2004: 4)

Each of these claims is, in practice, rather more controversial and contested than the statement suggests (a debate in part carried on in the Committee's report and the Cabinet Office's response: Public Administration Select Committee, 2005; Cabinet Office, 2005; see also Clarke et al., 2006).

The consumerist orientation, the growing salience of choice and the way in which choice functions as a proxy for processes of marketisation and privatisation have led some commentators to treat New Labour as the continuation of Conservative neo-liberalism or as merely another example of global neo-liberal hegemony (see, *inter alia*, Harvey, 2005; Marquand, 2004; Needham, 2003; Pollock, 2004). Though such directions do form a strong element of New Labour's politics and policy, there are problems about how to make sense of the complexities, contradictions and paradoxes of New Labour. The attempt to identify the 'core' elements of New Labour typically involves peeling away the layers of ideology, obfuscation and 'mere rhetoric' to lay bare the 'real' character. This strategy has also been used by political and media critics of the right who have been anxious to reveal New Labour's true character as a 'tax and spend' party of the Left. We are not wholly persuaded by such distinctions between rhetorical veneers and real truths. They tend to insist on an underlying unity or coherence to political and governmental projects – a unity that seems difficult to discern amidst New Labour's pro-market, anti-poverty, individualistic, communitarian and managerialist tendencies, to say nothing of their peculiar compound of modernising social liberalism and traditionalist social/moral authoritarianism. Treating political discourse as 'mere rhetoric' denies much of the significance of rhetoric as political-cultural work. We think that 'rhetoric' might point to the discursive labour of constructing the necessity, plausibility and desirability for some directions; of mobilising social forces (and de-mobilising others); and of negotiating divergent and potentially conflicting political-cultural perspectives that clutter up the conjuncture.

These concerns have led our analysis in two related directions. The first involves the questions of discursive work introduced above; the second addresses the conjunctural conditions of political and governmental projects such as New Labour. We have come to treat political discursive practice as an active process in which positions are negotiated, displaced, subordinated and co-opted. That is, we do not treat New Labour as 'expressing' a discourse: it does not exemplify neo-liberalism or advanced liberal governmentality, nor any of the many other discourses, philosophies or ideologies with which it has been associated (Newman, forthcoming). Rather, as a political project, New Labour appropriates, borrows and bends multiple discursive resources – assembling them into a complex (and shifting) form. Such resources are deployed in attempts to negotiate dilemmas and contradictions that confront New Labour. This active and negotiated sense of discourse owes rather more to the development of discourse analysis by social psychologists (e.g., Billig, 1995; Wetherell and Potter, 1992; Wetherell et al., 2001) than to the rather more integrated or coherent conception of discourse derived from Foucault's work on knowledge and power. In the following sections, we will be examining some of the ways in which 'consumerism' works to articulate different discursive resources (and the social imaginaries they invoke) into an apparently coherent model of public service reform.

These different discursive resources co-existed in the conjuncture in which New Labour rose to power. Conjunctures are particular formations of time and space in which multiple forces, pressures, tendencies and possibilities are condensed (Grossberg, 2006). Conjunctural analysis provides a way of breaking the assumptions built into linear histories and challenging their sense of inevitability. Taking conjunctures as containing multiple forces and multiple possibilities enables us to see how political projects attempt to construct coherence out of this multiplicity and create the apparent necessity of a particular future. Such political discursive work has different facets. Some tendencies must be emphasised (modernity as consumer culture) while others are obscured (deepening inequalities, deepening indebtedness). Some forces and conflicts may be engaged with and appropriated (as we shall see 'diversity' is a crucial symbolic resource for New Labour), while others are dismissed to the past, or de-mobilised as redundant. Some voicings (figures, languages, ways of speaking) are taken up, others dropped or disdained. In the process, the political and governmental project aims to construct a direction out of the conjuncture ('modernisation'), assemble the economic and social forces necessary to realise it, create the powers and institutional arrangements to make it come true – and manage the work of micro-political calculation to sustain the political rule that enables the work of the governmental transformation.

Assembling the citizen-consumer: equality, diversity and choice

The development of the citizen-consumer as a central figure around which reform and modernisation was mobilised has to be understood in the context of the strained and contradictory political and cultural landscape that New Labour encountered. In this landscape a variety of political-cultural forces had challenged and destabilised the 'public realm', dislocating institutionalised conceptions of the public, the public interest and public services (Clarke, 2004c). Among these forces were both deep-rooted, long-running trends and more immediate pressures. As a political project, New Labour faced choices about how to inhabit this landscape, how to manage or reconcile the contending forces and how to rework these conditions in order to inhabit 'the modern world' (Miliband, 2000). Here we wish to stress the multiple currents with which New Labour has engaged in its construction of a consumerist model for public service reform. They include:

- The displacement of social, political and institutional patterns of 'deference' by a demotic populism in which lay, popular or ordinary voices, experiences and views are increasingly 'authorised';
- The impact of social movements on normative orders of hierarchy, power and conduct, including challenging the 'institutional discriminations' inscribed within the policies, personnel and practices of public services;
- The impact of 'user movements' on established systems of public service provision and their distinctive combinations of authority and expertise, including the view that users of services are 'experts of their condition';
- Persistent desires for high quality public services, especially in the context of Conservative erosion of provision and financing combined with increasing 'conditionality' of services and benefits;
- Persistent concerns about forms of social inequality and their impact on public services.

Each of these contributes something distinctive to New Labour's approach to reform. We might suggest that each gives rise to a particular trope: demotic populism manifests itself as 'voice'; social movements as 'diversity'; user movements as 'lay expertise'; desires for public services as 'quality' or 'standards'; and concerns about inequality as 'fairness'. Each of these tropes is a site of discursive articulation between these social dynamics and New Labour's consumerist model of reform. Each becomes condensed in – and given voice by – the image of consumer choice.

The New Labour project certainly drew on some core inheritances from Thatcherite conservatism, and the transatlantic New Right more generally. Neo-liberalism had simultaneously challenged the form of service provision (the monolithic and monopolistic state/public bureaucracies); the cost of provision (excessive public spending unchecked by market/ competitive disciplines); and the collectivist image of the public (passive recipients rather than enterprising individuals making their own choices). Neo-liberalism had attempted to bring about a decisive ideological-political-discursive shift that involved remaking a whole field of relationships: between economy and society; between economy and politics; between people and states; between the public and the private; and between nations and the global, for example (see, *inter alia*, Cameron and Palan, 2004; Clarke, 2004b: Chapter 5; Larner and Walters, 2004). For New Labour, neo-liberalism manifested itself in the conception of modernity – a global economy requiring flexible labour forces and a consumer society in which freedom was closely associated with making (spending) choices.

But neo-liberalism was not the only register of changing relationships and expectations in the troubled intersection between the public and public services. New Labour's narrative of the societal shift from a rationing culture to a consumer culture also offered a potent shorthand for other dimensions and dynamics of social change. This narrative was strongly articulated to the 'markets versus states' position since it valorised market-based experience and expectation, treating them as the basis of new calculative norms. People, it was assumed, had come to view public services through a frame of reference grounded in the experience of being treated as consumers elsewhere.

The consumer culture narrative provided a way of 'voicing' dissatisfactions and discontents about the quality, accessibility and responsiveness of public services. Although New Labour gained substantial political support for its commitment to public services, this popular base was not uncritical of the standards and quality of services (reflecting the under-investment and fragmenting reforms of Conservative governments). While promising to reform and modernise public services, New Labour could not avoid addressing issues of equality, not least since it had to continue to speak to its traditional electoral supporters as well as win over liberal/progressive sections of the middle classes. 'Welfarism' has always been associated – albeit loosely – with social democratic or reformist images of social change, improvement and progress. To some extent, this implied mitigating the effect of social inequalities.

New Labour had worked hard to displace this 'Old Left' concern with material inequality. It substituted a concern with 'social exclusion' for more traditional party concerns with 'poverty', while also embarking on a programme of targeted public spending intended to eradicate child poverty. But it systematically residualised the concern with inequality as old-fashioned: a hangover from older ways of thinking. Instead, it offered an abbreviated concern with 'equity' as the guiding principle of social progress. In New Labour terms, a consumer-centred model of public services would both promote equity and overcome the problems of inequality associated with 'old' public services:

> Those on the left who defend the status quo on public services defend a model that is one of entrenched inequality. I repeat: the system we inherited was inequitable. It was a two-tier system. Our supposedly uniform public services were deeply unequal as league and performance tables in the NHS and schools have graphically exposed. ... The affluent and well educated ... had the choice to buy their way out of failing or inadequate provision – a situation the Tories 'opting out' reforms of the 1980s encouraged. It was a choice for the few, not for the many. (Blair, 2003a).

Critics of the choice agenda in public services were challenged by a characteristic New Labour device, the charge of elitism: 'It is frequently asserted – often by those who have a good deal of choice in their own lives – that users of public services do not in fact want choice' (Ministers of State, 2004: 4).

The idea of 'choice for the many, not the few' emerged as an anchoring point for the second argument about inequality: that by extending choice to active consumers of public services, equity would be enlarged:

> Extending choice – for the many, not the few – is a key aspect of opening up the system in the way we need. But choice for the many because it boosts equity. It does so for three reasons. First, universal choice gives poorer people the same choices available only to the middle-classes. It addresses the current inequity where the better off can switch from poor providers. But we also need pro-active choice (for example, patient care advisers in the NHS) who can explain the range of options available to each patient. Second, choice sustains social solidarity by keeping better off patients and parents within the NHS and public services... Third, choice puts pressure on low quality providers that poorer people currently rely on. It is choice with equity we are advancing. Choice and consumer power as the route to greater social justice not social division. (Blair, 2003a)

Equity here became a matter of dealing with forms of unequal access to, or treatment by, public services. This was a rather limited view of the relationship between public services and inequality, since it ignored the longer political debate about whether public services should remedy, rather than reproduce, patterns of social inequality. But even there, New Labour conceptions of social inequality were distinctive. In relation to public services, two conceptions of inequality dominated. The first was the 'postcode lottery', an idea that combined the idea of spatially unequal access to services with a model of chance – the lottery. It conflated active postcode allocative decisions with local variations in policy making which might determine local health or public provision priorities. As the Chancellor put it 'Local autonomy without national standards may lead to increased inequality between people and regions and the return of the postcode lotteries' (Brown, 2003).

Secondly, since the 1960s, other inequalities (generated by the dynamics of 'difference') had pressed onto the reform/progress agenda: most obviously inequalities of gender and race/ethnicity. Social movements had challenged the inequalities apparently embodied in 'difference' and had some success in constructing an 'equalities' orientation – gaining legislative and governmental institutionalisation for (uneven) commitments to equal treatment and the prevention of discriminatory behaviour. To some extent, normative expectations had been established that public services would seek to remedy inequalities; and that they would not reproduce such inequalities in their own policies and practices (in the form of institutional sexism, racism and so on). This had been institutionalised as the political/policy terrain of 'Equal Opportunities' (locally, nationally and supra-nationally, especially through the EU and European Court of Human Rights).

The challenge for New Labour was to continue to draw on the language of equality but to redefine this for the 'modern' conception of nation and people by a focus on 'equity', 'opportunity' and 'choice'. This was accomplished by the transformation of 'diversity' in New Labour discourse. For the most part, New Labour treated such equality struggles as belonging to an earlier era – and viewed them as having produced successful outcomes. Instead a more 'person-centred' view of diversity replaced the list of categoric differences. Although forms of socio-demographic difference were sometimes referred to (a list of women, minority ethnic communities, young people, old people and the 'hard to reach', for example), these were rarely seen as the site of structural inequalities. The dominant meaning of diversity in the New Labour lexicon was of a nation rich in individual differences of needs, wants and expectations. It was this diversity that must motivate public services.

> The challenge for public services is to provide universal services that are also personalised to individual need, in a consumer driven age ... we won't have a fair society if we don't face up to these challenges. (Blair, 2003b: 2)

> Since every person has differing requirements, their rights will not be met simply by providing a 'one size fits all' service. The public expects diversity of provision as well as national standards. (Office of Public Services Reform, 2002: 13)

This conception of diversity flattened structured difference (and its inequality producing effects) into a field of idiosyncratic and individualised wants, needs and desires. These individuated members of the public closely resembled the individuals-as-consumers imagined in neo-classical economics. What located or motivated their differences did not matter – what did matter were the desires that they brought to market (and the money needed to satisfy them).

The rise of neo-liberalism, struggles over poverty and class inequalities and the challenges of social movements around equality and citizenship were broad forces that played across public services during the late twentieth and early twenty-first century in Britain, and influenced the policies and strategies of other centre and centre-left governments in Europe (and the EU itself). Their specific power and effectivity clearly varied – but their combined effect unsettled the public realm and the place of public services within it. We want to stress their *combined* effect, since there are too many accounts that take one of these as if it was the main or even only story. Despite these widespread discontents, disturbances and dislocations, the other critical feature of the landscape that New Labour entered was the surprising persistence of public enthusiasm, and demand, for public services (Taylor-Gooby and Hastie, 2003).

The figure of the citizen-consumer provided one focal point for the attempted resolution of these contending forces into a political and governmental project. We do not mean to suggest that it was the only one, but it provided a sort of coherence that linked different domains of the public realm and public interest (including information, media and communication policies: see the discussion of the citizen-consumer in

Hesmondhalgh, 2005 and Livingstone et al., 2006). The citizen-consumer underpinned an approach to transforming public services that engaged public demand (for public services); constructed political support (within the electorate for investment and improvement); addressed political doubt (in the public and the party about New Labour's values and ethos); and embraced 'modern' conceptions of diversity, equity and service.

The dominance of this meaning of diversity was closely coupled to the idea of choice. Like the market/private sector, public services are needed to enable people to choose. As will become clear, choice here meant the public making choices in the context of the public services they consume. This is different from an older (New Liberal and social democratic) view of the role of public services being to enable citizens to make choices in their lives by providing the services and resources needed to create the conditions of, and capacities for, choice making. Choice could mean a rather inchoate variety of things in the context of public services – choice of school, choice of curriculum in the school, choice of university, course of study, level of fees, etc. – but it was central to current New Labour discourse (see Greener, 2003).

But it leaves open questions about what sort of political calculation the choice agenda represented. Was choice a proxy for electoral ambition and popular mobilisation? Choice has been a focus of popular ambivalence, evoking both desire and scepticism (Clarke et al., 2006). Promising to extend choice 'from the few to the many' was a characteristic form of New Labour's populism and anti-elitism. Alternatively, choice could be seen as a way of addressing the political problem of the middle classes: 'Offering choice is one way in which we can bind into the public sector those that can afford to go private' (Byers, 2003). By promising choice in valued public services (especially education and health), the defection of the affluent to privately purchased choices could be averted and their votes secured.

Whichever was the dominant political calculation, what was being presented was a conception of choice that had been thoroughly colonised by the market model. People had wants, needs or desires and they could choose the (commodified) goods or services that would satisfy them. Choices could be realised (or enforced) through the medium of money: the cash-nexus connects producer and consumer. Two points stand out here. First, this is a relatively impoverished (or, at least, very specific) conception of choice and the means through which choices might be realised. As Bevir and Trentmann (2006) have argued, there are other models and practices of choice that have been occluded by this dominant model of the rationally choosing market based individual. As many studies of consumption practices have indicated, market-based shopping does not resemble the rational choice-making model very closely. Second, people also formulate many choices in their lives that never come near the marketplace, and have many modes of trying to realise such choices (power, negotiation, seduction, compromise, collaboration, brute force, emotional manipulation, voting, for example). This raises a distinctive question of

power or, more accurately, a question of modes of power. In their celebration of 'consumer society' New Labour often draw attention to the
consumer power of the private sector. This is a specific and unequally distributed form of power: it is literally 'spending power' in the form of
money or credit. In the absence of money, it is not clear what other mode
of power can ensure the realisation (or enforcement) of choice in public
services. We will return to this question of power later.

In our name? The citizen-consumer as governmental project

Earlier in this chapter we highlighted the importance of understanding
consumerism in the context of particular national formations, and posed
the question as to whether New Labour simply represented a continuance
of the generic New Right project of neo-liberal governance, or whether it
has to be understood as a specific political and governmental project with
its own inherent tensions and instabilities. We have identified several
ways in which New Labour's policies drew on, but reworked, other
movements and discourses, at the same time as installing a new emphasis on choice supported by an extension of competition between service
providers. The citizen-consumer, then, formed a means of reconciling
potentially antagonistic conceptions of the public realm, the public interest and the future of public services (Hughes, 1998).

The paradoxical co-existence of apparently divergent political positions
was a recurrent, if not quintessential, feature of New Labour. It is one that
figured in attempts to characterise the political and policy directions, for
example, 'neo-liberal humanism' (Andrews, 1999); 'liberal conservatism'
(Driver and Martell, 1998) or 'post-social communitarianism' (Fitzpatrick,
1998; see also Clarke et al., 2000). It is also a feature that New Labour
attributed to itself in conceptions of the Third Way as a politics of reconciling and transcending apparently contradictory political positions –
between Left and Right (or Old Left and New Right); between market and
state; between freedom and equality (see Blair, 1998 and Giddens, 1998).
In this spirit, New Labour's invention of the hyphenated 'citizen-
consumer' is hardly surprising. The hyphenation of those two apparently
counterposed identifications marks the site of intense political discursive
work to announce, accomplish and secure governmental change.

This governmental project had two core aspects. One was the continuing programme of state reform (sometimes referred to as modernisation)
in which the apparatuses, agencies, agents and practices of governing are
being revised (Newman, 2001). The other was the reconstruction of the
'social' – the work of imagining and constructing a new 'modern' British
people (Clarke and Newman, 1998, 2004). State reform since the 1980s has
involved multiple dynamics – privatisation, marketisation, contractuali-
sation, pluralisation, managerialisation, decentralisation, overlaid by a
more recent enthusiasm for 'partnership' (Glendinning et al., 2002). In this

context, however, we would want to emphasise the dis-integration or dispersal of the state: processes of organisational fragmentation and proliferation combined with the intensification of centralised powers of control and direction (Clarke, 2006b; Clarke and Newman, 1997).

The emergence of a dispersed state form was accompanied by new systems of governing public services 'at arm's length' (Clarke et al., 2000; Clarke, 2004b: Chapters 6 and 7; Newman, 2001). These involved new alignments of centralised control in decentralised and devolved systems with quasi-competitive relationships between multiple 'providers' (constructed around target setting, performance management, evaluation and regulation, for example). But the 'arm's length' was also a discursive space: it separated government from the provision of public services, allowing a representation of government as the People's Champion against the Producer interest in public services. Here government (and its regulatory and evaluative agencies) simultaneously grasped the public as consumers, and identified themselves as the collective embodiment of the consumer interest. This marked a profound continuity with the neo-liberal tendency of Thatcherite conservatism and with the wider global project of neo-liberalism and its view of the public realm (see Hall, 1989, on Thatcherism as a distinctive form of populism; and Frank, 2001, on market populism).

This populist representation of government was also institutionalised in a distinctive set of practices in the performance management and scrutiny systems whose reach was enlarged by New Labour (Clarke, 2005c). In Daniel Miller's study of New Labour's 'Best Value' inspection regime for local government, he identifies the 'virtual consumer' as central to the conceptualisation of evaluation. The 'virtual consumer' is always represented by, or spoken for, by some other authority, while that authority in turn gains 'the authority of the consumer' (Keat et al., 1994). Miller argues that:

> The starting point was the rise of consumption as an increasingly important source of political authority… The consumer was becoming the ultimate arbiter of what should exist in the world. I argue that just as actual consumers seemed about to be, in some sense, empowered by being accredited this authority, it was in effect taken away from them by a whole series of institutions that usurped this authority. This leads to what might be called a fetishism of the consumer parallel to Marx's argument about the fetishism of the commodity as hiding its source in labour. Obvious examples of this seemed to me to include: first the power accrued to lawyers standing on behalf of consumer rights, second the power of the modern economist asserting academic models such as that of the free market that governments are supposed to conform to based on the claim that this is the best way the economy can serve consumers; third the huge increase in management consultancy and its claims to deliver clients and customers to those it advises …
>
> This logic seemed quite explicit and clear in the development of recent audits that seek to justify themselves as being carried out on behalf of 'patients as consumers' or 'students as consumers' or consumers more generally …
> (2005: 235)

Audit and inspection regimes such as Best Value position themselves as 'virtual consumers' – trying to represent the consumer point of view. But how do we understand 'the people' who New Labour claims to represent, and whose interests they seek to defend against unruly producer power? Here New Labour's conception derived primarily from the economics of neo-liberalism, specifically the critique of public services articulated in public choice theory (Finlayson, 2003b). Public services (as state/hierarchical/bureaucratic monopolies) were seen as being dominated and driven by the Producer interest, because the disciplining effects of market forces were absent. Producer interests were viewed as antagonistic to Consumer interests; in the marketplace, however, the (aggregate) effect of consumer power would keep Producers in line. In the process, public choice theory articulated a moral economy of 'mistrust', evoking a sceptical or cynical view of the 'public service ethos' as a smokescreen for venal and self-serving producer interests. New Labour's approach to public services took up this distinction between the Producer and Consumer as a key feature of the reform programme:

> All four principles [national standards, devolution, flexibility, choice] have one goal – to put the consumer first. We are making the public services user-led, not producer or bureaucracy led, allowing far greater freedom and incentives for services to develop as users want. (Tony Blair, Speech to Public Sector Workers at the British Library, London, 16 October 2001)

Although New Labour's consumerism drew on multiple voices, this neo-liberal conception of the sovereign consumer appears to be the central element around which the other, subordinate, elements were articulated. It was this that linked the consumer to the project of 'state reform' – connecting 'the people' to processes of privatisation, marketisation, systems of multiple providers, workforce recomposition and regulation, and systems of audit and inspection.

Hyphens and hybrids: New Labour's articulations

In the New Labour discourse about public service reform, then, the figure of the consumer dominated the reworking of ideas of the citizen. However this did not mark a wholesale dismantling of more collective terms: notions of the public, communities, service users and so on continued to appear. So, too, did more service specific terms, such as patients, passengers and parents, when health, public transport and education were being discussed:

> In reality, I believe people do want choice, in public services as in other services. But anyway, choice isn't an end in itself. It is one important mechanism to ensure that citizens can indeed secure good schools and health services in their communities. Choice puts the levers in the hands of parents and patients so that they as citizens and consumers can be a driving force for

improvement in their public services. We are proposing to put an entirely different dynamic in place to drive our public services; one where the service will be driven not by the government or by the manager but by the user – the patient, the parent, the pupil and the law-abiding citizen. (T. Blair, quoted in the *Guardian*, 24 June 2004: 1)

Nevertheless, these other identities were increasingly subordinated to – or articulated around – the idea of the consumer. It was this interlocking net of themes and identities that enabled the consumer to play such a central and organising role in New Labour discourse of public service reform in the UK. But how do we understand this process in which multiple identities (and the social relations they imply) were brought together in this uneasily hyphenated assemblage of *citizen-consumers*?

Some writers have used the idea of hybridity to analyse both New Labour and neo-liberalism. For example, Hesmondhalgh argues that:

> ... it is important to see the British Labour Party as having invented its own distinctive governmental project; one which undoubtedly involves neo-liberal elements, but on different terms from the neo-liberalism of the New Right of the Reagan and Thatcher governments of the 1980s. Labour represents a new hybrid. Such hybridity on the part of Labour governments is not new, but this does not mean that the Labour government is simply accommodating itself to capitalism in the same way as previous Labour governments ... there is a strong neo-liberal element to this hybrid governmental formation that takes for granted marketisation and the erosion of the public domain. (2005: 99)

But what are we to make of such hybrids: how does hybridisation work in political and governmental projects? Do the elements – whether neo-liberalism or communitarianism – retain their essential character, or are they transformed in the encounter with other discourses and positions? In a cross-national study of neo-liberalism and welfare reform, Catherine Kingfisher (2002) has drawn a distinction between the 'preliminary grammar' of neo-liberalism and its materialisation in different forms in different places. The 'preliminary grammar' of neo-liberalism (its general elements) is always embedded in hybrid formations: 'It is, in fact, only in the circulation of neoliberal related meanings and their articulation with other meaning systems that neoliberalism takes on its multiple and contradictory lives' (2002: 12).

Such a view draws attention to the contradictoriness and instability of political projects. They are alliances: assemblages of political discourses that are articulated *unities-in-difference*. They are forged in the face of paradoxes, tensions, incompatibilities and contradictions, rather than being coherent implementations of a unified discourse and plan (Clarke, 2004b: Chapter 5). This suggests two important features of the hyphenated citizen-consumer. The first is that the hyphen denotes the focus of political work: the effort to give the 'citizen' new meanings through its articulation with the image of the consumer. The second feature of this hyphenated articulation is that neo-liberalism comes to take on a particular local/national character precisely through its necessary encounters with other political discourses, oppositions and projects.

Stuart Hall has added to this view of articulation in describing this complex negotiation of neo-liberalism and other discourses as New Labour's characteristic 'double shuffle' (2003). He has argued that:

> New Labour is confusing in the signals it gives off, and difficult to characterise as a regime. It constantly speaks with a forked tongue. It combines economic neo-liberalism with a commitment to 'active government'. More significantly its grim alignment with the broad global interest and values of corporate capital and power – the neo-liberal, which is in the *leading position* in its political repertoire – is paralleled by another, *subaltern* programme, of a more social-democratic kind, running alongside. This is what people invoke when they insist, defensively, that New Labour is not, after all, 'neo-liberal'. The fact is that New Labour is a *hybrid* regime, composed of two strands. However, one strand – the neo-liberal – is in the dominant position. The other strand – the social democratic – is subordinate. What's more, its hybrid character is not simply a static formation: it is the process which combines the two elements which matters. The process is 'transformist'. The latter always remains subordinate to and dependent on the former, and *is constantly being 'transformed' into* the former, dominant one. (2003: 19)

The citizen-consumer provides one example of this discursive 'double shuffle' – working to subordinate and transform other conceptions of citizenship through the imagery of consumer choice and 'market populism' (Frank, 2001). It draws on, and gives voice to 'older' or 'residual' conceptions of citizenship (as well as more recent or emergent challenges to the state and public institutions). But it does so by voicing them through the figure of the consumer. The consumer appeared as the dominant identity by being able to represent all these other positions. They could be reconciled in the figure of the citizen-as-consumer – a figure deeply implicated in the neo-liberal, public choice and market populist discourses.

As a result, the citizen-consumer named new forms of relationship: between producers and publics, between government and service providers, between those commissioning services and those making choices in a marketised field of services. In its attempt to reconcile conflicting forces through a discourse centred on the citizen-consumer, New Labour can be viewed as attempting to articulate a national interest, purpose and sense of direction that 'took account of' other positions and projects, such as those associated with the movements and interests we mentioned earlier in this chapter. But it did so while articulating them as subordinate and supporting voices – tying them into the 'mission' and attempting to dissolve their differences (and thus status as alternatives) in the process. In the following chapters, we will address some of these issues in relation to three public services that demonstrate some of the diverse conditions, contradictions and consequences of reforming public services in a consumerist direction.

3

Delivery Problems? Consumerism and Institutional Variation

Our focus now moves from political discourse about the citizen-consumer and public service reform to the remaking of specific public services. The language of 'public service' tends to disguise the fact that there is no public service in general: our own study examined three services – health care, policing and social care – which have different characteristics and have been subjected to different reform pressures. In this chapter:

- we explore these differences of institutional and policy formation;
- we examine how New Labour's consumerist orientation was translated into the specific services;
- we use four core themes – Challenge, Choice, Inequality and Responsibility – to frame patterns of similarity and difference.

Each service involves specific forms of relationship between providers, the public and individual users. The three chosen for this study embody some critical differences about both the nature of their provision, and the forms of relationship that they involve. Health care has long been at the centre of debates about 'choice', the 'expert patient' and the de-centering of medical knowledge (Newman and Vidler, 2006a). Policing involved a distinctively 'authoritative' relationship between the service and the public, based in and involving the exercise of the law (Innes, 2003: 42). Central to the process of moving from police 'force' to police 'service' had been re-branding the organisation and re-thinking the relationships between the police and the public (Westmarland and Smith, 2004). By way of contrast, social care for older people had often been viewed as a 'Cinderella service', but the combination of demographic changes and the challenges to institutional care through the 1970s and 1980s made it a publicly and politically more visible domain of policy (Clarke, 2006c).

Each of these services was already in transition – engaged in the process of negotiating shifting conditions, pressures, demands and expectations (including those of central government). This changes how we might approach questions of institutional adaptation to consumerism. Institutional analysis highlights the power of embedded norms and rules (DiMaggio and Powell, 1991) or 'logics of appropriateness' (March and Olsen, 1989) to shape action. New stimuli – policy imperatives, user demands, societal shifts – are seen to be interpreted in line with existing norms, values or constructs, producing 'path dependent' trajectories of change. Adaptation over time can occur as a result of social agency; however emphasis tends to be placed on the role of agency in shaping continuity rather than change. We are not sure that our case studies fit this model of stability and adaptation. Far from being solidified institutional formations – a basis from which organisations or occupations might adapt to the demands of consumerism – the three services were already 'unsettled', already engaged in processes of change driven by other forces and pressures, already encountering questions about how to relate to the public or those who use/might use its services.

For instance, the medical profession has been a constant focus of complaints about its oppressive use of the combination of authority and expertise (expressed as failures to consult or communicate effectively in the practice of 'bio-medicine'). The institutional formation of the National Health Service had been subjected to waves of re-organisations since the 1980s that changed the internal 'architecture' of the service, revising the distinctions and relationships between different occupational groups, redrawing geographical and organisational boundaries, and reconstructing relationships with patients and the public.

In policing, arguments had raged since the 1970s about the appropriate forms of accountability that might link policing and different publics, some addressing local dimensions while others focused around discriminatory policing (Goldstein, 2005; Innes, 2005; Loader, 1999). At the same time, organisational and occupational reforms had taken place, ranging from the rise of a 'performance culture' based on tighter central government control and direction of the service to the police's more recently defined role as the key agency in community safety and community safety partnerships (Hughes and Edwards, 2002).

In social care, there had been significant challenges around issues of 'user empowerment' and the development of user centred services. Social care for older people had been marked by troubled relationships between needs, rights and resources (especially the question of who should pay for care). A long history of reorganisation of services, including the changing role of local authority social service/social work departments, was dominated by tendencies towards marketisation (the sub-contracting of service provision) and personalisation (the construction of individualised 'packages of care').

In these sorts of ways, the services we studied need to be seen as institutions that were already in a state of flux or transition before the arrival of specific policy initiatives emphasising the consumerist imperative. For us, then, the question for analysing these services was not merely the 'institutionalist' concern with how consumerism produced an adaptation to existing institutional norms, but how it encountered other trends, forces and pressures in the transitions that these services were undergoing. We need a sort of institutionalist analysis that makes sense of institutions that are unsettled, in flux and in motion. In developing this sort of analysis, we borrowed from a number of divergent sources. These include the work of Dorothy Smith on the processes of *mediated co-ordination* that regulate institutions, in which she emphasises the role of documents or text in creating institutional orders:

> Institutional texts are designed; they are ... interlocking (rather than intertextual); setting their categories, concepts and frames is highly politicized, not only in those settings ordinarily thought of as political. Texts are key to institutional coordinating, regulating the concerting of people's work in institutional settings in the ways they impose an accountability to the terms they establish. (2005: 118)

This points us to the 'text work' involved in institutions. Smith emphasises the way in which texts mediate interests, objectives and sites. In our case, the latter is particularly important for the relation between central government, specialist departments (the Home Office and the Department of Health in particular) and specific, localised, service organisations (and their internal order). There is a growing body of work that explicitly explores policy as discourse (Fischer, 2003; Marston, 2004), while many other studies have drawn on discourse analysis as a way of making sense of aspects of the intersections of politics, policy and organisational or institutional change (Clarke, 2004b; Clarke and Newman, 1997; Newman, 2001). As will be clear from the preceding chapters, our view of discourse in this study tends towards a concern with discursive practice, rather than the more formal identification of discourses as distinct and settled formations. In the move from policy to institutional practice, we are particularly concerned with processes of *interpretation* and *translation*. How do organisations 'make sense' of governmental imperatives? How do they weave them into existing trajectories? Through what existing discursive resources do they 'read' consumerism?

There are connections here to Smith's interest in 'text-reader conversations' in the activation of institutional discourses. She suggests that this phrase makes three linked processes visible:

1 It enables us to recognise the reading of a particular text as something that is being done in a particular local setting by a particular person.
2 It proposes that the reader, engaged in a text-reader conversation, plays two parts: first, she or he activates the text and, in activating it, becomes the text's agent; secondly, she or he responds to it in whatever way is relevant to her or his work.
3 It makes it possible for us to see the text, activated by a reader, as participating and playing a part in organising definite sequences of action. (2005: 120)

Our own study did not trace specific texts and their activation with the sort of precision implied in Smith's account. But we were interested in the ways in which policy discourses around consumerism were activated and responded to in the specific institutional settings of the three services. The importance of the institutional context for us was that such contexts are already awash with 'existing discursive resources'. New political or policy imperatives do not arrive in empty spaces – they arrive in the middle of already crowded and contested spaces where other discourses jostle for dominance (or at least credibility). We also borrowed from recent sociological work on public service professionalism and its difficult relation with managerialism (see, for example, Clarke and Newman, 1997: Evett, 2005; Exworthy and Halford, 1999; Gewirtz, 2002; Kirkpatrick et al., 2004). In thinking about public services as institutions, we think there is some merit in seeing them as combinations of organisational and occupational formations in which 'professional' cultures of practice have come under increasing pressure to conform to organisational/managerial direction since the 1980s. The 'internal world' of the three services is, then, characterised by sets of strains and tensions around the role, ethos, function and control of work and workers.

We found it useful to think about public service institutions as fields of adaptation, interpretation and translation – and as shaped by sets of dynamics that can be represented as a diamond (see Figure 3.1). The vertical axis in Figure 3.1 (governmental–public) locates two of the primary sources of pressures or forces acting on public services. Governments articulate views of reform, identify lines of social development, lay claim to particular conceptions of the public and how it is changing and, of course, develop and administer policies for public services. The double meaning of 'representation' is central to thinking about this axis. On the one hand, governments are constructed through the processes of representative democracy (they have to engage in the business of electoral calculation, positioning, etc). On the other, they are

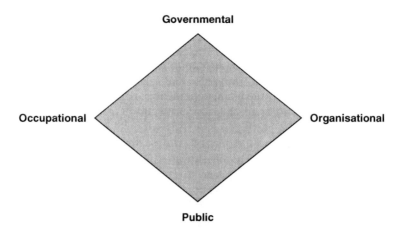

Figure 3.1   *The dynamics of institutional adaptation*

engaged in the symbolic work of representing themselves as the public's representatives. This involves constituting the public and themselves as particular types of social actor. As we argued in Chapter 2, both Conservative and Labour Governments have announced themselves as the 'People's Champions' against the Producer Interest in public services.

At the other end of this axis, the public is also a complex entity (Newman, 2005a; Warner, 2002). It is an 'imaginary unity' with which (some) people identify – seeing themselves as members of the public (this is discussed further in Chapter 7). But the public is also a highly differentiated entity, traversed by systems of inequality and differentiation that have been profoundly consequential for the politics, policies and practices of public services.

The horizontal axis of our diamond relates more directly to the sites of professional formation in public services. Public service professionalism is formed at the conjunction of occupational and organisational dynamics (Johnson, 1973, on mediating professions). We use the term 'profession' loosely in this context to identify forms of demarcated and certified work (ranging from social work to policing) that are deemed to require specialist knowledge. Each profession has distinctive occupational characteristics (resulting from training and both formal and informal modes of occupational socialisation) and takes place in particular organisational locations. The forms taken vary substantially – medicine is clearly different from policing and social work – but all public service professions are characterised by this mix of occupational and organisational dimensions, pointing to Mintzberg's conception of 'bureau-professionsalism' (Mintzberg, 1983). These occupational–organisational formations have been subject to different sorts of pressures for change during the last 20 years. Specific policy changes, the redefinition of the occupational dimensions (the contested changes in recruitment, training and career development, for example) and the 'redesign' of the organisational setting in the rise of managerialism have combined to transform public services (Clarke and Newman, 1997). This occupational – organisational axis has been the focus of many studies of public service managerialism since Pollitt's path-breaking work (1993). It is the site of struggles over the forms and limits of autonomy in the context of increasingly managerialised organisations. The dominant organisational logic has been the subjection of professional autonomy to organisational goals, values and missions (Evett, 2003). This does not necessarily mean that organisations seek to erode the whole field of autonomous judgement – indeed, most recognise the necessity of some degree of autonomy for the effective delivery of the service. But the aim is to specify the limits of such autonomy in organisational terms, rather than occupational ones. Autonomy in this view is that which is functionally necessary to the organisation's goals, rather than being referenced to some extra-organisational source (professional standards, ethos, regulation, etc). Such external sources are construed as 'narrow' professional interests that produce 'inflexibilities' into the rationally ordered world of the organisation. We will say little more about this – except to characterise it as the struggle to *corporatise* occupational cultures: making them part of the organisation, rather than tied to external orientations.

Using this diamond as a framing device organises this and the following two chapters in a particular way. In the remainder of this chapter, we concentrate on the upper part of the diamond – the relationships between government and the institutional formations of the three services. We look at how 'consumerism' was articulated in specific policies and guidance addressed to the three services and how it arrived in the institutional worlds. In the next chapter, we explore the lower half of the diamond, exploring the perspectives of staff and people who use services on the significance of consumerist developments. In Chapter 5, we focus on the views of managers in the three services. These 'represent' the organisation (at the right of the diamond), but do so in ways that attempt to reconcile the multiple pressures – governments, staff and publics/users – that bear on the organisation and its adaptation to consumerism. We begin in the following section with the translation of the consumerist orientation into policies for the different services.

Specifying consumerism: policy developments in the three services

Each service we have investigated has its own distinctive institutional formation and trajectory. They are located differently in constitutional and governance relationships. They have different organisational histories, cultures and capacities. They are also inhabited by different occupational or professional formations embodying distinctive notions of expertise, autonomy and discretion. Drawing on a mixture of policy texts and senior management interviews in each of the service organisations, the following sections trace some of the ways in which institutional histories and trajectories combine to shape how consumerism is encountered and given life in the world of 'delivery'.

Policy documents relating to each service present an image of the consumer as a rationale for institutional and cultural change. Policies may be developed in a way that loosely stitches together a range of different goals, and that attempts to reconcile multiple interests. However, they are presented as part of a 'story' that situates new initiatives, drives or targets into a history, and that draws on images of societal change and/or institutional problems to legitimate their proposals. Such an approach views policies – and the political speeches that surround their presentation – as drawing selectively on discursive repertoires that are in circulation. In the process, policy narratives organise such resources in particular ways. One example, discussed in Chapter 2, was New Labour's articulation of consumerism with discourses of universalist values, equality and diversity. In turn policy narratives – and the discursive elements they contain – provide a linguistic repertoire on which managers, professionals, user groups and other stakeholders can draw. In each of the public services we investigated there were texts that referred to the user being 'empowered' in the sense that challenging the service provider was acceptable, even to be encouraged. In the following sections we have used examples of policy text and political rhetoric to trace how consumerism has been addressed in each service. The chapter concludes by drawing out some of the differences and similarities across the three fields.

Health care: towards the 'standing up consumers of the future'

New Labour repeatedly asserted the need for health services to become more consumer centred, and the idea of the consumer represented the 'new' or 'modern' image of health in the narratives of change through which policy was explained. In the following extract the consumerist narrative is grounded in a particular historical account:

> Thirty years ago the one size fits all approach of the 1940s was still in the ascendant. Public services were monolithic. The public were supposed to be truly grateful for what they were about to receive. People had little say and precious little choice. Today we live in a quite different world. We live in a consumer age. People demand services tailor made to their individual needs. Ours is the informed and inquiring society. People expect choice and demand quality. (Milburn, then Secretary of State for Health, 2002a)

Here we can see the articulation of 'diversity' through the tropes of 'choice' and 'voice', grounded in a characteristic New Labour narrative of social change. The *NHS Plan* deployed a similar narrative to frame the problem that New Labour was seeking to address:

> The NHS is too much the product of the era in which it was born. In its buildings, its ways of working, its very culture, the NHS bears too many of the hallmarks of the 1940s. The rest of society has moved on. On July 5th 1948, the day the NHS was founded, the high street banks were open between 10am and 3pm. Today, the public has 24 hour access to banking services … In 1948, deference and hierarchy defined the relationships between citizens and services. In an era of mass production needs were regarded as identical and preferences were ignored. Today, successful services thrive on their ability to respond to the individual needs of their customers. We live in a consumer age. Services have to be tailor-made not mass-produced, geared to the needs of users not the convenience of producers. The NHS has been too slow to change its ways of working to meet modern patient expectations for fast, convenient, 24 hour, personalised care. (Department of Health, 2000: 2.9–2.12)

This sort of diversity required responsive services, here conceived as those which are geared to the *interests of users* rather than the *convenience of producers*. The image of the consumer stands at the heart of attempts to reform health systems to meet the demands of a 'modern' world in which citizens were assumed to have greater access to information and improved confidence in challenging clinician authority (Coulter and Magee, 2003; Goode et al., 2004). This conception of the consumer was a central feature of health reforms under both Conservative and Labour administrations. The White Papers *Working for Patients* (Department of Health, 1989a) and *Caring for People* (Department of Health, 1989b) attempted to introduce more consumer-centred services.

In New Labour discourse the key consumerist idea of choice was differently framed, and given very different weight, in each of the three public services under discussion. Of the three, health care has been very much to the fore of the government's drive to implement choice – a function, in part, of perceived electoral imperatives. The main shifts towards a consumerist or choice agenda in health are to be found in documents such as the NHS Plan (Department of Health, 2000); *Fair for All and Personal to You: Choice, Responsiveness and Equity in the NHS and Social Care* (Department of Health, 2003a); *Choosing Health: Making Healthier Choices Easier* (Secretary of State for Health, 2004) and *Health Reform in England: Update and Next Steps* (Department of Health, 2005a). We can trace across them the kind of narrative of change that resonates with the sociological theories of modernity described in Chapter 1: that is, the notion that people had changed (into more consumer oriented and reflexive subjects) and that choice was a necessary requirement for modern public services:

> For fifty years, the structure of the NHS meant that governments – both Labour and Conservative – defended the interests of the NHS as a producer of services when they should have been focussed on the interests of patients as the consumers of services. In today's world that will no longer do. People today expect services to respond to their needs. They want services they can trust and which offer faster, higher quality care. Increasingly they want to make informed choices about how to be treated, where to be treated and by whom. (Milburn, then Secretary of State for Health, 2002b)

The assumption underpinning the image of the patient as 'discriminating customer' was that people had become used to flexible, responsive, user centred services delivered in the marketplace and wanted the same when they came to the NHS. It is possible to identify a few difficulties inherent in such an assumption. The first relates to whether or not consumers do actually get what they want from the commercial sector – much of which is increasingly based on the decidedly de-personalised relations of the call centre and e-commerce. The second concerns whether people really do expect or want the NHS to behave like a company or whether it has a rather different place in the popular imagination. But the third, rather more serious difficulty centres on the role and status of choice in the reform programme and the tensions between this and other political discourses – notably those of 'equality' and 'need' – that remained significant in Labour's political lexicon.

The place of choice at the heart of consumerism had implications for equality that were politically troubling for New Labour. However circumscribed, the operation of choice in health opened up the possibility of growing inequalities between 'good' hospitals and health trusts (those in which middle class patients opt for treatment) and a residualised or 'second class' set of facilities. Equality/equity remained, therefore, a key issue for New Labour to negotiate. Political speeches and policy documents offered several different resolutions to this tension. Early policy texts repeatedly emphasised the importance of geographical consistency to overcome spatial inequalities (the so-called 'postcode lottery'). Later the emphasis shifted to the idea that the exercise of choice by some would raise quality for all:

> It is often said that choice and equity are in some way in opposition. I don't accept that argument. Consumers act individually but the effect of their actions is communal. The cumulative effect of individual choices increases choice for others. In this sense choice widely available is not inimical to equity, it is a driver for change for everyone. So often in state provision of services universal provision meant the equity of the mediocre. That might have been acceptable to those lying down patients of the past but it will not do for the standing up consumers of the future. What we aspire to is the equity of excellence and choice is a necessary, though not sufficient, part of that transformation. (Cayton, Director for Patients and the Public at the Department of Health, 2003)

Here we can trace a number of different themes in Labour's reform programme, but we want to focus on how equality was linked to the idea of the (defective) public services of the post-war welfare state – one based on scarcity, rationing and a strongly paternalistic approach. The idea of universalism was rearticulated as 'the equity of the mediocre'. This redefinition of equality – uncoupling it from its association with universalism and re-coupling it with the discourse of consumerism and choice – was a strong theme in both policy and political discourse on health. And, crucially, it was linked in the 2004 White Paper and 2005 guidance to a more competitive field in which money (resources for Health Trusts and Foundation Hospitals) would 'follow patients' who would be making active choices between alternative providers.

Policing: satisfying customers, securing communities?

In policing, similar tensions existed for a service that had traditionally relied on a combination of force and authority and that had not necessarily been designed with the convenience of the customer in mind. New Labour demands for partnership working as a result of the Crime and Disorder Act (1998) and an emphasis on 'citizen focused' policing had led to policy texts describing a responsive 'customer friendly' or 'consumer oriented' service which was to be offered to those who might have once been referred to as 'scumbags' or 'scroates' (Westmarland, 2001). Alongside the push for consumerist and rights based approaches to victims and perpetrators had been a continued pressure towards greater internal efficiency and organisational modernisation. Police services were also now expected to engage in new forms of partnership working around the theme of community safety, and subjected to new systems of performance management and modernisation. In 2001 a policy document published by HM Inspectorate of Constabulary (HMIC) considered these customer service issues and emphasised the need for 'visibility, accessibility and familiarity', stating that:

> Uniquely identifiable public/police interface points offering ease of access, convenience of location and high quality personal interactions are integral to a policing style that is rooted in the community and geared to its needs. (HMIC, 2001: 5.1)

Indeed, as an organisation the police were subjected to numerous managerialist pressures 'to make them more business-like', and were discursively represented as 'deliverers of a professional service (rather than a force)' (Loader, 1999: 375–6). The re-branding of the police as an efficient call handling service was described in the HMIC document *Open All Hours*:

> It is obviously very frustrating for callers who have used the correct non-emergency number to be left waiting many minutes for an answer. Many commercial companies set strict targets for answering calls, because this is crucial to their business – failure to answer the phone may mean that a customer goes elsewhere. Police service customers are more 'captive' but forces cannot afford complacency; if people are discouraged from calling, valuable intelligence may be lost or their confidence in police availability may fall. (HMIC, 2001: 7.26)

One of the aims of our project was to tease out to what extent the police had become 'consumer driven' or 'customer friendly' at the front line and in their boardrooms. The texts we reproduce here suggest tensions arising from the demand for police services to become more 'business-like'. So although the police had been familiar for some years with 'business case' approaches to finance, they were now viewed as marketplace providers, in a much more 'customer' focused sense than previously (Innes, 2005; Newburn, 2003). This approach can be seen in earlier government initiatives such as the Citizens' Charter (1991) and Victims' Charter (1993). In a climate of demands for increasing accountability for the police, Heward noted in 1994 that senior officers were proclaiming their similarity to 'supermarket bosses' and their market-like approach to goods and services. These demands on, and attempts by, the police to be more 'customer aware' however, can be set against research that shows the public have no dislike or animosity towards the police until they have some reason to be in contact with them and that 'personal contact is the most important determinant of satisfaction' (Dowler, 2002: 237). This contrasts with findings from health service research which indicates that although people are generally supportive of the idea of a national health service, they have fairly strong loyalty and positive feelings about health care professionals when they have had an encounter with their doctor (Calnan et al., 2003). One of the more interesting points of difference between the three services studied, then, is that the police were not simply seen as 'helping' or 'caring', but also have an enforcement role. As Walklate observes, although the 'relationship between the citizen and the state has changed in emphasis since 1945 in the UK … the principle of less eligibility and the notion of the dangerous classes' (Walklate, 2000: 61) still exist, and have implications for perceptions and practices of police and policing.

For police officers, crime victims and suspects, the issue of choice is different from that in health and social care in a number of ways. Essentially it is not about which service provider to choose (as there are few alternatives), but whether to become a customer at all. As the notion of choice became one of New Labour's drivers prior to the 2005 election, the problem for policing was that in an ideal world few people would choose to use their service. To some extent, however, the police had to buy into New Labour's choice agenda. A number of studies that described low or falling levels of public confidence in the police (Home Office, 2001, 2005; MORI, 2002) created some of the conditions for new plans of action. According to the Home Office, part of this dissatisfaction was because a 'clear gulf exists between the level of patrol the public want and what is being delivered' and the 'nature of the insatiable demand for "bobbies on the beat"' identified by the Home Office (2001; Bradley, 1998). One policy response was to introduce 'community' policing, as a fundamental aspect of the Strategic Policing Plan 2004–8:

> Firstly, we want to revive the idea of community policing, but for a modern world. That means a big increase in uniformed patrol on our streets but linked to 21st century technology to make sure they have the biggest possible impact on crime and the public's fear of crime … And we'll give local communities a real say in deciding the priorities for the new neighbourhood policing teams. (T. Blair, Prime Minister's Foreword to the Home Office Strategic Plan 2004–8 (Home Office, 2004))

Does giving local communities 'a real say' equate with the consumer model of choice in other services? Given the police's understanding of their central mandate being to 'uphold the law', the idea that they should hand over some choice and control to the populace they police illustrates tensions around power and knowledge that we discuss later. The *2004–8 Home Office Strategic Plan* and the White Paper *Building Communities, Beating Crime* set out a 'vision for policing which is accessible and responsive to citizens' needs' (Association of Chief Police Officers [ACPO] – Centrex, 2006: 5) where the 'purpose of neighbourhood policing' is described as follows:

Neighbourhood policing has to take its place within the larger national strategy for policing, involving objectives for reducing both crime and the fear of crime but with a local focus. The ACPO Centrex guidance on neighbourhood policing identifies three key requirements that would enable to the community to have its expectations met in relation to 'access, influence, interventions and answers':

- The consistent presence of dedicated neighbourhood teams capable of working with the community to establish and maintain control – to be visible, accessible, skilled, knowledgeable and familiar to the community;
- Intelligence-led identification of community concerns – prompt, effective, targeted action against those concerns;
- Joint action and problem-solving with the community and other local partners – to improve the local environment and quality of life within the community. (ACPO Centrex, 2006: 4)

At the core of this conception of neighbourhood policing is the commitment to the discovery of, and engagement with, public concerns and priorities. Rather than individual consumers, policing has to deal with more elusive collective identities (communities, neighbourhoods, the public):

> Neighbourhood policing is based on genuine community engagement and collaborative partnerships in identifying, addressing and solving local problems. The participation of the public and other agencies in finding solutions to problems means that strategies will need to be flexible, adaptable and reflect local conditions. (ACPO Centrex, 2006: 10)

The appearance of that strange word 'genuine' in this description of neighbourhood policing perhaps hints at the problems of managing the encounters between police and public (and the processes by which the public's concerns might be known). Later, this concern is echoed in a warning about the risk of over-managing these encounters:

> There are many ways in which a decision can be made on prioritisation, ranging from a vote at a public meeting to a representative panel of local people. In whatever way priorities are agreed, it is essential that they are chosen by representative members of the community and not unduly influenced by police and partners. (ACPO Centrex, 2006: 34)

At other points, the document talks about working 'directly with local people in identifying the problems that are most important to them, thereby giving the public direct influence over local policing priorities' (ACPO Centrex, 2006: 12). We want to draw attention to two key issues in this conception of setting policing priorities. First, such priority setting is understood as establishing the agenda for local policing, subject to an indeterminate qualification: 'Police and partners have a responsibility to engage with and, unless there is good reason, to respond to identified community priorities' (ACPO Centrex, 2006: 14). 'Good reason' is an interesting qualifier, underspecified in terms of what sorts of reasons might be good enough to override community priorities: resources; competing national strategies or targets; alternative police intelligence; or even unrepresentatively constructed local priorities? As we will see in later chapters, public services face particular versions of this dilemma centred around responsiveness: how does it intersect with other concerns about resources, professional judgement, national political or policy demands?

Second, the rise of community/neighbourhood policing involves ban is insistent view about placing the public/community/representative people in the dominant role in voicing priorities. This does imply a sort of 'collective consumerism' in both setting objectives and evaluating performance in local policing. As we hinted above, this 'collective consumer' proves elusive: it is difficult to name (citizens, the community, local people, the public, representative people) and problematic to activate. How to get local people engaged is a key issue, not least because some sections of this public are 'hard to reach/hear' (ACPO Centrex, 2006: 14).

Social care: promoting independence through choice?

Unlike health and policing, social care did not come to the forefront of New Labour's consumerist agenda until well into its third term. The dominant policy, organisational and occupational directions for adult social care had been established in the 1990s, in the National Health Service and Community Care Act, 1990 (whose social care elements were introduced in 1993). Since then, social care had been subject to extensive reform with changes in policy, organisational design and substantial new systems of regulation that were all marked by distinctively New Labour approaches to 'modernisation'. A range of initiatives were taken to modernise or reform the provision of social care, beginning with the 1998 White Paper that established a dominant theme for the future:

> We believe that the guiding principle of adult social services should be that they provide the support needed by someone to make most use of their own capacity and potential. All too often, the reverse is true, and they are regarded as services which do things for and to dependent people. (Department of Health, 1998: para. 2.5)

Eight years later similar principles, though now expressed in the language of user 'control' rather than capacity, underpinned the 2006 White

Paper on community based care. It set out three 'simple themes' that underpinned the new strategic direction for such services of which the first was 'Putting people more in control of their own health and care':

> People want to have more control of their own health, as well as their care. There is solid evidence that care is less effective if people feel they are not in control. A fundamental aim is to make the actions and choices of people who use services the drivers of improvement. They will be given more control over – and will take on greater responsibility for – their own health and well being. (Secretary of State for Health, 2006: 13)

> We will move from a system where people have had to take what is offered to one where people have greater control over identifying the type of support or help they want, and more choice about and influence over the services on offer. (ibid.: 81)

These statements framed some of the key dimensions of change. They took up the established social care issue of independence which had been a central concern in professional cultures and policy since the 1990 National Health Service and Community Care Act, and made it the dominant guiding principle for services to adults (while neatly linking it to the newer ethos of 'responsibility'). In a strongly neo-liberal formulation, the desired independence is contrasted with the stigmatised (and stigmatising) status of dependence (see also Leeson et al., 2003 on the salience and complexity of the concept of 'independent living' in later life). This binary distinction – which assumes that the 'normal state' of adulthood is independence – has been much criticised for the way that it conceals questions and relationships of interdependence (Williams, 2000). But New Labour consistently articulated independence and the diversity of individual need to a critique of 'producer power':

> Everyone deserves to be treated as an individual, and to have the system geared to their needs, not vice versa. Although social services help many people to live fuller and more active lives, they sometimes provide what suits the service rather than what suits the person needing care ... (Department of Health, 1998: para. 1.4)

In such policy statements we can see the traces of a series of struggles by different user movements. Such movements challenged relations of domination and dependency and contested the normative exercise of professional power over service users. And we can see ways in which government policy drew on such claims in challenging professional power and seeking to address practices that led to dependency by 'putting users first'. But more than other public services, social care has been dogged by the question of 'need', and this consistently skewed arguments about choice in peculiar ways. The 1998 White Paper was organised around the *specificity of need*, proposing that:

- care should be provided to people in a way that supports their independence and respects their dignity. People should be able to receive the care they **need** without their life having to be taken over by the social services system.
- services should meet each individual's specific **needs**, pulling together social services, health, housing, education or any others needed. And people should have a say in what services they get and how they are delivered. (Department of Health, 1998: para. 1.8, emphasis added)

Need has an uncomfortable relationship to the 'choice' agenda, since need is never simply a matter of 'what people want'. Need (rather than want) implies the existence of an objective condition. In social care, such conditions are discoverable through processes of 'needs assessment' (Barnes, 1998). Because of this implied objective character, need has been a contested concept in at least two different ways (Langan, 1998). First, there are contending perspectives on the definition of need – most notably in the profound tension between 'professional' and 'lay' standpoints, in which user movements have challenged the objectivism of professional knowledge (and assessments deriving from it). Instead, they have articulated the claim that users – not professionals – are the 'experts of their own condition'. Secondly, for many groups, the centrality of the concept of need occludes questions of rights, making services conditional and contingent. The right to receive services cannot be universal while filtered by 'needs assessment'. As we will see in the following sections, this tension around needs persists as a central feature of consumerism in social care. However, we should note how independence has been increasingly equated with 'choice'. For example:

> … those who work in social care services need to ensure that the way they do business becomes a force for independence rather than a force for dependence. They need to transform their services into modern, user-led services capable of delivering real choice and empowering individuals to exercise those choices themselves. (Social Services Inspectorate, 2000: para. 4.5)

Connecting independence and choice was critical for the project of introducing a more 'consumerist' orientation into established professional cultures. Despite many criticisms, social work had, since its nineteenth century origins, always espoused the concept of the autonomous individual/family as the goal of social intervention (Clarke, 1993). More recently, social work had adapted such established orientations to challenges around autonomy, user-centred approaches and empowerment. So the policy discourse of autonomy and empowerment was already well established within the organisational and occupational cultures of social care. But this 'open-ness' exposes an ambiguity in New Labour's approach to public service reform which requires a critique of the 'failings' of public services as a legitimating condition for 'modernisation' (Langan, 2000). The 'dependency inducing' or, worse still 'producer-centred', practices of social care were identified as stumbling blocks to reform:

Social work is not about dictating how people should live their lives. The role is to empower people and support them to live the life they want, not the one we think they should have. (Social Services Inspectorate, 2002: para. 1.3–1.5)

Although the reform agenda recognised that there may be constraints on the ability and capacity of social care organisations to deliver 'what people want', there was a suggestion that some of these limitations might be overcome by greater clarity, better information and a more positive disposition:

Much more flexibility needs to be built into the way that services respond to individual people's needs – departments need to encourage and support their staff to think laterally, when assessing people's needs, about what the solutions for them might be. (Social Services Inspectorate, 2002: para. 1.8)

Independence and choice became increasingly closely linked, particularly through the development of Direct Payments as an alternative to provision of services. Direct Payments were the outcome of struggles waged by movements of disabled people to enable 'independent living' (rather than professionally dominated services). They were subsequently extended to other groups of social care users and emerged as a model for rethinking social care:

When councils make Direct Payments to service users or their carers they establish a completely new relationship with the people they serve: a relationship of equality, offering support for the service users' own choices and futures, rather than one of control. (Social Services Inspectorate, 2003: para. 2.73)

In the Green Paper *Independence, Well-being and Choice* (Department of Health, 2005b), choice appeared as the mechanism that could guarantee both independence and well-being:

4.21 People at the centre of assessment have the opportunity to choose what services and support they think would best meet their needs . . . we want to create a mechanism that will allow individuals to keep control and choice over their situation and the support they actually receive. (Department of Health, 2005b: 33)

Direct Payments came to dominate the direction of policy, both as the favoured instrument and as the model on which a related model ('individual budgets') was based:

4.35 Giving people an individual budget should drive up the quality of services. The ability of people to 'buy' elements of their care or support package will stimulate the social care market to provide the services people actually want, and help shift resources away from services that do not meet needs and expectations. (Department of Health, 2005b: 33)

Needs and wants (or 'expectations') continued to be interwoven in complex and shifting ways in these policy statements. However the process of needs assessment remained a potentially contentious site where conflicting conceptions of have might meet, and have to be reconciled:

> Of course, the individual's own assessment of their needs might conflict with those of their professional assessor. At present, this is too often hidden. The individual's personal assessment must be transparent in this whole process. That is what happens in the rest of our lives. We work out what we want and then, in trying to achieve it, we may have to negotiate because of limits to resources or other factors. (Department of Health, 2005b: 31)

This image of 'negotiation' rather than the exercise of individual choice disrupts the model of consumerism being developed in social care, though it is a subordinate element in the Green Paper (Clarke et al., 2006). But by 2006 the language of independence and choice had entered the lexicon of the White Paper on Community Services in a way that almost completely displaced the language of need. Choice in social care was to be accomplished not only by 'giving people more information' but also by 'putting people at the centre of the assessment process', 'increasing the take up of Direct Payments' and 'introducing personal budgets that will give people greater freedom to select the type of care or support they want' (Secretary of State for Health, 2006: 81).

Conclusion: challenge, responsibility, choice and inequality

The three services discussed in this chapter are clearly differentiated in a number of ways. The specific institutional formations and existing trajectories of health, policing and social care made a difference to how 'consumerism' was imagined in relation to each of them. The same general point would hold true for other public services: the consumerist orientation – and the specification of mechanisms like choice – are differently worked out in education (and different sectors of education), housing and the benefits system, for example. Such differences matter in a number of ways. They highlight the diversity of institutional forms, relationships and practices in public services. They make visible the different sorts of relationships between publics and public services (e.g., the difference between the focus on the individual patient/consumer in health and the 'community' in policing). And they indicate some of the problems that governments face in trying to deliver or install a reform programme that seeks to 'modernise' public services.

However, while such institutional and policy differences are important, we can also detect some important commonalities across the policies for all three services. The first is that they all clearly bore the marks of New Labour's consumerist orientation. Even the policies addressed to

policing, while they might be centred on processes of community involvement and 'collective choice', were nevertheless shaped by an understanding of the public in what we might call 'service industry' terms: a public
composed of demanding, sceptical consumers with high expectations of
service delivery. In health and social care, this conception was more consistently articulated as a matter of individualised expectation, experience
and aspiration. The 'standing up consumers of the future' have replaced
the 'lying down patients' of the past (and the same may be true for the
dependent social service 'clients' or the passive communities of policing).

In Chapter 1 we suggested that the conjunction of consumerism and
public services was associated with four key themes: challenge, choice,
inequality and responsibility. In these diverse policy documents we can
see each of these themes being deployed in the development of a consumerist approach to reform. *Challenge* was a consistent theme: policy
documents identified the more demanding consumer as a driving force
that required change in the 'producer-dominated' cultures of all public
services. Challenge in these contexts is always a term with a double life –
it both refers to an external social 'reality' (the changing public) and
installs the government as the representatives or champions of that
public. Government both brings that challenging public to voice and
becomes the 'virtual consumer' (Miller, 2005), standing for a consuming
public.

Choice was both a core feature of all these policy developments and surprisingly elusive. We have noted how the 'agent' of choice varies from
the individual patient/user/consumer in health and social care to the
community as collective agent of choice-making in policing. The same
commitment to choice can be traced across other services. In public or
social housing, for example, both individual and collective choice making
was promoted (in the policy of 'choice based letting' and in tenant votes
on choice of 'provider' for transfers from local authorities to housing
associations, for example). In education, choice (the expression of parental
preference) has continued to dominate both policy and the controversies
surrounding it in relation to the change from primary to secondary
schooling. In the course of our study, the meaning of choice shifted in a
number of ways. Overall, we think there was a move from an early New
Labour conception of choice as meaning choice of ways of accessing or
engaging with public services (e.g., by telephone, in person or through
electronic means, see Jones and Williams, 2005) to a more 'marketised'
view of people making choices between multiple or competing providers,
and about the content or substance of the service they receive. Both health
and social care had developed these more substantial versions of consumer choice by 2005–6, culminating in the introduction of the ethos of
'money following patients' in a competitive field of health service
providers (Department of Health, 2005a).

One consistent part of the controversy surrounding New Labour's consumerism (and the growing centrality of choice in particular) was the

contested relation between choice and *inequality*. As we saw in Chapter 2, New Labour's articulation of consumerism had, from the outset, tried to disarm critics focusing on inequality. The claim that choice could drive equality/equity remained a core issue, and became the focus of substantive critiques. For example, one critic of education plans went so far as to claim that Labour's proposals would effectively restore the 'institutional apartheid based essentially on class' of the 1930s (S. Jenkins, 'Blair and Adonis are taking our schools back to the 30s', the *Guardian,* 25 January 2006: 27). Discussion of other axes of inequality was more muted, although the Commission for Racial Equality organised a seminar drawing together research on the racial/ethnic implications of the Choice agenda (December 2005).

Finally, *responsibility* was a rather less obvious theme in the specific policy documents though it was a dominating element in more general New Labour discussions about citizenship (see, for example, Clarke, 2005a; Dwyer, 1998 and Lister, 2002). In these service policy discourses, responsibility was more muted though there were clearly expectations that the combination 'independence' and 'choice' would produce people who were more self-sufficient and less of a cost, whether this was the safety-promoting community, the self-managing patient or the independent older person. As we will see later, responsibility came to take on another meaning in the context of the citizen-consumer: the expectation that such consumers would make 'responsible' choices.

In this chapter, we have traced some of the service policy similarities and differences. We have tried to draw out the distinctive institutional formations and trajectories that characterise the three different services, while remaining attentive to the common themes that link them in New Labour's modernisation or reform programme. In the following chapter, we explore how these issues – particularly the dimensions of challenge, choice, inequality and responsibility – are thought about by front-line staff in the services and by the people who use them.

4

Unstable Encounters: Users, Staff and Services

We now explore the emergence of a consumerist orientation from the perspectives of both staff and service users in health, policing and social care. In this chapter:

- we begin by locating some of the wider pressures that were at work on the encounters between publics and public services;
- we then explore staff and user views of consumerism in relation to our four key themes of challenge, choice, inequality and responsibility;
- finally, we link these themes back to political and policy discourses about choice and consumers.

This moves our focus of attention from the policy domain to the points of intersection between publics and public services, focusing on the lower half of the diamond that we introduced as a framing device in Chapter 3 (See Figure 4.1).

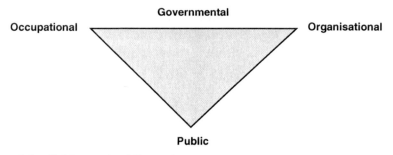

Figure 4.1 *Publics and public services*

In doing so, we are conscious that people – as staff and users – are actively engaged with discourses about choice, challenge, responsibility and inequality in public services. A central part of our interest is to see how they 'make sense of' the connections and disjunctures between these themes – and what discursive resources they draw upon in the process. This orientation has drawn us close to the perspective constructed by Malpass and her colleagues in 'problematising choice':

Our starting point is the suggestions that far from 'choice' being straightforwardly championed and promoted, it is increasingly circulated in policy discourse and public debate by being problematized. In particular, the problem of how to ensure that the choices of putatively free individuals are exercised responsibly – in terms of both individuals' own good and the good of broader communities – has become a recurrent theme of concern. (Malpass et al., 2006: 3)

While their analysis focuses on the articulation of choice and responsibility, we think it helps to orient our concerns with the multiple aspects – and discourses – of public service consumerism.

Knowing the public?

The relationships between service providing organisations and the public have been increasingly characterised by an uncertainty expressed around two key questions. The first is *who knows what the public wants?* Organisations have an interest in maximising their knowledge of what the public want, both to organise services, and to use the knowledge as leverage with central government. They also have an interest in trying to stabilise their encounters with the public in order to manage resources and performance. But the problem here is that their relationships with the public combine predictability and unpredictability. It is the new 'common sense' that public service users have shifted from the deferential to the assertive; from the ignorant to the knowledgeable; from the passive to the active voice. This set of changes has, of course, been narrativised as the transition from citizens to consumers. But, in practice, such shifts have proven to be profoundly uneven – they may be socially distributed (shaped by class, by age or generation, by ethnicity); but they may also be distributed experientially (shaped by involvement in previous struggles or movements, for example). They may be distributed between different sorts of people – but people are themselves neither stable nor unitary in their encounters with services. The same person may combine being a knowledgeable expert of their own condition; a rights-bearing and assertive citizen; an anxious dependent and a seeker after professional help and advice across a series of encounters with the health service. These are 'unstable encounters' (Clarke, forthcoming a) in which the possibilities of getting it wrong have multiplied as both the public and service organisations try to manage each other in more uncertain times.

The other line of relationship at stake here is between the public and public service professionals. We can identify this as organised by the question of *who owns the definition of need?* It is here that the contested character of knowledge/power (or combinations of authority and expertise) becomes most visible. Certainly in health and social care, the assumed dominance/deference relationship has been disturbed by alternative claims to be knowledgeable – the capacity to be 'an expert of one's own condition'. The extent to which such claims are made, and the extent to which they are accepted or recognised, remains highly variable. And it remains the case that, for many people, professional expertise is highly valued; though whether the desirability of expertise also means a toler-ance of professional authority (or paternalism) is more doubtful. This field of relationships operates in a range from 'collision to collusion' (to borrow a delightful phrase from Janine Wedel, 2001).

It will be clear that a whole range of governmental initiatives have played a part in reconfiguring the professional-public relationship and disrupting the claims of professional expertise and authority. 'Choice' – in both health and social care – is a critical element here, dislocating the pro-fessional control of assessment, evaluation and specification (diagnosis and treatment) as an integrated structure of decision-making. While we might note that the mythology of professions always overstated the inte-grated (and untainted) character of such decision-making, the rhetoric and institutionalisation of 'choice' is (and is intended to be) disruptive. 'Choice' as a governmental agenda includes a belief that people can define their own needs (Clarke et al., 2006). We return to this issue later in the chapter.

Staff and user perspectives: orientations to consumerism

In this section we consider some of the findings drawn from question-naire responses by front-line staff and users of the services in the three services. The questionnaire operationalised 'consumerism' as active on four dimensions: *challenge, choice, inequality, responsibility*. The main results are shown below. They are mapped on scales which run from +100 to –100 where all respondents giving 'strongly agree' responses to four state-ments on the theme would produce a +100 score (see **Appendix** for further details). Scores are derived from 268 returned questionnaires, weighted to balance differences between return rates for different groups. Some differences between services, staff and users are visible on each of the dimensions.

Challenge

Turning first to *challenge*, we were interested in whether people were becoming less deferential, less trusting, more willing to challenge authority and to make demands. In the service organisation, we explored whether staff welcomed the challenge posed by informed, empowered consumers.

The scores here are unevenly distributed (see Figure 4.2). Police users are by some distance the group who value challenge most highly, followed closely by social care staff. There is little 'mirroring' of staff and user orientations: social care staff's open-ness to being challenged is not matched by an enthusiasm on the part of social care users for being

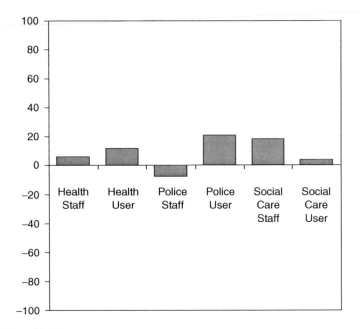

Figure 4.2   *Challenge*

challenging. Health users appear more enthusiastic about challenge than health staff (though this is the closest pairing). Police staff are not disposed to welcome challenge, even though police users appear most enthusiastic. We have touched on some of the conditions that might explain this lack of fit in Chapter 3. For example, police officers have to embody authority in particular ways, and interviews with both front-line staff and managers suggested that this sort of embodied authority makes 'challenge' a difficult mode of relationship between the police and the public. Users gave voice to frustrations about the level and focus of policing – and about their relationship to local voices:

> I wanted to say that, the police surgeries they are a joke because for those few hours, they are all standing there and they talk to you like they've got this service that they are providing you with and a couple of times I've challenged them on a political front, you know you're an organisation. Two things – don't you ever feedback within your organisation to some kind of structured liaison group where you are telling them what is working on ground level and what the people need? Don't you do that? They keep pushing it back on us. … They talk as if they are there but they are not. Even if you get through to them on the phone they don't provide the service people in this country need. (Newtown police focus group 1)

For officers, challenge may be experienced as personal, as much as organisational:

Oh, I see what you mean. Um, again, the younger generations, the youths will directly confront me. They will say to me that – they can be quite rude and aggressive and say 'you can't do that to me, I know my rights'. Um, 'that's not illegal, you're just picking on me', um, those kind of comments that – I usually say to them 'well if you go to [the] book shop in Newtown and you look in the road traffic manual you will see that yes, what you are doing is illegal. I've read the books and you haven't mate! (Newtown police front-line staff 05)

There is something powerful here about the relationship between embodied authority and expertise. This officer talks about deploying knowledge of the law as a counter to challenges. We can see this dynamic being worked out in a longer exchange between the interviewer and another officer about the significance of challenge and of different sorts of knowledge:

Respondent: Yeah, people question your decisions all the time because invariably they're not gonna be happy with it because they're not gonna get what they want. A lot of people ring the police and expect their problems to be sorted when the officer turns up on the doorstep when in actual fact it's gonna be a long-term problem which we're not gonna be able to deal with in one visit and they can probably help themselves sometimes in solving their own problems. Um, then of course you'll always get people who'll complain about the service they'd had. Um, and there's various reasons for that. Sometimes it's because they've got into trouble and they think by making a complaint against a police officer they're gonna get themselves out of whatever trouble they got into. Um, then you just have serial complainers who just like to complain, um, and then you know, you will get the person who has an original complaint, a serious complaint which is investigated. I think it was something like 99 per cent I was reading recently in one of our force gazettes that 99 per cent of complaints are dismissed, no further action because they're unfounded or can't be proven. But the report process is there, um, and it's a good thing. It can only go to improve the service.

Interviewer: Are you saying that you're willing to be challenged?

Respondent: Yeah. One of the biggest things that they tell us is, um, if you make a decision that's fine as long as you can justify the reason for why you made that decision. So if someone on the street wants to challenge my decision that's fine, they can do that, it's not gonna change it.

Interviewer: So it might not necessarily have much impact on what happens?

Respondent: Um, no.

Interviewer: To change slightly – um, just like people can buy anything there's increasingly a wish to buy extra policing from sort of private security companies and alarm systems. Um, I mean do you think – do you think this sort of choice is desirable that people can buy security if they want to? And do you think this increases their choice?

Respondent:	Yeah, I mean a local village close to me I've seen a private security vehicle, um, sitting there of a night time near the shops where the youths are. Um, I suppose it could go to help the police. But I mean the – the public will never have another place to go to apart from the police if they want the law enforced. Um, we would be their only recourse apart from civil action. Um, I mean yes, they have the options to buy these private security firms with their patrols and what have you. Um, all they're gonna do is patrol around. Um, it might deter some people, um, but if they come across a crime the chances are they're gonna ring us anyway. It just provides an extra pair of eyes out and about on the street and someone willing to stand up and provide a statement, um, as opposed to Mrs Miggins who might ring up and say 'I don't want to get involved' and put the phone down and then we're stuffed.
Interviewer:	Do you think … if they start buying more security services where they're obviously in a bit more of a powerful position as a customer, do you think they'll start expecting more from Police? Um, or expecting a different relationship with the police?
Respondent:	Um, they may expect it but I doubt if they'll get it.
Interviewer:	What would be the reasons why they might not get it?
Respondent:	Er, because we're – the police service is established for quite a long time – er, then we get these private security companies who are all sort of quite new and I suppose because the field's growing for them there's more demand for private security, um, but the police have been there, we're established, we know what we're doing and we have the information, the intelligence if you like, um, to be able to spread out the resources that we have. We only have a limited resource and I know the public wants to see more police officers back out on the beat but that's not gonna help reduce the crime, um, because nowadays, you know, with the areas that we cover we have to be in patrol cars to get to those areas, it's not gonna help if we're out on foot and have got to run a couple of miles to get to a fight that's going on. (Newtown police front-line staff 01)

In this exchange, challenge begins to blur into questions of choice (and the relevance of other providers). But it is clear that authority is both embodied (the person of the constable) and linked to the possession of specific sorts of knowledge (the law; local intelligence; and managerial calculation about resources and effectiveness). These are constructed as different from the knowledge of the public and the expertise and capacity of private providers.

Responsibility

In a second theme, we explored how staff and users felt about shifting attributions of *responsibility* for health, security or care. Did users and staff expect individuals to take on greater responsibility, for example, for their

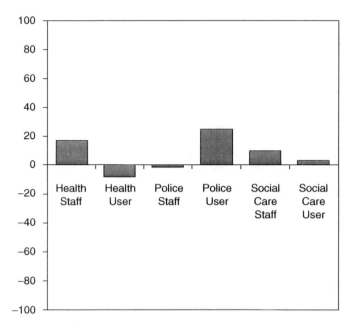

Figure 4.3　*Responsibility*

own health and well-being, for organising their own care, or for local crime and disorder issues?

Here, too, we can see some mismatches between staff and users (see Figure 4.3). Again police users were more enthusiastic about individuals and communities taking on greater responsibility than were police front-line staff. They expressed concerns about the capacity of the public to perform policing tasks knowledgeably and effectively. But equally striking was the difference between health staff and users, where users (in aggregate) seemed to reject the individualisation of responsibility. In interviews, however, both staff and users struggled to articulate the complex conditions and consequences of 'being responsible':

> I don't believe that if you have abused your body for 60 years you should be refused treatment when you get sick. But I do think you ought to, you shouldn't expect to sue because you can't be cured, you should take some responsibility for your own state. And I think most people would, but there are some who seem to expect that whatever they do it can all be made good, and it can't. ... Bad things happen and we've got complacent and think we can be insulated from bad and we take it out on the health service perhaps, when it's our health that is on the line. But the health service should treat us as sentient beings and ask us what we want, if we're interested. (Newtown health user 5)

> Well we have, um, we have the Expert Patients Programme so we have started haven't we around looking at, um, how patients can actually, um, you know, manage their own chronic diseases. And I know that, you know, there's – there'll be certain people in society that can do that and can do that very well. I think around

management of diseases I think health has to have perhaps more of an owner-ship around that and maybe prevent this, you know, somebody being out in the community, getting to the point where they're at crisis and then they're accessing hospital care. ... So I think it's a bit of both. I think there'll be people that can man-age their own chronic diseases and manage them very well, um, but I think there'll be others that if we want them to be managed then we've got to – we've got to be there to help them as well and support them. (Oldtown Health front-line staff 01)

Responsibility was clearly a focus of ambiguity and ambivalence for both staff and users (see also Malpass et al., 2006). Both of these interviewees can be seen negotiating public and professional discourses (and contro-versies) about the nature of responsibility. There is some anxiety, evidenced in the first quotation, about where NHS and individual respon-sibilities do – and should – intersect. In particular, the notion of the 'responsible' citizen who manages their life style so as not to be an 'unrea-sonable' burden on the NHS (and who might be disbarred from treat-ment) was clearly of critical concern. But for staff, the knowledge and capacity to be a responsible, if not expert, patient was – at best – unevenly distributed. In interviews, that distribution was seen to vary between types of condition (people with chronic illnesses might become 'expert patients'); between types of location (people in residential institutions were seen as having less opportunity to control their life styles); and between social groups (where material deprivation was seen as linked to both bad health conditions and poor health 'choices'). Such issues recur in relation to both choice and inequality, as we will see.

Choice

Given the growing political and policy centrality of choice at the time of the research, our survey of staff and users examined how they saw the relationship between choice and services, focusing in particular on whether respondents saw choice as likely to drive service improvement. As Figure 4.4 shows, there was a strong positive disposition to choice in five out of the six groups – with police staff taking a more sceptical view of its benefits. Police users were more optimistic; while social care staff and users were the most enthusiastic about the likely benefits of choice.

However these for/against survey results were opened up to more divergent and complex interpretations in the interviews and focus groups. These were located in different views of people and their rela-tionship to services as well as modulated by both political and profes-sional discourses.

I think choice preserves people's dignity and their sense of being in control of their own lives. And with older people believing in yourself is perhaps the most crucial thing I think, you know. When you stop believing in yourself then you doubt very quickly sometimes almost everything that you have to do. Can I cope with this? You lose your nerve. Now as long as people have still got choices and

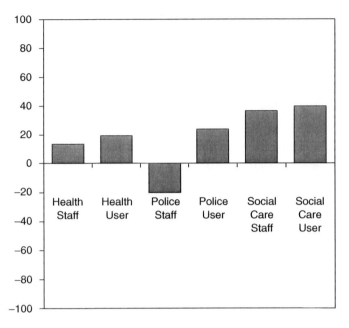

Figure 4.4   *Choice*

feel that they can exercise choice they feel in control of their fate and it maximises their confidence. And along with the consumer business and the business of choice which now both main party leaders are trumpeting about this week, you know, in all sorts of areas. Along with that, um, there is – the latest culture that we have from central government and the Department of Health, that we're here to promote independence. Now I think we have always thought of it that way. ... I think promoting independence nudges us more towards taking more risks with people. But again I think I welcome that, you know. And choice and promoting independence I think go very much together in terms of helping people to maintain their belief that they can still direct as much of their own affairs as possible and make choices of one thing against another and they're still in control. That matters. (Oldtown health front-line staff 03)

Here the respondent weaves an argument about the value of choice through a mix of professional, political and policy discourses – but always returned to a professional focus on what difference choice might make to users. However in many of our interviews an interest in, or even enthusiasm for, choice was tempered by more material and organisational doubts about the possibility of making the ideal materialise:

Yeah, they should have the choice. You know, it's – it's in a lot of the literature that I had to read when I was a student, as I said to you, you know, I've studied about it and read about it, you know, you read about it in the community care magazines etc. and the government, you know, going back years to when, you know, community care legislation as coming through, very keen on this idea of choice. I mean they're still talking about it nowadays. And you talk about it in the National Health, you know, with the hospitals and choice as to where people go for treatment. Um, but in reality, I'm not going to comment on that particular thing, but the reality for our clients, um, the choice is not necessarily there and it should be. . . . It would be – in an ideal world you should be able to arrange home care for people just when they want it, that's the ideal. Because if we're saying you should have the choice then that's part of the choice. Um, and they should perhaps have a choice of agencies. Now that's in the ideal world. I understand if you know they are so busy that they can't take on new clients, I can understand that. But then the time issue can be a big one for somebody who's an elderly person and is losing control of their – you know, they're not in control of their life and they're at the whim of you know, carers coming in to look after them and they can't get up and get – be ready for the day till the home carer's come in to do whatever it is that they do for them. And it could be – well it will be very frustrating for people. (Oldtown Social Care front-line staff 04)

For individual service users, in such circumstances choice might materialise as a choice not to take up specific forms of service being offered. But such considerations were in part shaped by users' reflections on the material and organisational circumstances that constrain service providers. In this example, one of the classic 'choice' issues in social care – the timing of personal assistance – was the focus both of disappointment and reflections on the conditions of that disappointment:

Respondent: Um, again I think it's funding, organisation and the number of people that are actually available to work to provide that service. One example with choice – I used to have evening visits, I no longer have them. Um, I wanted a visit after nine o'clock. I'm old enough not to go to bed before nine and I also have a life, I'd like to go out and enjoy myself, particularly at weekends. And I wanted to choose a visit say half past ten so that they would help me in going to bed at half past ten, get me ready for bed and help me get in to bed at half past ten. Um, and I felt that was a reasonable time, um, for a visit but the service stopped at nine o'clock. And, um, they tried to put me as the last patient or client. But most of the time it would be half past eight or half past seven and I would be put in my pyjamas or whatever at that time of night and I might have friends coming round and it would be really embarrassing. I would have to phone them up and say 'I've gotta cancel tonight cos the carer's coming round early and I don't particularly want you to see me in my nightclothes'. And so I don't think they're capable of providing a wider service or, um, changing things to be honest. I think, um, it's gotta be limited so that they can manage it. Basically. And what people want has gotta fit in to what they can provide. I mean they did later on try and put a later service on but by then I'd got fed up with being done so early that I decided to cancel the evenings and struggle myself.

Interviewer: Right. So that would be a choice you'd like but...

> *Respondent*: It never came to fruition so yeah. I'd – you've got a choice but I had to make the choice in the end not to have that service 'cos they couldn't provide me with what I actually wanted. And so, um, I don't think they have the capability of being able to expand a service to a certain extent. (Newtown social care user 01)

User reactions to choice and services were often refracted through this discourse about capacity and capability; and individual frustrations and disappointments were framed by considerations about resources and other priorities. Such representations of collective and institutional domains dislocate the individualism of the consumer choice model. People thought that such issues were part of inhabiting the world of public services – the mix of resource limitations and other people's needs was considered to be a key element of their 'publicness'. Choice was also modulated by questions about who knows what is needed. The concept of 'need' is a vital one in both health and social care, where it is activated in professional discourses of diagnosis and assessment. Both staff and users recognised this as unsettled ground where both parties have potential claims to know 'what is needed'. However, this was rarely resolved in favour of a consumerist version of choice. Instead, professionalised knowledge was *conditionally* desired and seen as necessary:

> Well, again that's the bit that boils down to the trust, isn't it? I mean if I go to my GP with a problem and she said to me well, you could have this treatment, or these tablets, or these tablets, or these tablets, and explained why there were three different sorts – probably to do with side effects, maybe, I don't know – that would be why she was giving me the option. I would still say to her, well, what do you think I should have? Because I'm not a professional and I don't know any different. (Oldtown health user 01)

> Well, hah, I think that anybody would like to have choice but in order to have that choice you need to be tremendously well informed of people, places, conditions, everything that is involved in order for you to make that choice. Because you can't make it with a lack of knowledge. (Newtown health user 02)

While some users clearly saw themselves as more active and extensive choice makers than this model implies, others saw themselves as well served by the professional processes of needs assessment:

> *Interviewer*: Would you want more choice in that sort of way?
> *Respondent*: No, I'm quite happy as it is. When they assess what you need, according to that you get what hours you need, don't you?
> *Interviewer*: Do you want more control and choice, and if you do, what would you like to be able to control better?
> *Respondent*: It suits me, how things are. I don't think we would be able to control it as well as whoever does it now. Some perhaps would, some have more intelligence than others.
> *Interviewer*: But you are happy with the system working as it is?
> *Respondent*: Probably, I would get more worried about it if I had more control. (Oldtown social care user 04)

This speaks to the conditional and contextual character of how users felt about choice. They saw it as hedged with a variety of conditions: about knowledge (and who has it), about geography (and the 'localness' of services) and about the specific situation in which someone needs a service:

> Now I suppose if you lived in the country, miles away from anywhere, and your nearest hospital was a little cottage hospital, which, you know, didn't have any facilities at all hardly, they may want the choice of going to a big general hospital, the nearest big general hospital which may be a few miles further away. I mean I understand that. But I think to generalise on the thing and say, you know, everybody should, I think it's ridiculous. I do really, I think it's daft. . . No, no, I think it's absolutely ridiculous I have to say. If you think you are dying, you know, and somebody says to you, well, which hospital do you want to go to, well [*laughs*] it would be just take me to the nearest hospital. (Oldtown health user 01)

We have argued that the promotion of choice takes place in a field of encounters between providers and users that is already unsettled. Anticipating who might be knowledgeable, assertive and empowered (and through what means) is a site of potential difficulty for organisations and their staff to negotiate. Indeed, users reflected on the problems that providers have to confront in the face of such unpredictability:

> But you do sometimes think that they [health staff] assume that you're not interested in the detail, and you might be, because a lot of people aren't, as I said like my mother-in-law. She just wants to be cured, she doesn't want to be asked about what she would prefer. But some people do. I've talked to quite a lot of people about it, and quite a lot of young people don't want any choice. It's not an age thing, which I thought it was once, it's perhaps a personality thing. And it's difficult for the health professional because they have got to judge, I suppose, what sort of person they are faced with. Because obviously some people would be upset by being told that there was choices and it wasn't as simple as all that and others are obviously upset if they are told this is what we are going to do and that is it. And I don't see how, I suppose training in bedside manner might help to some extent, but I don't think they are ever going to get it right every time, because they can't tell. (Newtown health user 05)

The uncertainty and unpredictability of user orientations is a significant dynamic in the current relationships between services and the public (Clarke, forthcoming a). This is, however, not just a matter of mapping different dispositions in the public (assertive/passive; knowledgeable/ innocent; independent/dependent). While people may have such dispositions, they are variably evoked – at some points, in some conditions, they may be either assertive or passive. Even if they are 'knowledgeable', they may wish to surrender to professional expertise. Even if they are inclined to be 'patient patients', specific circumstances may make them assertive, angry or aggressive. In return, organisations need something more than a 'bedside manner' – they need to find ways of being adaptive to both the needs and the orientations of particular users. As we will see later, they might have to find ways of seeing themselves in varieties of 'partnership' with people who use services. We return to this issue in Chapter 7.

Inequality

Finally, we turn to the problematic relationship between consumerism and *inequality*. In our study we were interested to discover how staff and users of services perceived this. Did they believe that increased choice and voice would disproportionately benefit those with either the skills to negotiate the system or with the loudest voices?

Figure 4.5 suggests relatively high levels of concern about inequality and choice in four of the six groups in the study. Police staff seemed less exercised by this issue, with health staff falling somewhere between the police and other groups. It may be that concern among police staff was lower because of the relatively 'thin' presence of the choice agenda in policing policy. For the other groups, however, this was one of the most consistent set of returns with all user groups, and social care staff, all recording levels of 20+.

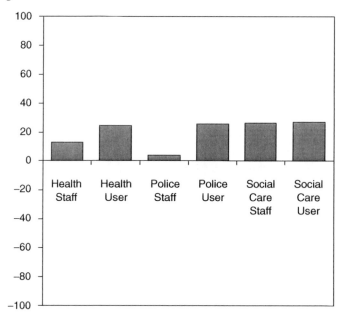

Figure 4.5   *Inequality*

It is important to say a little about how inequality was constructed in the questionnaire. We deliberately asked questions that were about capacity to 'work the system' and to 'shout loudest', rather than about socio-economic position (class; rich/poor). We did so partly because the absence of the cash nexus in the co-ordination of public service removes the most direct or visible link between economic resources and choice outcomes. Instead we tried to capture more indirect forms of inequality – in particular the unequal distribution of social and cultural capital that has historically enabled the middle class to benefit disproportionately from public services. We were also interested in the relationship between *voice* and responsive services. Voices vary both in volume and in audibility – a phenomenon recognised by both users and staff in interviews.

Indeed, the discussions of 'inequality' in our interviews represent something of a masterclass in analysing dimensions of inequality and their implications for public services. Respondents deployed different conceptions of inequality, reflected on how they intersected and puzzled about their likely interrelationship with choice. It was not that they saw the choice agenda as creating inequality, rather as creating a new terrain on which existing inequalities might be played out. We traced a number of different inequality discourses, of which the most basic was the 'problem of the middle class':

> I think there's always going to be those, er, middle class educated people who do well out of a system. And, er, they're the majority aren't they really? Er, but it is this group, yeah. I mean the group we're seeing at the moment, the new systems, are the people who can't ascertain the new systems, er, because they're vulnerable. And they're vulnerable because they're ill so they're the very people we should be helping. And they're a sort of neglected group. (Oldtown health staff 02)

This is a conventional analysis of the class distribution of social and cultural capital, identifying the people who have the capacity 'to do well out of the system'. Interestingly, these were contrasted not with the 'working class' or even the 'poor', but with a category generated much more from professional and policy discourse – the 'vulnerable'. The vulnerable and the neglected were seen as at risk of missing out in new systems even though 'they're the very people we should be helping'. The systemic character of class/education/capacity blurred into discourses that addressed the unequal distribution of information, knowledge and choice-making capacities. In this example (as in studies of educational choice making, see Gewirtz et al., 1995; Tomlinson, 2001), the class distribution of these capacities was highlighted:

> Yes, and certain people would be handicapped because they wouldn't know how to weigh up, well they wouldn't know how to get the information in the first place, but they wouldn't know how to weigh it up when they had got it. They would be in the hands of friends and relatives, who had either knowledge or prejudices, it wouldn't necessarily be an informed choice. Again, it would be the chattering classes who would grab the best and that isn't necessarily a good thing. So it leaves the health service able to fob certain sectors off. (Newtown health user 05)

In the following extract, material inequalities (affluent and deprived people) were mapped geographically (suburbs and poor areas) in ways that drew out connections between the unequal distribution of health needs and the unequal distribution of health services. The well-established connection between high need and low provision (sometimes known as the 'inverse care law') was itself the focus of government policy in the 2006 White Paper (Secretary of State for Health, 2006). But this extract introduced a further twist, linking poor areas, their high needs and low provision with the implications for professional practice in enabling choice. It is interesting that, as far as we can tell, New Labour's policy agendas on choice and on social exclusion were not, in practice 'joined up'. This extract suggests reasons why they should be:

> I think it's all down to – especially if we just think of the Choice Agenda, I think it's down to, again, awareness with the GPs as well. Because if you're in a poor area which is sometimes staffed by a poor number of GPs then, you know, you've got a small number of GPs dealing with a population who's probably got the highest need so they don't really input the amount of time that they should do because, I mean, they just – they're on that treadmill and they're just churning people through the system all the time. So it'll be those type of practices that are not aware of choice, that are not aware. So to me you'll always find that those people that are deprived and don't have access to what they should have may always stay in that sort of like rut if we don't help them out of it. So I think we've got to really look at where we need to invest in – practice wise certainly to help GPs and to help that population because otherwise, you know, the affluent people of [suburb] will always access, you know, care a lot sooner won't they? Because they'll have knowledgeable GPs who are not working with the most deprived people in the society so I think we've got to really look at where we put our investment and time and resources into helping people. (Oldtown health staff 01)

In one of the police interviews, this geographical conception of inequality was itself inverted. This may owe something to the different character of the service (and the professional/managerial calculations of the need for it). But it also hints at questions about how professional priority setting and voice intersect:

> Well funnily enough I was only saying the other day, what I see as a big inequality actually isn't the way round that you might think it would happen. The people who are suffering the worst are probably the most deprived, they're actually getting most of the resources thrown their way, not only by the police but you know, by the local authority and by the government. And the people who are sort of middle of the road, they're not getting those same attentions. And one of my big worries although it's not only my worry, it's other people's worries, I think it's obviously been identified as an organisational problem, is that if say we throw a load of resources into a particularly bad area, you're probably just gonna end up displacing the problem to the area next to it and unless you actually strengthen the area next to it as well to have some resilience you're actually going to make life better for one set of people who are the worst served but you're gonna make life slightly worse for the people next to them who up until then have been quite happily just living their lives. (Oldtown police staff 01)

As we noted, this may have something to do with the distinctive character of the service, but it raises important issues about the dynamics of resource allocation and the effects of policy. The 'displacement' effect of policing (moving crime from the focus of intervention) has been the subject of much research and professional attention. More generally, it raises questions about the nature of the equity that public services are expected to produce. 'Targeting' resources (whether in policing or other benefits and services) is legitimated as a means of focusing on the worst areas or most needy people. But this assumes that the target is clearly defined and that there are no displacement or ripple effects. More importantly, it cuts across other public service principles of equity, especially those associated with universalism.

In some sense, each of the services in our study was engaged in trying to balance different (and competing) conceptions of equity and equality. 'Targeting' (in some form of priority setting, rationing or the strategic deployment of resources) was common to them all, as we will see in Chapters 5 and 6. In addition to such social and spatial discourses of inequality, all three services provided accounts of what might be called 'volume related distortions' of allocative choices: a view that 'voices' have different volume levels, power and reach. In particular, respondents pointed to the capacity of some people to 'work the system' locally through contact with local councillors or local media. Such contacts may not be distributed structurally – respondents pointed to the networking effects of friends and relatives as crucial but situationally specific resources. Nevertheless, the capacity to generate both volume and pressure was seen as interrupting efforts to produce rational and accountable procedures for rationing resources:

> It is a very grey world that we live in, and even with the best or the most thorough thought out and legally sound eligibility criteria and even with the right balance in terms of people who make assessments and so on there is always the political dimension for those who know how to shout loudest and who know where to go and to press the right buttons to still get what they're looking for which doesn't necessarily fit with policy. (Newtown social care staff 02)

In some of the accounts given, the capacity to generate and apply pressure on service providers appeared to be contingent. But for others, the volume issue was woven back into the discourse of social and cultural disadvantage:

> Oh yes. But I think that happens anyway doesn't it? It's always the eloquent people who know their rights who, um, get what they want. And it's the less secure, um, sometimes poorly educated or people with special needs who don't get what they need. You know, I think that's the imbalance of life and I don't think in this context it's any different. (Newtown voluntary worker 01)

We end this section with an extract from an interview in which the choice agenda was specifically connected to questions of social inequality and responsibility. The individualism of a consumer choice model is here contrasted with a conception of inequality as social and structural:

> ... Although it's consumer choice so then it comes with consumer responsibility and it also comes with consumer faults in some respects if things don't go right. But society out there isn't very fair and it isn't very equal so how you can just, you know, look and focus in. Sometimes you have to focus at the wider level. There's a lot of inequality out there and that isn't solved by just solving – not always solved by looking at that individual, is it? (Oldtown social care staff 01)

This reminds us that staff draw on a range of discourses, not all of them easily reconciled with simple notions of 'professional' concepts of personalised care, protection or service. The extracts in this section also overturn any neat binary between 'professional' and 'lay' publics: each may come with a range of social and ethical – and even political – commitments and identifications that inform their understandings of the possible impacts of consumerism.

Consumerism at issue

In this chapter we have explored the views of both front-line staff and users about consumerism and its implications for the reform of public services. The four key dimensions that we derived from the academic literature in Chapter 1 provided a framing device and clearly evoked strong responses from those who filled in questionnaires and took part in interviews and focus groups. Overall the chapter has highlighted key differences between services, with issues of choice and inequality being less central in policing than in the other two services, and notions of responsibility being more significant in both health and policing than in social care. We also found important differences between the responses of staff and of users. Users were more prone to feel confident about challenging providers than were staff welcoming of such challenges. Users were, however, less enthusiastic than staff about possible transfers of responsibility from providers to individuals and communities. Users were more likely to think that providing increased choice would bring about service improvements, but were also more likely to see increased choice as bringing with it a higher risk of inequality.

Treating consumerism as having several dimensions (rather than just 'choice', for example) enables us to see why it has been and remains a controversial approach to public services. It touches on the shifting and unsettled relationships between providers and users, crystallised in the question of 'challenge'. It poses problems about where and how the distinction between public and personal responsibility is being redrawn. And it bumps directly into concerns about both equity and inequality in the provision of public services. Both the quantitative and qualitative data on these themes suggests that this is not a landscape where everyone is ready for consumerism. On the contrary, doubts about whether this is the best way forward abound.

In one sense, this is not surprising. The people we talked to (whether staff or users) are 'reflexive subjects' in sociological terms. They are capable of reasoning about politics, policy and practice, and of making links to their own and others' experiences. In that respect, they might look like the 'active sceptical citizen-consumers' celebrated by New Labour. The trouble is that while being both active and sceptical, they also apply their scepticism to the consumer choice agenda. As Malpass et al. note in relation to responsibility, people 'might be articulating justifiable scepticism towards the whole frame of "responsibility" that is being addressed to them' (2006: 13). In Chapter 7 we will look at the relationship between being active and sceptical and the identities of citizen and consumer.

In the meantime, we are struck by two things about the interviews we have reported here. The first concerns the rich discursive repertoire on which people draw in discussing aspects of consumerism. Being 'reflexive subjects' marks our respondents as something other than the bearers of cultural change, dominant political ideologies or dominant discourses. Rather, they work with discourses as resources for reflection; political and professional discourses clearly play a role here for both staff and people using services. But we have also seen a diverse set of popular 'sociological' discourses about equity and inequality being put to work in discussions about the consequences of choice. In these interviews, we see people in the process of 'making up meaning' by drawing on (and not just reproducing) discursive resources that form part of the stock of popular knowledge (Malpass et al., 2006; see also Clarke, 2004a; Holland and Lave, 2001; Wetherell and Potter, 1992). This elaborate and complex stock of knowledge can be seen as Gramsci's concept of 'common sense'. For Gramsci, common sense was not merely backward or conventional thinking, but a complex of 'traces' of many different ways of thinking:

> Every philosophical current leaves behind a sediment of 'common sense'; this is the document of its historical effectiveness. Common sense is not rigid and immobile but is continually transforming itself, enriching itself with scientific ideas and with philosophical opinions which have entered ordinary life. (1971: 362, footnote 5)

This brings us to our second point. New Labour consistently glossed some of the aspects of the orientations here as characteristic of the move to a consumer culture: in particular, the willingness to challenge professional authority, and the expectation that increased choice will improve services. At the same time, it tried to subordinate or repress the more uncomfortable or discordant elements of those movements and tendencies. It insisted throughout that independence and autonomy (and citizenship rights) necessitated 'responsibility'. It also claimed that the consumer choice orientation could promote equity. Neither of these two claims seems to have effectively colonised 'common sense': they remained grounds for doubt and sceptical distance for some of our respondents. Most strikingly, respondents seem to be keeping alive complex discourses about inequality and the challenges that inequality poses for public services – articulated through a variety of key words: class, disadvantage, deprivation, poverty and the unequal distribution of need, services and capacities. We return to these questions – and whether such reflections are 'merely residual' – later in the book. In the next two chapters we explore some of the dynamics and problems of managing institutional change in the three services.

5

Managing Consumerism: from Policy to Practice

The consumerist policies we traced in Chapter 3 produced a new set of dynamics within public services. Rather than viewing this in terms of the conventional separation between policy and implementation, this chapter draws on extensive interviews with senior managers in health, policing and social care to trace the processes of institutional inflection and translation that were taking place at the time of our research. The interviews explored how managers saw pressures towards consumerism in their service and how these processes intersected with other changes, pressures and demands. In this chapter:

- we consider how managers approached the process of adapting their organisation to consumerism;
- we explore the implications of such changes for staff and people who used the services;
- we assess the possibilities and problems that such developments created for the services.

The institutional shifts in public services over the last three decades have placed such service managers in a distinctive position. The processes of decentralisation and devolution have given managers increasing 'freedom to manage', albeit in very particular and constrained ways (see, *inter alia*, Clarke and Newman, 1997; Kirkpatrick et al., 2004; Pollitt et al., 1998). One element of this managerial relative autonomy is the task of negotiating the organisation's intersections with different sorts of 'stakeholders'. In terms of the institutional diamond framework that we introduced in Chapter 3, managers represent the 'organisational' corner. Managers identify the organisation's needs and interest and speak for its mission, values, purpose and direction. They negotiate, juggle and try to reconcile the different pressures from other stakeholders visible in that diamond: government (in its many facets); the staff of the organisation (multiple occupational groups); and the public (a complexly differentiated field, including roles as users, taxpayers, voters, citizens and even employees of public services).

Public services are settings where active translation, transformation and enactment take place. Each of the three services we studied is marked

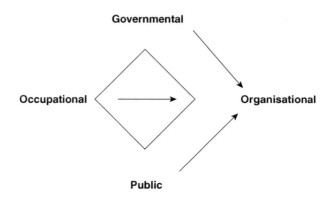

Figure 5.1　*Multiple pressures*

by distinctive *institutional formations*, and by distinctive *institutional trajectories*. By institutional formations, we mean the composite of organisational and occupational cultures and dominant (and other) patterns of relationships within organisations, between organisations and between services and the public. In the process of turning policy into organisational practice, managers occupy this distinctive position of trying to make policy fit the organisation, and the organisation fit the policy. This does not mean that managers form a neutral conduit through which policy passes into practice. On the contrary, the process of 'implementation' is an active one in which policy is translated into the institutional environment (see Newman, 2005b). Nor are managers disinterested observers or witnesses whose views can provide a transparent reflection of these processes. Managers are also 'stakeholders', trying to establish organisational directions, purposes and values in the face of competing conceptions of what the organisation might be. Although we see managers as occupying a privileged position in the processes of enacting policy, we need to read their descriptions, analyses and evaluations as discursive practices in which they articulate the views of policy, staff, the public, government and 'the service' purposively. Our primary interest, then, is in how they construct consumerism and its relationship to the possibilities and problems of providing the service.

Policing: different voices, different choices?

As we saw in Chapter 3, the ideas and languages of consumerism are less apparent in police policy texts than in either health or social care – a reflection, in part, of the comparative difficulty of realising the key consumerist idea of individual choice-making in a police setting (see, for example, *Policing a New Century: A Blueprint for Reform* and *Policing: Building Safer Communities Together*, Home Office, 2001 and 2003). Compared to health care it is much more difficult to envisage a scenario whereby police consumers could be given a choice of provider, facility or type of treatment, a point attested to by one of our interviewees:

> We think the thing is … that the public actually as a rule have to take the service that they get, they can't actually go out and say, we don't actually like the way (*Local Force*) Police do this so I'm going to see if we can phone through and get (*Neighbouring*) Police to come and do it, because on such and such scales they deal with my type of incident in a far better way. (Newtown police senior 02)

In place of individual choice, police policy texts have tended to draw upon an alternative set of discourses focusing upon different aspects of the local, including conceptions of community choice, partnership and devolution (see Hughes, 1998, for a discussion of the discourses of citizen, consumer and community). Our interviews suggest that it is these conceptions that dominate the discursive landscape of senior police officers. While police policy texts may have minimised the idea of choice, they nevertheless incorporated some aspects of New Labour's consumerist agenda, aspects that senior managers have felt compelled to address:

> There are some cases now that are starting to happen where people do have a choice and the kind of things I'm talking about is if they're reporting racist issues and things like that, because say for example in (Newtown) there's something in the region of about 30 reporting centres and some of those will be police, but there'll be areas of worship, there'll be schools, there'll be other areas, housing offices etc. and they can actually choose who they report those to and what we're finding is that some of the communities would prefer to report it to their area of worship rather than actually report it to the police because they think that they'll be dealt with more sensitively. (Newtown police senior 01)

As Crawford notes (2006 and forthcoming) the police have had to respond to a market where 'reassurance has become a commodity to be bought and sold' and they are not the only 'providers' responding to the public demand for security. It was clear that the senior staff we interviewed were well versed in the discourse of consumerism and could confidently discuss Government policy, having recently met with the Prime Minister, Tony Blair, for breakfast, been in regular contact with David Blunkett, the then Home Secretary, or were on first name terms with Hazel Blears, then Police Minister. We asked interviewees about the ways they had incorporated 'consumerist imperatives' into their strategies. Most officers were clear about the meaning of the term but were less sure that it was being used, or was potentially useful for their organisation. As one explained:

> ... in some ways, we're trying to open up the debate about looking at the public as consumers and having an understanding of what their needs are, and then in return for that being able to move from being what I describe as an ill-informed community to an informed community, then you can actually have some logic to your debate with them. (Newtown police senior 02)

Another explained that although the 'more senior people within the organisation' would 'appreciate' it:

> ... we don't use the term consumer or consumerism but we all have our own ideas of what it means and to me, as a senior police officer, as the Divisional Commander, I do see our key partners, and the community, as people who consume the services that we can provide. (Oldtown police senior 03)

However, another senior officer explained the difficulties with regarding some of their users as consumers:

> Interestingly ... if we're talking about certain sets of consumers, if we're talking about those that don't, wouldn't want to engage, i.e., the offenders that we deal with, our service has to be lawful, everything we do has to be lawful and so we've concentrated very much on that element of it whereas now we're starting to look at adding quality to that ... (Newtown police senior 02)

This officer also reflected on whether – in the longer term – consumerism might turn out to have more far reaching implications for how policing might develop. Here there is a sense of disjuncture between the immediate focus on 'the core business' and what the business might become:

> ... and for me the only thing is...you know...what is our core business and how do we crack on with getting things done and there may well be things within this world of changing use of consumerism that are very fundamental to how we police and that therefore become quite systemic and not just another flavour as it were. (Newtown police senior 02)

Treating the public as consumers and 'giving them what they want' presents the police with a number of problems. One critical element of many of the discussions of consumerism in this context was the senior managers' perception that the relationship between provider and service user in policing is quite different from that in either the private sector or other public services. In particular, they pointed to the uneasy intersection between consumerist ideas and the processes under which some people are *obliged* to receive services. Although such 'coerced consumers' are not only visible in policing – in social care, for example, statutory powers exist to enable public agencies to intervene in individual and family lives, where people are deemed to be a risk or at risk – our interviewees' preoccupation with this issue undoubtedly reflected the institutional centrality of the powers of arrest and detention:

> [S]ome of the actual business around consumerism, there's difficulty in transferring it from one arena to another ... you know, squaring up to somebody in a situation where they don't want to talk to you as opposed to somebody selling them a tin of beans or trying to sell even double glazing. That is very, very different, and you know, there are lessons to be learnt but can't transfer directly. (Newtown police senior 01)

Senior managers' responses to the consumerist agenda were articulated in relation to its perceived 'fit' with other, ongoing processes of change. Again, the picture is a complex one, the consumerist agenda going 'with the grain' of some processes of change but colliding uneasily with others. An example of the former was the (ongoing) shift from 'force to service' (Johnston, 2000: 43). Our interviewees' acknowledged how this change facilitated recognition of users reconfigured as *customers* of the service:

> I think what the police are trying to do is to look upon the service that we provide, and compare it to what industry does in modern day, so we are trying to find a parallel to where we fit in with that. So whereas a few years ago we might have said we don't have customers, we are the police force, and that is what we do – we police the streets and keep order, we did not necessarily look upon people as providing a service to them and that they consumed our service. The changes have come, I think, the government stance, certainly in very recent years, sees the police, like any other public service, as strictly providing a service. (Oldtown police senior 01)

If the shift from force to service appears to have contributed to a 'consumer-oriented' re-conception of the relationship between the police and their users, the consumerist agenda's relationship with other aspects of reform had proved rather less straightforward. The following example demonstrates this clearly:

> [I]t's very hard to reconcile that idea [of consumerism] to the, sort of, performance culture that the police currently find themselves in, because, you know, I mean, I know we jokingly mentioned that there's nothing worse than a satisfied customer, and you know, police officers know that that's something that leads, compromises their business imperatives if you like, because in fact what happens is you can get swamped with all the problems of your satisfied customers, so in some ways, you know, ways we're trying to open up the debate about looking at the public as consumers and having an understanding of what their needs are and then in return for that being able to move from being, what I describe as an ill-informed community to an informed community, then you can actually have some logic to your debate with them. (Newtown police senior 02)

This extract reveals a perceived conflict between consumerist ideas and the *performance culture* established by the political centre (Clarke, 2005c). As Crawford and Lister report (2006) the purchase of a 'public good' such as policing, as in an initiative they describe in New Earswick, North

Yorkshire, not only leads to potential inequalities, but creates conflicts and tensions. In this experiment, residents believed they had their own 'dedicated' or 'purchased' officer and when local police managers had to move the officer from the 'duties specified within the commercial contract' for their own operational needs, 'purchasers felt they were not receiving the anticipated level of service'. For the officers we interviewed, the pressure on the police to meet government targets was seen as sitting in a problematic relationship to the application of a specific interpretation of consumerist ideas: a mix of community voice and community choice. In particular, our interviewees were unsure how, in the world of delivery – and in the context of nationally set performance targets – 'collective public consumerism' might be achieved. Certainly their frequent reference to 'community' speaks to the weight of that discourse in policing, and yet senior managers were extremely hesitant about the wisdom of listening to community voices or acting on community choices. Our interviewees returned to worries about 'ill-informed' communities' wants, expectations and choices – as opposed to the police's interpretation of needs – driving change. As in the field of health care, there were persistent issues about the relationship between different sorts of knowledge – in particular, organisational and occupational expertise – and decision-making power:

> Because sometimes what you can have, is you can have consultation with a community that in fact don't know what they're talking about and therefore you know, if that's the validation of your policy you can actually be very, very compromised later on by going down an avenue which you have actually responded to maybe a pressure group, or maybe a group that's totally ill-informed. So it's a way in to a community but you've got to be really careful about how much leverage you allow that to have on the organisational goals until you've got a really stable relationship with them. (Newtown police senior 02)

So it seems from these discussions that Government directives about public or collective choice did not figure at the head of the local police agenda. We were interested in how institutional adaptations of Government agendas was communicated to the people on the ground and one of the Oldtown officers explained:

> It works in the simplest of ways, by very senior officers from this force very often having to go to London to find out what the brief is, what is expected of us, coming back and briefing people like myself as divisional commanders, we have to go then and make sure that our division delivers, we are answerable at a performance review process in the force, that every month we look at our performance across the board, and likewise the Chief Constable is answerable to the Home Office … So you've got a very critical, a very close monitoring of performance, and performance against targets … it actually relates to burglary dwellings going up or are they going down, where are the worst places in the city, where are the worst areas for it, what are you doing about it, who are the worst offenders and what are you doing about them, have you targeted them, and we are expected to

know that detail then, whereas a few years ago somebody in my position would be seen as the strategist who sits above it and wouldn't need to know all that detail ... Whereas now that personal lead is given by the Prime Minister, and even this debate in the last few days about his health, many would say it is because he is too intrinsically involved in all the minor issues, about what is going on, but this reflects down to Chief Constables and Chief Superintendents. (Oldtown police senior 01) (The interview refers to a period in which the Prime Minister had a much discussed minor heart operation.)

This officer saw organisational objectives as being more directed by the choices of Government than by those of local residents. If the shift from force to service appeared to have enabled a 'consumer-oriented' re-conception of the relationship between the police and their users, the consumerist agenda's relationship with other aspects of reform had proved rather less straightforward. One of these difficult intersections occurred between the consumerist imperative and the attention New Labour was (during the middle part of 2003) paying policing and its 'performance':

But we are judged more on leadership, and my division has recently had a HMIC inspection, via ... Her Majesty's Inspectorate of Constabulary, it has already been published this week, and the two main issues that they are looking into are performance and leadership, both of which are critical ... it is a pressure, the pressure to succeed, the pressure to reduce crime, because the feeling is that if you don't reduce crime there is always somebody who is ready to pounce upon you and literally, the power to remove Chief Constables and ultimately BCU commanders such as myself if we don't do our job correctly. Now, that might not be something that is involved every two minutes, and it clearly isn't, but it is the sort of thing ... we are under intense scrutiny. (Oldtown police senior 02)

These pressures seemed to be more focused on traditional 'core' policing issues such as reducing crime, rather than customer service in a public problem-response sense that was emphasised in the policy texts cited earlier. Being judged by quantifiable 'results' still seemed to be at the heart of the message New Labour was delivering to police via senior strategy officers, or at least this is the one they were hearing. Perhaps the choice agenda was too nebulous a concept to be measurable in police performance terms, or perhaps, as the extracts above suggest, the gap between 'them and us' (the unwilling customer, the unreasonable demanding, 'uneducated' public or the undeserving victim) is still a large gulf to cross. Culturally perhaps, the public service 'crime fighters' as opposed to the healers or carers may have further to move if their view of the customer or consumer is to be altered radically.

Social care: supporting choice?

Social care has its own distinctive institutional formation and trajectory. Its organisational dimensions have been dominated by its place within local authorities (social services departments, or social work departments in Scotland). Occupationally, social care has been dominated by the mediating or bureau-profession of social work, even though most of its staff were not professionally qualified (Clarke, 1996). Both of these axes have been the subject of extensive and persistent challenges and pressures for change since the creation of local authority departments following the Seebohm and Kilbrandon reports (Clarke, 1993). However, social care has also had a less distinct institutional identity than either health or policing: problems of defining social care, social services and social work have a long history. It has also had rather more blurred relationships with the public (as potential users of its services).

In common with health, social care has seen an increasing emphasis on a consumerist or choice orientation (see, for example, the shifts from *Modernising Social Services* through *Fair for All and Personal to You* to *Independence, Well-being and Choice*, Department of Health 1998, 2003a and 2005b). Asked in broad terms about a 'consumerist imperative', our interviewees agreed that this was something to which social care organisations have had to adapt. At the same time, however, they argued that this process of adaptation was not a recent phenomenon but part of a longer term trajectory of change, beginning with the 1990 NHS and Community Care Act. For some, the idea of choice – here articulated as the diversification of provision – had played an important role in shaping this changing relationship:

> Well choice is not new you see. With the 1990 NHS and Community Care Act and what the then government was pushing was that they gave the local authority, um, the task of assessment, didn't they, for private nursing and residential care. Now all that was about choice, so basically what I think social services, um, we've accelerated this really, um, yeah. You could say, um, in the past most of the services that we've delivered have been in house but certainly that act exploded the situation … That act I think triggered the beginning of the end in terms of the majority of services from Social Services… So people, um, will be able to choose from the private, the voluntary or our in house services or any combination … (Oldtown social care senior 02)

Others identified the significance of the 1990 Act as a critical turning point in relationships between service users and providers:

> Er, I think that imperative has been around for a long time. Um, I would say since the – in social care terms – since the NHS and Community Care Act 1990, where I think there was a focus on listening to the views of service users and carers in doing new assessments. And within that legislation there was the choice directive – for example, for residential care. So, and I think similarly in um, you probably can't say when it started but that's been a growing thing throughout the nineties, probably in the eighties as well but especially nineties. And certain other bits of legislation – Disabled Persons Act, Carers legislation, our policy like the valuing people, people with learning disabilities. Um, a lot of mental health policy and guidance – nearly right up to national service

frameworks for older people, mental health etc., they all have this emphasis on putting carers at the centre. I think particularly in the last three or four years where we've used terms like person-centred care, person-centre planning, um, so I think that focus has been there for a long time but it's got more focused and more specific in recent years. (Newtown social care senior 07)

In their observations, people constructed different readings of this history that begins with the 1990 Act. But questions of challenge and responsibility were identified as things to which social care organisations had (more or less) successfully adapted. As a result, current initiatives were, to a large extent, seen as going 'with the grain' of the institutional formation and trajectory of social care. One dominant theme was that – even if the language is difficult – social care services had been substantially transformed to a more user/person/customer centred mode of working during the last decade. These managers viewed this as a positive development. But it was not a story without problems or disjunctures. There were some recurrent themes in how social care managers spoke about delivering social care in a more consumerist environment that centred on the difficult relationships between resources and priorities (taken up further in Chapter 6). Social services departments have, since their inception, encountered problems about managing the relationship between demand and resources (as do most public services). But they perceive the will to create more choice or more options as unreasonably constrained by the availability of resources – frustrating both them and (would-be) users. Many of our interviewees circled round how choice was to be exercised in a context where resources were perceived as always falling short of need. One manager expressed it pungently:

I'm saying that this thing about choice, when you don't have any resources to deliver choices, is a complete red herring because quite frankly there isn't the choice. The choice is you take it or leave it really … And you know, I've got a budget and I've also got government guidance that really encourages choice, you know, positively encourages it but I think what I was saying is there is certain areas of provision where there isn't the choice. You're so constrained by resources. There's also things like you know, you can't really choose what time somebody comes round to get you up because you're so constrained by the lack of people. And especially in [Newtown], you've probably heard people talk about it being an economic hotspot, there simply aren't the workers to be able to deliver that choice. You know, you're setting up things to fail. (Newtown social care senior 07)

As a group, the senior managers we interviewed were preoccupied by the ways in which resource shortages were constraining their ability to offer choice to users of the service. In turn, this preoccupation shaped their approach to the choice agenda in various ways. First, there was a great deal of emphasis on the need to be 'honest' with service users about what they might reasonably expect from the service. Our interviewees clearly perceived it as necessary to expend significant amounts of time and energy – both managerially and on the front-line – managing expectations and demand:

> [Y]ou have to be up front and honest with people, and say that's within a financial envelope, so the world is not our oyster, we can't say you can have what you want, but what we can say is that, that is what we can spend, or what we can allow you to spend through direct payments if that is the road they're going down. These are the services that we have got available. (Oldtown social care senior 01)

If expectation management constituted one response to the difficult relationship between choice and resources, an emphasis on individual needs assessment was another. Our interviewees were very preoccupied with the question of needs and had clearly spent time pondering how responding to needs – rather than wants – had a constraining effect on the implementation of the choice agenda. The following extract explicitly recognises that it was only when individual assessments were put together – again, on the basis of needs rather than wants – that offering choice became a consideration:

> Yeah, what I am always clear to say to staff is that when we talk about choice, we need to be clear about what those choices are and particularly I find it difficult with elected members when they are responding to constituents. I want a home help, I want this, I want that, and they keep saying to them nobody can have anything until we have done the assessment, we have to identify that there is a need. Only once we have done that and recognised that we need to put a package together, then that is when the choice comes in. (Oldtown social care senior 01)

A further complication noted by our interviewees stemmed from the inevitability of different definitions of need and the associated question of rights. Definitions of need have, of course, been long contested by groups using social care services; at the same time they have pointed to the conflict between needs and rights whereby the process of needs assessment renders rights to services conditional and contingent, rather than universal and absolute. This leads us into the problem of inequality. Talking about this issue, our interviewees frequently echoed their health care counterparts in drawing a clear distinction between the wants of the informed, articulate consumer and the needs of the relatively disadvantaged. In the following extract, consumer demands were represented as a threat to the objective assessment of need; if demands took precedence over need assessment the likely result, it was argued, would be inequitable distribution:

> I think the problem at the individual level is that the more articulate and the better informed who are often the more middle class and wealthier consumers, um, are able to advocate for a better deal. And that, um, you know there's no reason why everyone shouldn't advocate for a better individual deal but given

our job is to manage to provide the best possible service within, um, available resources, part of a local government job is trying to use the available resources equitably. And there is the possibility that by individual consumers advocating strongly that they actually upset that equitable distribution which is meant to be based on need, you know targeted based on their need which is where assessments is meant to be a sort of objective judgement of different levels of need. And if someone with er, less needs advocates more strongly and gets more resources then inevitably other people get less resources somewhere along the line. So I think there's that pressure – those competing aims really. Um, I think there's a similar potential pressure in relation to different, um, service user groups because clearly children's services to a certain extent because of public scandals, have – are able to claim more resources. And I think, um, certain strong consumer movements which may well be carer and professional advocacy led, um, are always trying to increase the sort of percentage of overall resource available to their particular group and so there's … almost this competition between different groups in terms of, you know, where the resources should go. (Newtown social care senior 04)

As with policing, there are issues about the relationships between services and unwilling 'service users'. Our interviewees pointed out that not all users of their services actually *choose* to be such at all, but rather find themselves obliged to receive services. Although compulsion is certainly less visible in social care than in policing, the existence of 'coerced consumers' – deemed to be at risk or a risk to others – was repeatedly highlighted. Likewise managers pointed to the existence of 'reluctant customers' whose decision to access social services is not so much a positive choice as a reflection of constrained financial circumstance:

[T]he concept of customer assumes that somebody is coming to you because they wish to. In the mental health field, in abuse situations, people are not always coming because they want to, they're being forced on their doorstep. (Oldtown social care 03)

Consumerism, well, I suppose consumerism, again, is about having the money to buy what you want. And, um, although growing numbers of people who use our services have the money to take different paths and use different choices they don't come to social services through choice in a sense. They come to social services because they have certain things happening which we can work with them to help them either understand or to organise services that will help them through that period of time. But, you know, if you've got half a million quid in the bank you don't necessarily want to come anywhere near social services. You just go and sort it out for yourself and pay the bill. (Newtown social care 06)

These last extracts return us to questions about equality raised in Chapters 2 and 4, and suggest other limitations of consumerism as the dominant template for reform. They also remind us that other dynamics and relationships have to be reconciled in professional responses in a myriad of what, in Chapter 4, we termed 'unpredictable encounters'.

Health care: making choices?

Interviews with senior managers in the two Primary Care Trusts (PCTs) demonstrated that they had by far the greatest preoccupation with the idea of choice. PCTs had a double function in the NHS. They provided non-hospital health care services – coordinating General Practitioners and other providers. They also took responsibility for the health strategy for their locality, including commissioning hospital services from Hospital Trusts on behalf of the public of their area. These managers clearly felt compelled to address the idea of choice, but were nevertheless busy reframing and reinterpreting it in a variety of ways. The unresolved tensions at stake in these processes of translation were summarised thus by one interviewee:

> It depends… what you mean exactly by choice, whether there is a choice to be had in that particular area, and actually who that choice is ultimately going to benefit. (Newtown health care senior 02)

The meaning of choice varied considerably in our interviewees' reflections, with managers emphasising different aspects of the choice agenda and relaying different accounts of motives, means and ends. Accounting for these differences, one might point to a range of factors – not least, for example, interviewees' divergent professional backgrounds – but particularly significant was how they conceived the interaction between a consumerist agenda and other, ongoing processes of change within health care. Take, for example, choice of hospital, a central plank of the government's choice agenda, and one flagged up by several interviewees albeit in a way which routinely failed to echo the government's consumerist discourse. Policy texts consistently advocated choice of hospital as a *powerful tool for increasing responsiveness and consistency of high quality care* (Department of Health, 2003b: Chapter 3, Para. 49). In practice this aspect of choice tended to collide with – and be reinterpreted against the background of – senior managers' ongoing preoccupation with government targets on waiting times:

> Obviously, the first requirement for patient choice is, any patient that has been waiting more than six months, at the end of April should be offered a choice of provider… this is almost a punitive measure, to make sure that patients are seen within six months, so we think it is a backdoor way of decreasing waiting times even further. (Oldtown health care senior 03)

> [T]here is a government initiative at the moment called choice and that's for patients who have been waiting for longer than six months for surgery, they are then given a choice as to where they would like to go to have that surgery… The hospitals benefit because they don't breach their targets, or the PCTs don't breach their targets. You get severely penalised if you have patients waiting for longer than six months, your Chief Exec's job's at risk … that's the sort of thing that you would be star rated against. (Newtown health care senior 02)

Such comments may be read as a calculating evaluation of one of the government's key initiatives on choice, but we do not wish to paint a picture of cynical resistance to the consumerist agenda (cynicism and foot-dragging reluctance being charges often levelled by New Labour at public service workers and professionals). Indeed, while interviewees clearly rejected the notion that introducing choice would be in any way straightforward – or without potential drawbacks – they were nevertheless engaged in serious attempts to respond to the consumerist agenda. On the one hand, interviewees were busy dealing with the practicalities of introducing choice, reorganising commissioning processes, redesigning internal systems and realigning their organisations to compete in the new environment. On the other hand, our interviewees were actively re-conceiving the relationship between professionals and patients, often appropriating particular aspects of a consumerist agenda in the process, in order to secure the professional goal of improved clinical outcomes.

Here we wish to focus on just two key re-conceptions of the relationship between professionals and patients. The first centres on a fundamental reworking of the choice agenda away from choice of hospital and towards the idea of patient involvement in treatment decisions:

[I]f you talk to people about choice, a lot of people will think it is about choosing whether you go to this hospital or that hospital. But from my point of view it is around choice right down to the patient level, and it is a bit greater than which hospital you go to, it's around how do you want the service delivered to you, so once you have been diagnosed with cancer it is around saying that there are these options available for your support which will fit you best? There are these options available for treatment, which one fits you best? (Oldtown health care senior 01)

[P]art of, um, part of delivering any choice agenda well has got to be also to provide patients with information about the... different options that are available to them. And I'd like to think that the options available to them aren't always just that you have to – you've got to have an operation and here's the choice of where you go to and these are the outcomes in these different hospitals for what they do. It's even more than that. It's about 'Well Mrs X you've got – you know, you've got this condition, you've got this problem and the options are we work with you to manage the pain better or we work with you through diet and exercise to minimise the damage that's been caused. Or alternatively you can opt for surgery and if you opt for surgery these are the risks, these are the benefits, these are the outcomes and the different providers that are offering this care'. So I think it is much more sophisticated than perhaps it's projected in the newspapers. (Newtown health care senior 04)

These extracts reveal ways in which senior managers were attempting to engage with the government's choice agenda, and to render it meaningful within a particular service context. Our interviewees had moved away from the idea of choice as being about a choice of provider, and towards a more professionally established – and acceptable – notion of choice as involvement in treatment decisions. The hoped-for relationship between patients and professionals was described by one respondent – using a (very consumerist) shopping analogy – as a partnership:

> [W]e all know the shops we enjoy shopping in and it's ones where the, um, assistants get the right balance between offering to help but not intruding too much and sort of like frogmarching you round the dresses or the tins of beans or whatever it is. And, um, so in health care I think that's what we've got to work at, getting that right, getting the partnership between patients and their care givers right as opposed to what was previously a rather patriarchal or matriar- chal way of doing business with them. (Newtown health care senior 04)

Interviewees understood this conception of the relationship as a partner- ship in very specific ways. As the above extracts imply, the role of 'ideal' health professional was to act as a helpful (knowledgeable) guide around the various treatment options; here, partnership was certainly not used to imply *equal* partnership. Likewise, this model of the patient as involved partner stands at a significant conceptual distance from the figure of the demanding consumer. The latter rarely surfaced in our interviews – and when it did, interviewees tended to view it as a source of difficulty:

> The old adage is that we shouldn't be going down to a medium level. We should be trying to raise everything to a higher level. So as soon as you start taking resources away from somewhere else, they are going to start shouting, the self- empowered consumer in that area is going to start complaining. (Newtown health care senior 01)

Interviewees' concerns about the best ways to deploy finite resources and set priorities also extended to other anxieties about the implications of the choice agenda. Whereas New Labour policy promoted choice as a way of raising standards across the board, senior managers retained very real con- cerns about the relationship between choice and inequality in their locality:

> I mean my slight worry with this is that choice will only be exercised by people – well, from the middle classes. I hate using that term but it's the best quick description, um, because they will be able to articulate and demand what they want. (Newtown health care senior 04)

These concerns about how to balance choice, needs and resources were voiced repeatedly across all the three services we studied. For service managers, one of the critical differences between public services and mar- kets was that demand implies costs, not just income – accordingly, demand was something to be managed, rather than stimulated. Similarly, the history of class advantage being reproduced in and through public provision suggests the anxiety about who gets to exercise choice – or whose choices are realised – was a reasonable concern to raise in relation to the consumer/choice agenda.

The concept of choice, then, provided a bridge between professional and consumerist discourse. It was welcomed where it could extend or amplify a pre-existing professional ethic, especially ones associated with the empowerment of particular groups such as people with learning disabilities or mental health service users. However this was rather different from the idea of choice as elaborated in government policy. In professional discourse, choice meant involving patients in decisions about appropriate treatments in the interests of more effective health outcomes (rather than giving a choice of provider, for which, as several of our interviewees pointed out, service users had inadequate information in any case). Any more expansive conception, linked to patients expressing wants or demanding particular treatments, was viewed as a source of difficulty since it raises the problem of how clinical definitions of 'needs' might be aligned with the 'wants', 'preferences' or 'choices' of the service user. One respondent told of how a storyline on the popular TV series *Coronation Street* about a woman who had not had smear tests dying from cervical cancer had led to a distortion of clinical priorities, with patient demands displacing the service's focus on 'need'. In another interview 'giving patients what they want' was equated with the approach of some GPs in the past who (reputedly) gave repeat prescriptions on patient demand. The attempt to change this practice had met with strong patient resistance.

'Needs' and 'wants' then, are contested concepts, and form a point of conflict between clinician and patient. The tension between them was a frequent theme in the interviews.

> *Interviewer*:   So how do you think issues like choice and consumerism apply here?
>
> *Respondent*:   It slightly goes against the whole culture of the NHS being free and in society and not excluding people because consumerism can be – it's a contentious thing isn't it because if people are able to choose then what they must understand is they might be taking choices away from other people, so it kind of goes against the whole citizenship and social stuff. (Oldtown health care senior 02)

The 'whole citizenship and social stuff' mentioned here stands as the antithesis of consumerism. The trajectories of change in Oldtown were geared towards the shift of emphasis to primary care and the establishment (through public-private partnership) of four new multi-disciplinary health centres that were about 'redefining' health care to meet the complex *needs* of those living in an area of high deprivation, and to attract GPs in response to severe shortages. This was a very different narrative of change from those highlighted in the policy statements: community needs, rather than consumer demands, were viewed as the driving force and staff were acknowledged as a critical resource.

Managing consumerism: different trajectories, common themes

We have explored how service organisations are adapting to consumerist imperatives in different ways. To some extent, these differences reflect the different policy injunctions from central government, but these injunctions are made sense of, interpreted and translated within the particular institutional formations and trajectories of the three services. One important element of this study has been making these differences visible, rather than talking about public services in general. At the same time, however, we can trace some common themes across the services. We will take up some of these in the following chapter, but before doing so we return once more to the diamond framework to consider the dynamics of institutional adaptation (see Figure 5.2).

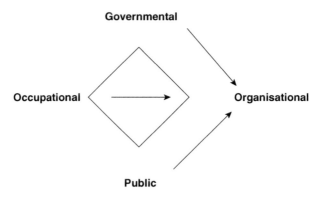

Figure 5.2   *Managing multiple pressures*

In this chapter, we have been foregrounding senior managers as representing the 'organisational' point of this diamond and negotiating relationships with the other points – the 'stakeholders' of public services: government, staff and the public. Most also bring with them occupational identities and professional histories that shape the ways in which they seek to influence the process of institutional adaptation (Newman, 2005c). But their capacity to do so is in turn shaped by other dynamics as they relate both to government and to the public itself. In relation to governmental pressures, we have seen two dynamics of adaptation: the process of translation of policy into practice; and the reconciliation of consumerist imperatives with other governmental demands for service 'performance'. Each organisation was the site of active interpretation of governmental initiatives, attempting to bring them into alignment with the institutional mix of local, occupational and organisational trajectories. Such processes of inflection, interpretation or translation are also sites of recurrent governmental frustration, leading to a search for the 'levers' that will ensure the implementation of governmental objectives. The multiplication of control devices (legislation, guidance, incentive systems, reporting systems, inspection and audit) is, in part, a testimony to the 'loosely coupled' nature of implementation, not least in an era in which devolution, decentralisation and local autonomy are also supposed to be key elements of modern systems of governance (Newman, 2001).

The space for interpretation in the process of implementation can be seen as arising from the coincidence of several features of public services. First, the complex system of apparatuses, agencies and agents through which policy is delivered involves such spaces. The organisational complexity of systems of governance in public services – combining different layers or levels, different spatial formations, different sorts of organisations and different sorts of expertise – produces an institutional architecture in which 'levers' have a hard time connecting central government and front-line staff. If anything, the last three decades of public service reform have made this architecture more, rather than less, complex through processes of marketisation, contracting and partnership that produce multiple organisations engaged in service delivery (Clarke, 2006b).

Secondly, the 'wriggle room' for interpretation is opened up by the existence of multiple objectives demanding the attention and resources of public services. The literature on public service management treats this as a characteristic feature of public service organisations, marking their difference from the 'bottom line' focus of private sector bodies (e.g. Ferlie et al., 1996; Flynn, 1997; Pollitt et al., 1998). Some of these multiple objectives derive from explicit policy imperatives – visible in discussions of crime or waiting list reduction targets, for example. But these governmental objectives have to co-exist with others: more informal, local or organisational pressures for results, requiring organisations to promote their own legitimacy and 'success' to other stakeholders. Organisations have been quick to understand the potential value (as well as risks) of discourses of decentralisation and devolution. They also recognise governmental ambivalence about local autonomy – and how constrained it is by the growth of national evaluative systems (Clarke, 2005c).

Our analysis also shows how each of the services has concerns about how to align the occupational axis with the demands and pressures of consumerism. Staff – their skill mix, their orientation to the service and to the public, and their engagement in the corporate culture – form a critical focus of organisational management. Managers are conscious of the different demands – the need to 'modernise' the organisation; the need to 'get people on board' to ensure a successful, high-performing, organisation; the pressure to engage with the public in more productive ways; and – by no means least – the pressure to engage with the professional values and ethical orientations of public service staff. As we have seen, consumerism is both a pressure for some of these developments and a disruptive force.

Finally, all of these organisations were in the process of reviewing, rethinking and remaking their relationships with the public. None of them were wholly at ease with a conception of the public as 'consumers' of their service but all recognised that consumerism marked something more than just another governmental 'initiative'. Relationships with the public were in flux – uncertain and unsettled. Encounters between services and their users could not be framed as the providential meeting of expert authorities and grateful supplicants. We are not wholly convinced that this was ever true – but the dynamics of deference, compliance and dependence may have formed a potent cocktail that kept people in their place. Organisations providing services know that the apparent stability of provider-user encounters cannot be relied upon. Some users are now 'experts of their own condition'; some are assertive 'rights bearing' subjects; some are insistent 'consumers' – while others may be patient patients, quiescent users of services or compliant in their relation to professional expertise. The possible dynamics that govern provider-public encounters have multiplied, and make for a more unpredictable field of possibilities. We will return to some of these issues in the following chapters.

6

Sites of Strain: Consumerism and Public Services

New Labour's enthusiasm for the consumer/choice model for public service reform treated slow or imperfect implementation of new policy and organisational reforms as the result of institutional reluctance or professional back-sliding. Our interview data might be read through this lens: senior managers seeking to resist or deflect consumerism in defence of organisational or occupational privilege, or merely the 'good old ways'. However, this would miss both the complexity of adaptation and the anxiety about how change is to be accomplished, especially about how it is to be achieved without deleterious effects.

In this chapter, we deal with three renewed sites of strain that featured as recurrent objects of concerns in our interviews with managers:

- the tensions between *choice and equity*;
- the problems of reconciling *needs, wants, rights and resources*;
- the tensions emerging in challenges to professional power and the attempted unravelling of the *knowledge/power knot*.

In the final section, we examine how these three sites of strain come together in a potent image – the 'responsible consumer'.

Negotiating choice and equity

In the previous chapter we explored different interpretations and translations of the consumer orientation, especially the dynamic of choice. Like the staff and service users (in Chapter 4), the managers we interviewed were exercised by the difficult relationship between choice and equity in the development of services. For example, in health care, managers talked about two different approaches to reducing health inequalities. The first was what one respondent termed a 'global' strategy, focusing on improving health inequalities through programmes to persuade people to stop smoking or eat more healthily. A second was to target resources to particular 'vulnerable' groups – travellers, asylum seekers, young people with drug or alcohol habits and so on. For some, consumerism risked reproducing inequalities because of its passive mode:

> Is it equitable that everybody is treated the same? Is it equitable that those that can ask should get it? Is it equitable, or should there be some way of making sure that those people who are most in need, and perhaps not asking, get it? (Newtown health senior 02)

The smoothing over of the tension between choice and equity in the policy documents discussed in Chapter 3, where choice was viewed as driving up standards for all, was clearly not convincing those who had to deal with the reality of resource decisions on the ground. The tensions stubbornly refused to go away. But although the source of these tensions lay in the general programme of modernisation, they were experienced as problems for the *specific* authority, the *particular* practitioner, the *individual* budget holder or commissioning manager. This can be understood as the combined effect of consumerism and devolution. As such, we can see how consumerism serves to individuate the tensions between needs or demands on the one hand, and resources on the other. Despite oscillations and inconsistencies as consumerism was overlaid on different trajectories of change, and interpreted through different professional discourses, the move towards a more consumerist, choice-based conception of health serves to mask the continued need for rationing and priority setting at the local level. In this extract, one manager reflected on the tension between individualised claims on services and the commitment to equity:

> A lot of people are much more informed than they used to be, feel that they've got rights, um, can be very vocal in trying to achieve those rights ... Some people have very realistic demands in saying 'if I've got this need it should be met and I ought to have these choices and I ought to have this quality of service' and that can be very realistic and you think 'yes, if that was meant for me, my family or myself I would have those same requests' and so that's fine although it's not always easy to meet. There's other people whose expectations have gone beyond what we can realistically afford. And I think that we have to be realistic with people about the cost of things. That's the other side about engagement – it brings with it responsibility. And one of the things that we've done with people during the engagement process is to be honest about money side of things, about 'this is a fixed budget – we can spend it in different ways but we can only spend it once, we've got to ensure some equity and fairness so that one person can't have the Rolls Royce and everybody else goes around on bicycles – we want to give everybody a little car then at least there'd be some fairness there subject to their needs'. (Oldtown social care senior 03)

In political speeches and policy documents the tensions between equity, need and choice were reconciled into a seamless narrative of the move towards modernity. The more material questions about resources, rationing and priority setting were passed on to the 'empowered' clinicians and managers responsible for delivering services. This was well recognised by many of our respondents who did 'joined up' reflections about the policy process and its implications for practice:

Respondent: Throughout, they [government] have got to realise the consequences, and I've touched on quite a few of them, but when the
government sets in train a policy I think they have got to think it
through and then they have got to acknowledge that even
though they've tried to think about it as much as they can, there
are going to be consequences they haven't thought of. That is
the purpose of piloting things, but what happens is that they
might pilot it, they might not, and even if they do they usually
don't wait for the pilot to finish or report before they actually get
everyone else to do it.

Interviewer: What do you think those consequences would be, if any?

Respondent: Choice combined with payment by results could easily lead to
bankrupt hospitals. It could also lead to hospitals saying we're
not going to carry out that particular treatment because it costs
too much. It could lead to patients travelling up and down the
country ... then any sort of green policy goes out of the window,
doesn't it? (Oldtown health senior 03)

In early 2006, such issues became publicly visible as some Health Trusts
attempted to deal with financial deficits by deferring medical treatments
following guidance from the Health Secretary that balancing the budgets
should take precedence over clinical priorities ('NHS told: put money
before medicine', the *Guardian*, 23 January 2006: 1). These recurrent anxieties about the impacts of policy and the problems of managing them
have sometimes been read as forms of professional or organisational resistance. We do not think that such analyses capture the many subtle ways
in which our respondents were attempting to install more user-centred
and customer responsive services. They were doing so in a way that
attempted to reconcile two very different imperatives. One was to meet
government targets and to reconfigure services in line with policy imperatives (as in the establishment of 'choice centres' in Oldtown). This was a
matter of redesigning systems and procedures. The second was to pursue
developments to secure professionally defined goals. The excitement
expressed by some respondents about the idea of the 'expert' patient or
the 'responsible' health user can be viewed as an attempt to secure more
effective treatment alongside moves towards better demand management. The interviews suggest how many of the professional developments taking place in health – more emphasis on health promotion, more
person-centred care, more effort to inform and involve the patient in their
treatment – were being elided with the idea of a more consumerist
approach. Expert, informed and 'proactive' users were seen by some as a
means of making the system more effective:

Going to the doctor and just standing there like a stuffed dummy and expecting
him to tell you what is wrong with you is, I think, almost a thing of the past. You've
got to be proactive whenever you go and see a health professional and there's no
better way of being proactive than learning about it before you go. Therefore you
have got to have patient involvement and public involvement.... It enables you to

be more self aware about your own body, about your own condition, and to try to get the best from the system you possibly can. (Newtown health senior 01)

But for others, the proactive or assertive user threatened the capacity of the organisation to maintain equity. In the following extract the business/customer model is clearly seen as promoting inequalities in the face of organisational commitments to equity:

Respondent: … when you're running a business and the customer is always right, the last thing you want is someone shouting around and saying that the service is terrible, you appease these people and do that.

Interviewer: Is that a big pressure?

Respondent: Oh it is a pressure because you've also got to be responsible for the people who like I say haven't got anyone to shout loud, the vulnerables people. (Newtown social care senior 01)

Here we can hear a more sceptical rendering of the consumer/customer image and the implications of the popular common-sense about the business model – that 'the customer is always right'. In service providing organisations, such a view of the customer is potentially troubling, given the clash of expertise it implies, since public services have tended to rest on the presumption that 'professionals know best'. But the respondent above also touches on the unequal distribution of voice or advocacy – a concern that recurs. For some interviewees, the move to a consumerist orientation had multiple implications: some beneficial, others more troubling. Here a reflection on the potential benefits of social care changes, especially direct payments, for minority ethnic groups is tempered by a more sceptical view of what happens 'in reality':

I think there's something about more equality if it's done properly. I mean certainly things like the choices that are available for people from ethnic groups are not great. And I think certainly things like direct payments are allowing – because before you weren't allowed to employ a member of your own family or a close relative or whatever. I think for people from ethnic groups it simply isn't appropriate to go somewhere and be done unto, to be able to employ someone that you know, I think that's good. I think that would mean that people would get services that they didn't before so I think that's good. But I suspect in reality, you know, unless people, unless workers stop listening to those who shout the loudest it will remain unfair. (Newtown social care senior 07)

That is a rather despairing conception of 'reality', in which the unequal distribution of the capacity to shout (and be heard) was viewed as likely to distort service priorities. This was a persistent concern across all the services and many of our respondents spoke about the unequal distribution of the resources and the need to make choices and make them effective:

If we do it correctly then we should understand where the inequalities are. But if we're just involving the usual suspects, those people that traditionally come to me … then those people that are suffering from inequalities … will just get further and further marginalised. (Oldtown health senior 02)

And it's the people who are very vocal who are educated and articulate that can demand. And they're – you know, that's not a bad thing and I think everyone should have responsibility and everyone should be aware. But sometimes that is at the cost of those people who aren't articulate, who are disadvantaged because they don't have access to the internet, to, um, journals or magazines, maybe they don't read, um, maybe they live a long way from the surgery so they would only go if they were really really ill. Um, and they are perhaps, well they are the group that we really need to be focusing on. But it's very hard when you've got a bunch of articulate people knocking on the door with their internet papers to actually work your way around those so that you can go and reach the other clients. (Newtown health senior 02)

Such a view of the social inequalities that might distort 'choice' is a significant connection between such organisational knowledge and academic studies. This is not an argument that poor or working class people lack the 'capacity' to make choices. What is at stake is the unequal distribution of the social and cultural resources that enable and empower choice: what Bourdieu calls the fields of social and cultural capital (Bourdieu, 1984; Greener, 2002). The ability of the middle classes to extract disproportionate value from public services is a well-established theme in policy research (e.g., Gewirtz et al., 1995; Le Grand, 1982). While most of the discussions centre on these dimensions of class inequality (and the unequal distribution of knowledge, articulacy, advocacy and assertiveness), in some contexts other dimensions of diversity and inequality become visible. For example, public or community 'demands' for more and better policing often focus on getting 'more bobbies on the beat'. But too many police in the wrong place can also be a source of public dissatisfaction, despite the Home Office, ACPO and Centrex observations in the policy texts (noted in Chapter 3) recording the public's 'insatiable' demand for visible presence police officers. Neither the public nor communities are unitary or homogeneous entities – and getting the balance right can be difficult, as the following extracts illustrate:

They irritate the kids on the corner who believe there's far too many police knocking around. But they don't reassure the public who are demanding them. (Newtown police senior 01)

Because when you think about it that's another thing that's regularly complained about. It is one, we are harassing young black males with stop and search. And the other one is that we're abandoning black areas as crime gets up. Now it's true in all of our black high crime areas, same as it is in all of our other areas of high deprivation that they're high crime areas, they're crime hotspots for street crime, burglaries…, and we have to use appropriate intervention as well in stop and search which is likely to get results. But the same people don't see any contradiction in complaining that we're abandoning an area to crime and we're harassing young black kids with stop and search. (Oldtown police senior 03)

Equity persists as a central concern for public services. Even if they were not 'in the business' of promoting greater social equality, the service managers we interviewed saw their organisations as having definitely *public* obligations and responsibilities – including that of upholding the value of equity. As we have seen, they remained concerned by the particular effects of choice as a mechanism for governing the relationship between the public and the service.

Reconciling needs, wants, rights and resources

In interviews with service providers, we saw a regular construction of a distinction about the process of becoming consumer/customer-centred. They accepted, and even endorsed, the idea of developing a stronger focus on the person using the service, and having a responsive approach to their expressed concerns, needs or wants. However, this was not the same as guaranteeing to deliver the service that the person wants. There were two reasons commonly given. One was that, despite the rise of the 'expert' user, providers believed that they knew something that the service user did not: personal experience is not the same as professional expertise. We explore this issue in the following section on the 'knowledge/power knot'. The second reason was the condition of limited resources. Interviewees made repeated reference to not 'being a business'. In this context, they emphasised that demand and supply were not connected in a way that made increasing demand a criterion of success. On the contrary, public service providers saw themselves in the business of *managing* demand. As a result, the empowering of user choice encounters organisational pressures to the control of (limited) resources, leading to processes of priority setting and rationing. In all the services, there was a sense that this was a dynamic environment in which public expectations had been changing:

Um, and you know, I think there's been a development over a period of time where um, we've actually started to look at the people who use our services not as receivers, grateful receivers of whatever we decide to give them, um, but people who've got views, rights, responsibilities and who actually want to get into a dialogue about, um, how their needs should be met rather than just having things put upon them which, I guess, you know when I first started in social work that was the way things were and nobody challenged it. I mean alongside that I guess again over a period of time – you know, I think one of the big – the biggest challenges for the public services, not just local government but public services generally, is increased expectation on behalf of the public so, you know, successive governments have played about with the health service, um, and, that you know have said you're not gonna wait more than however many weeks it is to see a consultant. (Newtown social care senior 06)

This positive gloss on changing expectations and changing relationships was not shared by everyone. For others, the process of raising expectations was viewed as unsettling or even counter-productive. In the following extract, it is possible to see the signs of strain located in a discourse of 'broken promises':

The other problem is raising public expectations. Um, and this has always been a problem with the NHS, particularly I believe, of course this is my own opinion, but the government is very very good at telling the public you can have this fantastic all singing, all dancing service but then not providing the money to, um, make it happen. An example of that was the Patient Charter. ... Everybody thinks the patient charter is lovely – was lovely and great. And nobody disagreed with it but actually it led the public to believe they would get stuff that actually was never gonna happen because the NHS couldn't afford to deliver it. ... So the sum total of what could have been a very good initiative was that people ended up more annoyed than they might have otherwise been because they thought this was their right, indeed it was their right but they couldn't have it. So that was raising public awareness in terms of an unhelpful way. And that is the danger of public involvement as well. (Newtown health senior 03)

We return to processes of public involvement later in this section. For the moment, though, we want to stay with the uncomfortable relationships between expectations, demands and resources. The sense of strain is – in part – located within the organisation as managers strive to reconcile meeting needs and balancing budgets. Each of the services has approaches to priority setting: for example in social care, it was the combination of establishing common eligibility criteria and performing individual needs assessment. The following two extracts indicate something of the dynamic nature of this process as managers tried to manage:

I think there's a constant battle for us between meeting needs and balancing budgets. And if you ask what's the greatest pressure on me it's those two things which are sometimes opposite ends of the spectrum. Um, if we have an eligibility criteria which we do, and we assess somebody within that eligibility criteria and they meet that criterion then we should provide a service. One of the pressures on us is that we don't always have the budgets to sustain that. I mean we are, on our external domiciliary care, um, we are at £270,000 pounds overspending this year. Now I'm the budget holder, you know, I'm the guy who's accountable for that. (Newtown social care senior 05)

In the following extract, the problem of reconciling demand and resources was ironically translated from 'problem' to 'challenge' by someone remembering their management training. More strikingly, this respondent saw how the strain was occurring both inside the organisation and embedded in more difficult relationships with the public:

> I think the problems or challenges if you're to be a bit more upbeat about it, um, I mean there is this expectation, er, that you will get what you need, you'll get it quickly and I think that applies to the services we provide. And, you know, you're paying your rent so you ought to get a good repair service, um, you ought to get your home care when you need it or get into residential or nursing home care if you need it. And, um, one of the big challenges for us is that we just haven't got enough cash to be able to do that. So what you have to do is you're pinning down your eligibility criteria more and more and more in order to be able to gate keep all of this which in itself produces pressures and quite often difficult relationships that have only become difficult because of that expectation and the lack of resource to be able to do that. (Newtown social care senior 06)

This business of 'expectation management' is clearly a critical element in these processes. Managers in all the services shared this anxiety about what people expect from services. Choice – or at least the promise of choice – disturbed such processes of demand management by creating the appearance of freedom from resource constraint. In health care, for example, choice threatens to disturb well-established practices of managing demand, as new expectations change patient behaviour by altering the calculations that patients make about access to treatment:

> Well, choice would only became more difficult if demands became even greater, so if more people, you know, because waiting times have gone down, some of them previously said 'Don't put me on the waiting list, 'I'll have to wait two years for it.' Well, they might think … 'I'll be done and dusted in three months, I might as well go for it.' So, that may well be that more patients end up on the waiting list or haven't been treated.' (Oldtown health senior 03)

For managers in the different services, choice and resources were mediated by different concepts: for example, demand can be articulated through ideas of needs and rights. One interviewee above hinted that the patients' charter had created rights, even if the public could not exercise them. Rights are an ambiguous part of British social and public policy, and often difficult to turn into specific service outcomes. However, there are points at which rights to services exist – and emerging legal decisions suggest that they may increase (particularly under the Human Rights Act 1998). Nevertheless, the establishment of legal rights to services (individual or collective) has a rather unpredictable and disruptive quality in relation to principles of public service that have framed processes of priority setting and rationing hitherto. One of our case study organisations was the subject of a Human Rights Act case that had challenged their decision not to provide a particular service. Their decision was represented as a rationing decision and the legal challenge as posing uncomfortable new problems for rationing processes and principles. It was viewed within the organisation as a 'pre-emptive' claim on a limited budget – pre-emptive both in terms of committing scarce resources, and in terms of taking a decision about resource allocation out of the collective consideration of claims and resources that the organisation saw as its proper responsibility:

> I haven't really talked about rights because I think one of the things that has been very difficult for us is this whole notion of rights/human rights act. Er, people going more and more down that legislative/litigation, judicial review. You know, these are our rights, our rights to services. And, er, you know, I think that has pushed the agenda, that's pushed the direct payments, that's pushed the charging policies, various things. Er, I don't think the Department of Health are always very good at handling these issues because they try to get a compromise with everyone and it turns out into a sort of mess, I think, often, there is lack of clear thinking. And I think that's – you know, it's very difficult – back to that public service ethos of trying to share out available resources on some equitable basis and I think that often the notion of rights – there's a lot of good things about rights, about the fact people deserve to be treated with respect and dignity and listened to, etc. But at the end of the day I think there still needs – you are then having to make judgements about levels of service provision which involves negotiation, etc. And that, the – some of the rights stuff, it doesn't fit very well with that. (Newtown social care senior 04)

One reading of New Labour's enthusiasm for choice is that it was intended to be a de-stabilising force as a means to challenge 'producer domination'. But it also had the capacity to disrupt established means of making accommodations between individual wants and collective resources without providing an alternative point of (re)stabilisation. As a result, both organisations and their users were experiencing increasing uncertainty about the prevailing, or proper, relationship between rights, resources and rationing. The idea of 'need' was often deployed as a way of trying to re-stabilise this process, since need promised a more 'objective' basis from which organisations could allocate resources:

> I think the problem at the individual level is that the more articulate and the better informed who are often the more middle class and wealthier consumers, um, are able to advocate for a better deal. And that, um, you know there's no reason why everyone shouldn't advocate for a better individual deal but given our job is to manage to provide the best possible service within available resources, part of a local government job is trying to use the available resources equitably. And there is the possibility that by individual consumers advocating strongly that they actually upset that equitable distribution which is meant to be based on need, you know, targeted based on their need which is where assessments is meant to be a sort of objective judgement of different

> levels of need. And if someone with er, less needs advocates more strongly and gets more resource then inevitably other people get less resource somewhere along the line. (Newtown social care senior 04)

This discourse of need is a means of restoring the organisation to a dominant role in managing the relationship between wants and resources. Where rights are located in the hands of the user, need is to be determined by professional evaluation. Need is indelibly marked by professional determination: while users may know what they think they want, only professional expertise can establish what is necessary. For this reason, the distinction between rights-based and needs-based models of social care service provision has been a constant focus of challenge from disabled people's movements. The objectivist conception of need also plays a critical role in the tangle of the 'knowledge/power knot' that we discuss in the next section.

As we saw in Chapter 5, the question of freely made choices was problematic in all three services. Sometimes this was because of forms of compulsion present in policing and, under the Mental Health Act, in health and social care. But more generally, people approach services in order to remedy an unhappy situation or condition. Rather than trying to access a particular commodity they are looking for their circumstances or conditions to be improved or remedied. This implies that public services are rather different from the domain of self-directed choice in pursuit of individual wants and self-realisation that is imagined as the dominant mode of contemporary consumer culture (this does not imply that it *is* the dominant practice, see, *inter alia*, Bevir and Trentmann, 2006; Gabriel and Lang, 1995; Hilton, 2006 and Malpass et al., 2006). In discussions of the consumer in public services, voice and exit have been identified as the two main means of exercising choice and influencing the output and behaviour of organisations. The distinction is derived from Hirschmann's trinity of exit, voice and loyalty (1970). Voice is typically taken to mean the capacity to be listened to by an organisation; while exit implies the capacity to take one's business (and/or money) elsewhere – to a competing provider. The 2004 National Consumer Council (NCC) Policy Commission on Public Services treated this as a distinction between 'choice and voice', both of which 'should be extended in order to rebalance services away from provider interests and towards the services of users' (2004:7; see also Public Administration Select Committee, 2005). In our interviews, however, voice was seen as both desirable and potentially problematic. Organisations hoped to hear from – and learn from – their users. Voices could help shape organisational direction and practices, and most organisations had developed an increasing array of 'listening devices' to bring user, and even non-user, voices into the organisation (Barnes et al., 2007). Here, too, different dynamics came together in the way public involvement was glossed:

> Well, at the end of the day we're all doing public involvement because the government says we should. Um, says we must and has passed legislation to ensure that we do. However, actually, most of us are doing it because we think it's the right thing to do. ... Certainly that's why I'm doing it. Um, being old and cynical I find that, you know, I don't care if the government says we're doing it, I think well I'm only gonna get involved if I think it's the right thing to do. And the reason why I'm in this job is because I think it's the right thing to do and the right way to go. ... But I'm very much not out there on my own. A lot of, um, people at senior levels also share that opinion. Um, a lot of people at junior level share that opinion and a lot of people at grass roots share that opinion. (Newtown health senior 03)

We can see here another version of the intersection of governmental and professional or ethical conceptions of expanding involvement. Like the translations of choice discussed in the previous chapter, this is a view of taking up policy because it can be aligned with other commitments. The extract opens with a self-consciously 'cynical' comment on the weight attached to public involvement in government policy. This cynicism is itself the focus of further reflection in a suggestion that there is a dynamic between 'lip service' and effecting genuine change:

> So there is a culture change going on in the public as well. And sometimes they're suspicious and sometimes they come in and say well you know this is all just lip service, you're not gonna listen to me, you're not gonna take it on board, you're just gonna do what you think. And sometimes that happens. But again, we are getting better at it and we are changing the perception and people now expect more in that line than they did before, simply because they're now getting it. (Newtown health senior 03)

Nevertheless, this process is something other than 'choice' – voices are registered, mapped and managed by organisations as part of their decision-making processes. But the involvement of such voices is, in an important sense, indeterminate (see also Social Care Institute for Excellence, 2004). There has been a proliferation of 'voices' in relation to public services as both individuals and collective movements have demanded greater recognition, respect and responsiveness. At the same time, governmental organisations of all kinds have been taking a greater interest in consulting a complexly constituted public – recognising forms of socio-demographic diversity. In the process, however, there is a potential tension between claims to voice and the voices that organisations are willing to recognise as legitimate. Governmental bodies are implicated in the process of constructing, as well as hearing from, their publics (Barnes et al., 2003 and 2007). In public service provision, organisations retain the capacity to weigh, judge and evaluate different voices. In the following extract, we can see the typical reflection of government drivers for public involvement combined this time with 'ambivalence' (rather than cynicism). This ambivalence derives from a compressed consideration of the 'representativeness' of those who become involved.

About the patient involvement, what do we actually expect? Why are we trying to do this? Well you could say, why, is because the government has told us so, but I think there is more to it than that, I think the government are quite right in trying to improve patient involvement, but I am again a little ambivalent about it, how far can you actually go? We have already mentioned that you will only get certain groups of people who are interested in finding out about health care, usually those who have a vested interest, either for themselves, or for a relation, or for a child or whatever. (Newtown health senior 01)

Service managers were aware of the risks of reproducing inequalities in this choice/voice mode. The articulate, the culturally competent, and the socially authoritative are likely to both speak louder (or more clearly) and be heard better by organisations. But it is not simply a matter of the distribution of such cultural capital between classes. Organisations deal in a complex field of individual and collective voices that work through – and alongside – the conventional processes of political representation. Increasingly, managers see the processes of participation, consultation and listening as a site of dialogic negotiation through which the 'public' can be remade. One police officer summed up the 'needs, wants, choices' tension in his concluding statement:

If...what they actually need isn't quite what you want to deliver, you try and influence either the way that you deliver or the way that they perceive their needs to match up. But most people don't actually talk about the needs, they talk about a solution...But they come up with this solution that we want more police officers on foot and in uniform, particularly during the evenings, that's what I want, that's the solution. Yet we know that that won't actually deliver the reductions in crime that the public think it will do. (Oldtown police senior 03)

The greater attention to diversity might be understood as requiring attention to many voices, but the question of the power, reach and audibility of different voices (and the significance of selective hearing) poses a much greater problem. At the same time, the balance between lay knowledge or expertise – expressed in this greater array of voices claiming organisational attention – and the established sources of organisational and occupational authority in public services was proving equally troubling.

The knowledge/power knot

One critical issue in the unsettled and uncertain relationships between publics and public services is the relationship between expertise and authority, or knowledge and power. Earlier in the book we discussed how the model for public services had rested on a distinctive model of expertise as authority which, for the most part, secured deference and compliance. Consumerism has been one way of trying to grasp the unsettling of such combinations of expertise and authority – the growth of a 'credibility gap' for public services and the professionalised workers they employ. But, as we argued in Chapter 2, there are many different sources of this loosening of nexus of expertise and authority – one of which has been the resurgence of alternative forms of knowledge as the basis for claims making and challenges to professional power.

Forms of knowledge variously described as 'lay', 'situated' or 'experiential' have disrupted the authoritative status of formal or objective knowledge. In public services, there have been different strands to this process. Challenges to the particularity and biases of professional knowledge and the discriminatory exercise of authority have been vitally important, linking feminist challenges to masculinised medicine; anti-racist challenges to the discriminatory use of police powers; and the disabled people's movement's refusal of the 'medical model' of disability in health and social care. More generally, there has been a reluctance to accede to the claim that 'professionals know best' – instead people have laid claim to being 'experts of their own condition'. Richard Sennett catches something of this character of public service bureau-professionalism when he argues that the welfare state had the effect of 'pacifying those whom it helped ... in practice these institutions, which sought to treat clients as whole human beings, made the great and glaring error of denying that the clients were competent to participate in the terms of their own dependency' (2003: 178).

Sennett's argument opens a different view of 'dependency' that drags it away from the binary independence/dependence (active/passive) that has dominated debates about the dependency inducing effects of welfare. Instead, it moves closer to recognising the active state of dependence that brings us to rely on the help, support or assistance of others. As we have suggested, this condition – actively seeking support or remedy – tends to be the condition in which people approach public services. Sennett catches the complex mixture that might characterise the relationships they seek: acknowledging dependency, while having their own competence acknowledged, and being active participants in the process. This complexity is also unstable as different people, at different moments, may give greater weight or emphasis to particular aspects of the active/dependent/competent mix.

We will return to this issue later in the book, but in this context we want to focus on the implications of Sennett's argument for the relationship between expertise and authority – or knowledge and power. The proliferation of ways in which people are seen, and see themselves, as active, competent participants disrupts the unity and stability of the connection of knowledge and power in the bureau-professional institutions of public welfare (Clarke and Newman, 1997). Instead, we see the relationships between knowledge and power as a tangled knot, in which many threads are wound together. We have borrowed the focus on knowledge and power from the work of Michel Foucault who explored the intricate interweaving of power and knowledge and the installation of particular forms of knowledge-as-truth in apparatuses and practices (see, for example, Foucault, 1977 and 1979 and the discussions in Marston, 2004 and Watson, 2000).

Our interviews highlighted the unsettled relationships between knowledge and power in the contemporary fields of public service. In Chapter 4 we looked at some of the tensions around 'challenge' to service providers. The relationship between knowledge and power is central to the question of challenge. In our organisational interviews with service managers, it became clear that changing services and their relationships with the public involved difficult realignments of knowledge and power: we were concerned about the role of professional expertise and identity in influencing the front-line response. Not surprisingly given the dominance of medical knowledge, this was particularly visible in the context of health care:

> And it is like therapy, the client is the main focus, and enabling and empowering the client to make choices that are right for them is my professional ethic, so that is where I come from. But the health professionals don't have that background, so won't come from that point of view so we have a big exercise if you will, with people who have been trained traditionally and in hierarchical ways around them giving up power. A lot of it is around fear, losing status, I suppose, losing control, but also I fear for the patient that they don't trust the patient to make the right choice, whereas from my perspective there is no right choice. (Oldtown Health senior 01)

> Um, certainly it's my perception that, um, there is the kind of 'knowledge is power' thing going on, particularly amongst the medical staff... there is the kind of well, hey I'm a doctor and we know the right thing. And it's not just applicable to doctors, that's applicable to lots of people in the NHS, in all different types of disciplines... it is the kind of, um, sharing of power that's the painful bit. (Newtown health senior 03)

The history and organisation of health provision is seen as a central structuring principle of power in these extracts: 'tradition' and 'hierarchy' are intimately bound up with power (bearing in mind that these interviews were conducted in the primary care sector, rather than in hospital settings). But both extracts speak to the sense of strain and tension around power, and to the ways in which new relationships with patients are difficult to construct. The same themes are visible in the other services. For example in social care:

> I think some staff have actually found that a lot more challenging than others. You know, I think some staff have actually seen it as you know, a sort of I don't know – a diminution of their skills, you know. Er, um, but, er, they're not the kind of all seeing, all hearing professional who knows best anymore, they have a certain set of skills and they need to negotiate with the person that they're working with in order to get the best for them. Um, so it's not you know, the professional knows best any more. I think that's been quite difficult for some staff to actually deal with. (Newtown social care senior 06)

These extracts point to ways in which public services are considered to be a site of hierarchically organised professional knowledge and power that has become unsettled and tangled into new knots as other forms of knowledge are asserted and other claims to power – or empowerment – are made. Managers and senior professionals (the two categories are blurred in most services) see themselves as responsible for undoing the 'knowledge/power knot' and reconstructing the relationships between staff and users. Organisations, embodied in the authority of managers, have been trying to find new configurations of knowledge and power that would take account of a more active, participating, competent public. To some extent, their attempts to disentangle the knowledge/power knot focus on staff: getting them to loosen their grip on knowledge, power, authority, status and control. But as we will see in the following section, they also see themselves as working on the users of the services.

Realistic, reasonable, responsible: constructing the ideal consumer?

In political and policy terms, it is clear that 'choice' is seen as a way of cutting the knowledge/power knot and undermining producer or professional power by putting choice in the hands of the consumer. As we have argued in preceding chapters, this may explain some of its appeal, promising services that are more responsive to user wishes and undercutting the subordinating and pacifying effects of professional authority. It has, though, two problems that bear particularly on the knowledge/power knot. First, it does not address the dynamic of active dependency in which people seek expertise because they want problems solved or conditions remedied. Second, it does not address the relationship between wants and resources discussed earlier. The discourse of choice was seen by many of our respondents as having created expectations that they will struggle to meet:

> So you do get some people who want the world on a plate. They expect everything, and of course it is limited resources, but they want the carer there at a specific time on the dot, they don't seem to understand that it is for everybody, there is limited resource, and that we are trying to do our best, but some people use it literally as a consumer, as they would out in the marketplace. (Newtown social care senior 01)

A similar sense of frustration about public expectations and what services could deliver was articulated in some of the police service interviews:

> And the more people get to understand not just what their problems are but the way we operate and the different, the level of demand. Because people genuinely think – because they say 'and you never bothered to send anyone', as if we've got a bunch sitting there playing cards and say 'we can't be bothered to

turn up for that'. But the reality is that everybody's out there and is this important enough to divert somebody away from what they're already doing? Which is what we do when something serious comes in. Now sometimes there will be people who are free but the majority of time there isn't anybody free so something gets stuck in one form of queue unless it's life threatening or we're likely to lose a prisoner if we don't go straight away so then people get diverted. But most people don't understand that. They think it's like the ambulance – although they're increasingly like us – or the fire service where the 999 happens and everybody rushes to the cars and goes off – not. They're already out there and they're moving from different places. (Oldtown police senior 03)

No doubt there have always been mismatches between what people want from services and the capacity of services to deliver. But in some interviews the government's choice and reform agenda was seen as promoting the rise of 'unrealistic' expectations:

Respondent: Oh don't ... resources. Especially in the NHS. You know, every day there's an announcement on the breakfast telly – that they're gonna chuck in another x billion pounds or whatever. You know damn well that everybody out there's thinking that there's gonna be masses of money sloshing round the system, they're gonna get to see their doctor within 24 hours, they're gonna have their operation next week and you know, what the government never says is that this money won't even keep the older, you know, population getting more frail ...

Interviewer: Does that impact on what's expected of you?

Respondent: Yes, oh yeah. It's hideous. (Newtown social care senior 07)

The government set in play a destabilising dynamic in the triangular relationship between themselves, the public and service organisations. It clearly expected that 'choice' would provide a lever of reform with the specific capacity to improve performance, not least through creating rising expectations of service quality and responsiveness. The intention was, presumably, to ensure that service providers should become 'responsibilised' in this process (see Malpass et al., 2006 on the problematisation of responsibility). Indeed responsibility for performance had been devolved to specific organisations whose performance could then be measured, evaluated and compared. It is less clear that the public believed in this division and devolution of responsibility, since it continued to hold government responsible for the performance of key public services (Clarke, 2005c).

We want to highlight two less visible features of the Labour government's approach to choice. The first concerns what we might call 'the small print': in policy and practice, choice had been hedged around by qualifications about who could choose what, and under what conditions (Clarke et al., 2006; Greener, 2003). For example, parental choice in education meant, in practice, the expression of preference; patient choice in the NHS denoted choice of GP (where available) or choice of hospital for surgery (after a specified waiting time); and choice in social care was constrained by eligibility criteria and subject to means testing. Of course, the 'small print' is not an exclusively public service phenomenon: market-place choice is also complexly hedged around and confined by various qualifiers and conditions.

The second feature of choice that is significant here concerns the ideas of 'reasonable' and 'responsible' consumers. The expansive and dynamic choice agenda encounters – or perhaps even produces – the 'unmanage-able consumer' (Gabriel and Lang, 1995). There have been recurrent cam-paigns about 'irresponsible' consumption of public services: most obviously around inappropriate use of the emergency (999) call numbers and calling out GPs to deal with non-urgent conditions. In health care, one of our case study organisations had developed what might be described as a diversion system to deflect some of the demand from GPs to nurses:

> Minor illness nurses they're fully – obviously fully trained at degree level, um, will see a patient, talk to them on the phone, will see a patient and examine that patient fully. And they are far less likely to prescribe than GPs. The whole idea is to educate the patient but if you wake up with a sore throat you don't need to ring the GP there and then. You can actually take some paracetomol, drink some extra fluids and see if it gets better. And if after three or four days it's not getting better than perhaps that's the time to come down to the surgery. But the first sign of a cough doesn't mean that you have a chest infection that you have to be seen. But what it means is that's your body's – a cough is a natural reflex, it's the body's way of getting rid of something, it could be something or nothing. You sort of wait and see. Um, if you have a cold or flu you don't have to go to the doctors the first day, you can self-medicate at home, use your pharmacist's advice, wait and see. So a lot of the minor illness nurse role is around educat-ing people. (Newtown health senior 02)

It is possible to see a variety of strategies in this innovation. One is the diversion itself, from GPs to nurses. The second is the likely implication for service delivery, implying reduced prescribing levels. A third is that the nurse system will put time delays into the process: 'sort of wait and see'. Finally, there is the process of 'educating people': getting people to know themselves medically and become experts of their own 'minor' conditions. All the organisations we dealt with saw the processes of involvement and engagement with the public as a means of constructing 'reasonable' con-sumers. At an individual level, provider organisations saw encounters with users as a site for remaking at least some of them into self-directing or self-managing subjects. In health, for example, 'expert patients' were a route to more autonomously self-managing patients that could be ensured through their participation in education and development programmes. In social care, the processes of assessment and support could also be a passage to more autonomy and less dependency.

In more collective forms, organisations treated forms of public involve-ment as a sites in which both organisations and the public could be 'educated'. Service providers could learn about user/public perceptions, wants and expectations while the public could become 'knowledgeable' in service terms – learning to appreciate the constraints, conditions and calculations of 'professional' or 'organisational' knowledge. One senior police officer memorably talked about this as constructing a shift from an 'ill-informed to an informed community':

> ... in some ways, we're trying to open up the debate about looking at the public as consumers and having an understanding of what their needs are, and then in return for that being able to move from being what I describe as an ill-informed community to an informed community, then you can actually have some logic to your debate with them. (Newtown police senior 02)

Bringing the public to an understanding of the organisational and occupational 'logics' of service provision is clearly a process through which more realistic and reasonable expectations can be constructed. Our study provided rich examples of how such 'educative' work could be done; for example in Newtown specialist police officers (drug squad or dog handlers) were encouraged to talk to the public about what they contributed as a counter to blanket requests for more 'bobbies on the beat'. Constructing an informed public may even have amplifying effects as members of the public come to represent the service to others:

> I'll give you examples of this ... The consultation groups that were set up under Scarman all those years ago, people come along to the first one they've been to shouting the odds and demanding this and demanding that and why this, why that. And you'll see the ones who've been coming on a regular basis are quite often – senior officers don't have to defend anything because they will explain. 'I waited two hours for a burglary, two hours'. And one of them said 'was the offender there?'. 'Well, no'. 'Well how long do you think you'll wait in casualty? That's reasonable. It's waiting two hours with someone physically breaking in that would be unacceptable'. (Oldtown police senior 03)

Organisations are edging towards more 'dialogic' relationships with the public, both in terms of individual users and collectivities involved in participation and consultation processes. Such shifts are uncomfortable and uncertain because they are shaped by each of the strains that we have discussed in this chapter. They are forms in which services try to negotiate choice and equity and the troubled intersections of needs, wants, rights and resources. They are both the product of, and responses to, the tangles of the knowledge/power knot. They are multi-tasked: potentially expansive learning experiences for the organisation, but they are also means of deflection or diversion (responsibilising and autonomising users) and the site of 'educative' work as organisations seek to create the responsible, reasonable and realistic 'consumers' of the future.

7

What's in a Name? In Search of the Citizen-Consumer

Our research started from the New Labour conception of a consumerist imperative for public service reform. Services should match the experiences and expectations associated with a 'consumer society'. The depth of social change involved in the move to a consumer society or consumer culture had left public services looking outmoded, out of touch and out of time:

> People grow up today in a consumer society. Services – whether they are private or public – succeed or fail according to their ability to respond to modern expectations … People today exercise more choices in their lives than at any point in history. Many can afford to walk away from public services which do not command their confidence. (Milburn, 2001)

In this chapter:

- we explore how people – as providers and users of services – think of this relationship;
- we begin with some of the reflections in provider organisations on their changing relationships with the public, and some of the difficulties of 'naming' people who use services;
- we then examine the ways in which people who use services identify themselves, exploring the connections and disjunctures with government discourse;
- we emphasise the ways in which people engage reflexively in 'relational reasoning' about their existing and desired relationships with public services.

Addressing the public

Rather than seeing the consumer as the all-powerful driver of a more accountable, responsive and user-oriented service, the interviews we conducted with service managers offered a number of different conceptions of the people who used their services. Indeed, the interviews suggest that the relationship between the public and public services was a continuing concern to service organisations as they tried to find ways of bringing together a changing public and changing public services. There were ongoing struggles to re-conceptualise the user in ways that drew on developments in professional conceptions of best practice, that responded to some of the challenges of user movements, and that acknowledged the need for maintaining or creating legitimacy in the eyes of possibly sceptical users of services.

A critical issue concerns the words that have been used to name preferred identifications. Almost everyone we spoke to reflected on the problem of 'naming'. They drew out the current uncertainty about what words to use to identify the members of the public with whom they came into contact. A couple of examples will indicate just how complicated they perceived this issue to be. First, a complex and ironic reflection on the mutability of terminology and the problem of the contextual appropriateness of specific words:

> In five years or something I think public involvement will be part of our everyday function. And I think that once the actual act becomes much more of a day to day [thing], the terminology comes with it because at the moment the terminology is scary, you know, the customer thing is scary 'cause that means we might have to, like, you know, ask some stuff and you know, treat them differently. Um, and similarly consumer, um, it's a bit like the British Rail thing isn't it? Stop calling you passengers and started calling you consumers, everybody just laughs because, you know, it's stupid because I'm still a passenger. But, um, if it's the right place I think – and that's the crucial thing for me. In the right place and not just because it's the buzz-word, not just 'cause the government says 'these are the words we should use now' and it's the thing to do because that's when it gets ridiculed. But in the right place as clients and users now are. And I can remember five years ago I suppose, not very long, when people absolutely ridiculed the use of the term client. And I won't tell you what they used to say about it because I thought it was quite rude, as in other places where they use the word client. Um, and now, you know, people don't turn a hair at that phrase. So I think that when – it's about changing the culture and the other stuff comes with the change of culture. (Newtown health senior 02)

This subtle tracing of pressures, contexts and changes over time links governmental and organisational dynamics. Elsewhere, people reflected on the difficulties of naming the sorts of relationships that form the everyday business of the service:

Respondent: Um, as an organisation more often we use the term 'service users, users, people who use services'. I think we're moving towards 'people who use services'. The reality is if you're writing a report or writing anything you tend to go for some kind of shorthand. We do tend to move towards service users and away from clients although there are just occasionally times when client feels the right term.

Interviewer: What times?

> *Respondent*:   I knew you'd ask me. Um, I suppose when engaging with people who don't want to engage with you. Um, particularly if you think of adult protection, child protection, um, when people are not necessarily willingly coming to us. Because again the concept of customer assumes that somebody is coming to you because they wish to. In the mental health field, in abuse situations people are not always coming because they want to, they're being forced on their doorstep … I think that, um …, the client you're getting involved with, in the main, because of them presenting some risk somewhere along the line whereby we need to exercise a degree of control. Um, they're definitely not coming of their own free will. I suppose for customers not coming of their own free will but in a bit of a different position, they know that they want a service, they know that if they want that service they've got to come here. It's like when – if you wanted a car from Ford it used to be black because they all did black cars but you could choose to have the cars. (Oldtown social care senior 03)

Our interviews generated an astonishingly rich set of reflections on a variety of terms: citizens, clients, consumers, customers, service users, members of the public, patients, people who use services, punters and more. Each of them was turned over and over to bring different facets into view for consideration. Here, for example, a social care worker (employed by a private provider, rather than a local authority) ponders on the word customer:

> *Respondent*:   Well customer really is what they are, aren't they, because they're paying for the service that they get. But I don't like using it, I don't think that's a nice word to use when it's so personal. I wouldn't be standing at a till in Tescos giving somebody a full wash down would I? You do that in the privacy of their own home.
>
> *Interviewer*:   Is that why customer is not a nice word to use?
>
> *Respondent*:   No I don't think so, no. And they don't actually pay me do they? They pay the company. They're not paying me. So they're not my customer are they? They're a customer to the service. (Newtown social care front-line staff 02)

Here we catch a troubled glimpse of the multiple relationships that might be in play in the process of providing and using a service. Customer, for this worker, registers one aspect – the payment for services provided. This is a relationship between the providing organisation (the company). It has a commercial referent (Tesco), but fails to grasp the particular nature of the relationship with the worker and the person receiving the service. For this relationship, customer fails on two grounds: the relationship is not a direct cash transaction ('they're not paying me… ') and it misses the 'personal' character of the service.

In health care, however, the conception of the relationship between provider and service user still tended to be dominated by clinical models of care, albeit models in which patient experience was accorded a higher value because of its impact on health outcomes. In Oldtown an initiative was under way to research patient experience of their treatment – the 'patient journey' - in order to compare this with best practice in terms of specific health problems. The idea of the patient journey offers a more person-centred concept of the service user, but this is still a long way from the image of the active, informed or empowered patient: it is a source of (aggregated and codified) data that can inform service planning in order to secure better treatment and health outcomes. The idea of the 'expert patient' signified rather different changes in the relationships between provider and service user:

> The idea is that these patients who are going to be sent on the expert patient pro-gramme are the patients that present, sort of every week, that they do have ... a chronic illness, but they just seem to need reassurance about all other aspects of their health and so will present week after week. So there is a place now where they can learn how to be more independent. Um, and that is a govern-ment initiative. (Newtown health senior 3)

The language of 'expert patient' was sometimes rejected in favour of a more professionalised concept of 'guided patient self-management' (Oldtown health senior 04: a senior clinician with a GP background). The aim was to secure better health outcomes, but the change of language explicitly rejected the linking of 'patient' and 'expertise': the challenge to professional power was thus minimised. Other shifts in language suggest ways in which policy discourse was being appropriated and reworked. In Newtown one respondent linked patient expertise not to individual dis-ease management but to a more collective sharing of knowledge and experience among patients. She spoke of how parents of children who had been cared for in the hospital's special baby unit, but who had recov-ered and returned home, came in and talked to parents of children cur-rently in care; and of how adults who had been in intensive care came in to explain to current patients what they could expect when they go home:

> And that's kind of my original definition of expert patient but it can happen in all sorts of fields, for example diabetes. And now the Expert Patient programme that the government is supporting [has come in] and it's a training course... it teaches them self-help skills, um, how to deal – different ways to deal with pain, different ways to deal with depression caused by pain, um, and so forth, improves their confidence, improves their ability to speak to health care professionals, all of which I think is terribly important, a jolly useful thing to happen. But I think calling it the Expert Patient programme was really unhelpful. (Newtown health care senior 03)

Here we have used capitals to signify 'official' policy usage of the term and lower case to signify the everyday usage amongst those we inter-viewed. The distinction between official and everyday usage suggests ways in which government and professional discourses are aligned in complex articulations, and how such articulations reflect particular points of institutional adaptation. But other contexts produce both innovation and problems of 'naming' (Newman and Vidler, 2006a). Primary Care Trusts have been one of the settings for 'cross border' working between health and social care – an encounter that generates its own language troubles:

> Some of the nurses are employed by the PCT, some would have a joint, um, post between PCT and the Council, and we could not agree on what to call them because they are patients – when they are in the surgery they are patients. They are clients, if you work for the council they are your clients. Service users sounded hard and not at all patient friendly, um, so we couldn't agree on a word that we all felt comfortable with because the, um, people who like to call them clients were saying 'well they're not ill really so they're not patients'. Nurses don't tend to use the word client, client they tend to feel is more somebody who is per-haps going for counselling. So it's all these different cultures about 'what do you call somebody'. So there is no easy answer to that and if you've got fifteen spe-cialist nurses in a room and they can't come up with a generic name it's, um, I mean customers, clients, patients, users … (Newtown health senior 02)

In policing, too, concepts of the consumer and customer gave rise to dis-comforts about the models of service and service relationships that they implied. One senior officer explained his reservations about consumerist ideas and the problems of describing his service as something similar to a 'business' model:

> … in business it is all about people, don't get me wrong, I'm sure that business people have very good contacts with people they've built up over the years, or even friends, but I think the difficulty with our customers is that some of them can be quite difficult individuals, some of them are very difficult to satisfy and you may disagree with some of them... (Oldtown police senior 02)

When asked by the interviewer whether this was because of a lack of a cash relationship with the users he went on to explain:

> I think we've got a far bigger duty to our customers than that, I mean … if some-one wants to make a complaint, but if I was in Marks and Spencers it is easier to give them vouchers, £60 worth of vouchers and then they go away and say 'thank you very much' and are happy, you know, whereas sometimes I have to say 'OK, I appreciate how upset you are about the way the officers dealt with that, but actually they are actually complying with the law, but we are sorry if it causes distress'. (Oldtown police senior 02)

Another Oldtown officer made a similar point about the 'customers' who come through the door:

> But the community, most definitely, they demand things of me, essentially to reduce crime and disorder, so they are my customer, and I need to deliver that.

> But in a different way, the offender who comes in through the door to the custody office, even though they have lost their liberty, they are still a customer ... (Oldtown police senior 01)

In a similar vein to the social care discussions earlier, this concept of the unwilling customer was taken up by most of the police interviewees, with one of the Newtown officers, in a discussion about the difference between public services such as the police and private business, stating:

> I think too, that the difference for us in some ways with Tescos is, you know is that we have some people who are not customers by choice. (Newtown police senior 01)

He added that in terms of changes in attitudes of the rank and file towards such people, that:

> They will use the word customer ... but almost in a sarcastic way ... Most of them. Most police officers are aware that there's something happening out there, that people are less tolerant of a poor service, so they do refer to them as customers ... (Newtown police senior 01)

This senior officer, in common with an earlier interviewee from Oldtown quoted above, who said that he thought it would only be 'senior people within the organisation' who would be conversant with the term consumer, is aware that front-line staff might not embrace the concept of the consuming public. This observation was largely accurate as the questionnaire data from the front-line police staff shows. Like other services, they were reluctant to take up the term consumer, though more willing than the others to think of people as customers.

Table 7.1, like Figures 4.2–4.5, suggests some key differences between how front-line staff in each service tended to conceptualise the publics with whom they interacted. For example the use of 'customer' was much more prevalent in the police service than in health and social care; but so

Table 7.1   *Who are the people who use your service?*

	Health	Police	Social Care	Total
Consumer	1 (1.4%)	4 (2.9%)	3 (5.0%)	8 (3.0%)
Customer	3 (4.1%)	25 (18.4%)	6 (10.0%)	34 (12.6%)
Patient	22 (30.1%)	0	4 (6.7%)	26 (9.7%)
Service user	24 (32.8%)	10 (7.4%)	21 (35.0%)	55 (20.4%)
Citizen	3 (4.1%)	15 (11.0%)	6 (10.0%)	24 (8.9%)
Member of the public	5 (6.8%)	54 (39.7%)	3 (5.0%)	62 (23.0%)
Member of the local community	15 (20.5%)	28 (20.6%)	17 (28.3%)	60 (22.3%)
Total	73	136	60	269

Note: Totals are for identifications checked on the questionnaire. Since respondents were allowed up to two answers, the totals are greater than the total number of respondents. See **Appendix** for more details.

were the terms 'citizen', 'member of the public' and 'member of the local community'. In the following sections we explore how people using services thought of themselves, and compare this with the data in Table 7.1. But we want to draw out two more general points about the issues of identifications and relationships suggested by the interviews and focus groups we used to unpack the 'snapshot' findings of the questionnaire. First, it is clear that, for all three services, the relationship of service providers to the public was unsettled. Each of them was engaged in processes of 'reinventing' those relationships, trying to deal with changing expectations, and problematic alignments of expertise, knowledge and power. At best, they saw 'consumerism' as merely one aspect of this larger field of unsettled relationships. More often, they saw it as carrying inappropriate and unhelpful implications that clouded rather than clarified the reinvention of their relationships with the public.

Secondly, the interviews and focus groups revealed an intense engagement of both managers and staff with the question of 'naming'. These are not just 'word games': rather they reveal just how troubled organisations and their staff are about relationships with people who use their services. These are sites of discomfort (words that don't fit or feel wrong), anxiety (about how to address people individually and collectively) and desire (about how to make things work better – for the public and for themselves). The phrase 'it depends what you mean by … ' is not a trivial comment. As we can see here, and will see more in the following sections, quite of lot of important things 'depend on what you mean by … ' consumers, citizens and the rest.

Who do you think you are?

Now we turn to the people who use services. How do they think of themselves when they engage with public services? In trying to answer this question, we will be drawing on three types of data from our study. The first is the questionnaire that we distributed to 50 randomly selected users of the three services in our two locations. The final question asked respondents to consider a number of possible identifications and relationships (citizen, consumer, member of the public and so on) and to select those that they felt best reflected who they thought they were when interacting with the service in question. People could select more than one category, and most did so. It produced data that parallels staff responses in Table 7.1 above. They were then invited, on the questionnaire itself, to add comments about why they had chosen particular categories. This gave us initial sets of quantitative and qualitative data.

We then used this data to design semi-structured interview schedules to test some of the emerging themes, and carried out follow-up interviews with respondents who had indicated their willingness to be interviewed. The interviews, then, are not based on a random sample – they possibly represent those with more time and commitment than the norm. However we found very similar themes emerging from the questionnaires and interviews: the interviews, then, allowed us to explore in further depth themes that were already emerging from the questionnaire data. Finally, we held focus groups in each case study site drawing on members of local patient and public participation groups. These were not 'representative' of the general population but individuals who were engaged in directly using services or acting as public representatives in various institutional forums.

The survey results suggest that, despite the current prevalence of consumerist discourse in policy texts and political speeches, ideas of consumer and customer appear to not be very significant as an identification for people who use services to talk about themselves.

The results in Table 7.2 are significant in a number of ways. The limited identification with consumer and customer was striking, but so, too, was the limited identification with citizen (less than 10 per cent of responses). Is it possible that the big binary distinction between citizen and consumer so central to political discourse (and political science) lacks any substantial popular reach around public services? By contrast, what we might call 'service specific terms' (patient and service user) – expressing a relationship to a particular service – had a much greater reach. Interestingly, when we compare this with Table 7.1, we can see that users of police services tended not to think of themselves as customers despite them being named as such by police officers; and, though less statistically significant, the data suggests that health service users were rather keener to hang on to the term 'patient' than were health professionals (see Table 7.1).

Table 7.2   *Who are you when you use public services?*

	Health	Police	Social Care	Totals
Consumer	3 (3.1%)	1 (1.6%)	0	4 (2.2%)
Customer	3 (3.1%)	1 (1.6%)	4 (22.2%)	8 (4.4%)
Patient	30 (30.9%)	0	4 (22.2%)	34 (18.9%)
Service user	23 (23.7%)	6 (9.4%)	6 (33.3%)	35 (19.6%)
Citizen	5 (5.2%)	11 (17.2%)	1 (5.6%)	17 (9.5%)
Member of the public	20 (20.6%)	19 (29.7%)	0	39 (21.8%)
Member of the local community	13 (13.4%)	26 (40.6%)	3 (16.7%)	42 (23.5%)
Totals	97	64	18	179

The other popular terms amongst people who use services were ones that invoked a sense of 'membership' – relationships of belonging in which people are part of something, and feel that being a member is a condition of entitlement or access to services. Larger collective imaginaries – the public and the local community – carry this sense of belonging and attachment. Ideas of belonging carry double meanings. Belonging can both locate an identity and express a relationship of ownership: I belong here; this belongs to me/us (see Cooper, 1998).

The questionnaires suggested that people are well able to hold different identifications alongside each other, but that these are mobilised depending on the context and nature of specific transactions. We looked at the different forms of hybrid identifications evident in the 'comments' section of the questionnaire. First, four responses from Newtown attempted to reconcile consumerist with other forms of identification:

> I find it very difficult to answer as I would like to feel I was a consumer as I have paid for my treatment. Unfortunately I still feel a patient and as though there is a long way to go before the general public realise we pay for this service and have rights to demand a better service. (Newtown health user 32: no selection)

> The NHS is like any other service provider, public or private. I am therefore a customer forced to use the service but with no opportunity to take most of my custom elsewhere. The private sector does not provide many of the products only available from the NHS. (Newtown health user 21: selected customer and service user)

> I have many relatively serious conditions, and, therefore, am most definitely a patient. But I am also a consumer, having paid NI contributions for many, many years. (Newtown health user 34: selected patient)

> I can and have been a patient and if and when I use my doctor or hospital I suppose I am a customer. As I have paid NI cons for 45 years I hope I'm a valued contributor and customer – there is a doubt in my mind though! (Newtown health user 11: selected consumer and patient)

Interestingly only one of these – the second – used the term customer to open up questions of choice; the others interpret 'consumer' or 'customer' as something linked to the rights of citizenship associated with paying NI contributions or taxes. This sense of contribution and entitlement is a strong one around the health service, though less visible in relation to the other two services. Indeed, in one response on policing, the connection of payment and rights to service was explicitly rejected:

> I am not the type of person who says 'well we pay for your wages so serve us'. When it comes to crime and disorder we must all be as responsible as we can and the police like the rest of us are also members of the public and a local community wherever they live. (Oldtown police user 3: selected member of the public, and member of the local community)

In social care, however, the consumer/customer positions were also glossed in terms of payment, but here the question of payment seemed to be located more immediately in the context of means-tested contributions to the cost of services:

> I am a service user dependent for my well-being on the care I receive. I am a customer because I have to pay a high price for this care. (Newtown social care user 1: selected customer and service user)

> I am a customer because I pay for a service set up by Social Services and so I am a service user as I use the service set up by the social worker and provided by the care service. A carer comes to my house on a daily basis to help

with personal care, which I pay for. (Newtown social care user 6: selected customer and service user)

In the health responses, the identification 'patient' was much more prevalent than those of consumer or customer. These two terms were often explicitly rejected in ways that addressed wider political discourses and implications:

Patient is the traditional term and I think it is still appropriate. The NHS is a service to users (in the local community). I know 'consumer' and 'customer' imply choice and that is what we are supposed to want. I would consider it an acceptable achievement if everyone could have what was best in the matter of treatment as of right. There are certain cost considerations but that is another issue. 'Choice' may be a political ploy to take our eye off the ball and confuse us as to what really matters. Choice sounds a good thing – but is it? Sorry, this is one of my hobby horses! (Newtown health user 8: selected patient and service user)

Consumer/customer do not fit as I do not 'buy'. Service user is politically correct psychobabble. Citizen is not a word that appeals to me. When I need treatment I am a patient, when I do not I am a member of the public. (Newtown health user 33: selected patient and member of the public)

The hybrid forms linking 'patient' (or 'service user') and 'member of the public' (sometimes 'member of the local community') were by far the most common combinations. But they expressed distinctive conceptions of 'patient' or 'service user'. Some registered conditions of dependence and need, while others suggested a more assertive, knowledgeable or self-reliant image, closer to that found in current policy and professional discourse:

I am a user of the NHS service when I am in need of it. I consider a patient to be someone who is more intensely dependent on the NHS. I like to be involved in making decisions about my healthcare, and question 'professionals' when I feel the need: yet I don't feel autonomous enough to be labelled a 'customer' or 'consumer'. (Oldtown health user 20: selected service user and member of the public)

Service user – this is a two way partnership between the person who is ill and the medical adviser. Member of the local community – because I am concerned about the quality of this public service for all its users in the community. (Newtown health user 16: selected service user and member of the local community)

1   I am registered as a patient with a GP practice and as such I am entitled to receive consultation and treatment and/or referral for health issues. The practice (I believe) received NHS funding for having me registered as a patient.
2   As a member of the public my relationship to the NHS extends beyond that of only a patient. As a long term (unpaid) carer for my elderly mother I had extensive experience of dealing with the NHS on her behalf when she became old and frail. I have been involved in voluntary work through the Carers Project on a GP initiative project. Also as a member of the public with a vote I consider a political party's policy on NHS issues when I cast that vote. (Newtown health user 13: selected patient and member of the public)

The last two quotations are interesting for the ways in which they combine an individual conception of patient-hood, closely based on a personalised relationship with medical practitioners, with wider collective identifications and – in some cases – active commitments. This was visible too in many of the combinations discussed by police users:

> Police matters should be consistent all over the country not just depending on where you live. I am a local tenant looking after myself but also my fellow residents. (Oldtown police user 08: selected member of the public and member of the local community)

> As a citizen and a member of the local community I have responsibilities for 'my actions' and to those who live besides me. (Oldtown police user 11: selected citizen and member of the local community)

Finally, we want to note how, in using the opportunity on the questionnaire to elaborate on their choice of words, many gave aspirational or normative responses – as in 'I am currently x but would like to be thought of as y', or a particular word should mean something different from what it currently seems to mean in practice:

> Fact – I am a patient – no fancy or alternative word is necessary, and I am a member of the public, but that is where it stops in terms of words.
> I need to be listened to; I have brains, access to the internet, know my body etc.
> Respected, i.e. separate wards, male/female.
> A person.
> I need to be trusted, i.e. that what I say is true to my best knowledge.
> That as a patient I am part of a team and care works both ways. I have expectations as a patient – that I will get the best and most up-to-date treatment in the cleanest of environments and as a patient it is my right to have this. The word patient should be used at all times in its truest, basic meaning. (Newtown health user 1: selected patient and member of the public)

The formulation here of a 'truest, basic meaning' tries to organise the plural, overlapping and possibly conflicting meanings of the word patient into a hierarchy of legitimacy. To explore ways in which the meaning of many of the words in question is being contested or re-negotiated we turn to an analysis of reflections that emerged in the interviews and focus groups.

Reinventing the patient

In interviews and focus groups, health users made it evident that they perceived themselves – and, indeed, wanted to perceive themselves – as patients, rather than customers or consumers. Here we focus more specifically on how they construed the identity and role of being a patient. This issue has a particular salience within our study, in part because 'patient' is always treated as the most professionally or medically defined identity. But it also catches a wider political and cultural significance of the National Heath Service as the embodiment of public services in the UK. The NHS, since its inception in 1948, has provided a symbolic representation of public service values. It thus provides a fertile terrain on which people reflect about their relationships to services.

> I think a patient is, er, I think a patient is more or less, er, you have a personal relationship between your doctor and yourself. There is a relationship between the doctor and yourself, whereas as a customer there is no relationship. You just walk in and do your business and walk away, whereas there is a continuous relationship between your doctor and you, probably till the day you die, do you see what I mean? ... [I]n my GP's surgery I'm like a stakeholder because my secrets are there, do you see what I mean? My notes are mine, my patient notes are mine, they are my problems, my illness, my concern, so again it's like a partnership, that is how I see it, do you see what I mean? Whereas if I am in a shop, if I go to Marks and Spencer, I am just there to buy something, I don't have any relationship with them ... No, I don't want to be a customer. I want to be a patient. I want to be a patient. I think once you become a customer you are lumped with customers in a shop, customers in a petrol station, customers in a travel insurance company, whereas as a patient you have that personal relationship which is very difficult to break. (Newtown health user interview 01)

This insistence on the relational connection to personified or embodied health care is a recurrent theme. In this extract, the relationship to the doctor is a nexus of complicated connections and is forcefully contrasted with the depersonalised transactions of the commercial customer. A similar juxtaposition is visible in the following extract:

> I am a patient and that's the word I understand ... I don't feel I'm a customer of the National Health Service, or any health service for that matter. I feel I am a patient and I would like to develop my relationship with my health care professional. Because the way I view it is, being a diabetic, and any other problem I may have health wise, I'm the one whose got it and I have to lead it. The people who are around me are my team who are helping me get there. And a healthcare professional is part of my team. But I am his patient or her patient ... I think customer is a very distant relationship. I don't think it is a relationship because I can walk into a shop over the road and be a customer, but not necessarily know the person who is serving me. But I think it's important that you know the person who is dealing with you as a patient. (Oldtown health user interview 03)

In these extracts, the word patient is not used as a default position. Instead it was perceived as a term that positively identified the processes of developing and maintaining meaningful and productive relationships with health professionals. Indeed we can see emerging constructions of the patient that incorporate or appropriate elements of professional discourses of 'stakeholder', 'partnership' and 'team' relationships, and, in the second quotation, of the patient as 'leading' the health care team. But we can also trace older inflections of the 'special-ness' of the doctor-patient relationship: as the first respondent above puts it, because 'my secrets are there …'. These two different constructions of the doctor-patient relationship – one as more open and team-based, another as private and special – are reconciled in the idea of the doctor-patient relationship as ongoing and personal, one based on deep and intimate knowledge.

The important feature of this knowledge is not the 'expert' knowledge of the professional in contrast with the 'unknowing' patient, but a more personalised knowledge both of the self – 'these are my problems, my illness, my concern … ' and of the other – 'I think it is important that you know the person who is dealing with you as a patient' (see Newman and Vidler, 2006b). This reciprocal knowledge is viewed as the basis on which successful relationships are based. We might tentatively ask how far this knowledge might be the basis of the 'responsible health care user' or 'expert patient' central to contemporary policy texts, and how far it might be in the process of being dismantled in contemporary reforms such as the modernised appointment systems in GP surgeries and the introduction of choice of hospital or treatment centre. Both, while cutting down waiting times, disrupt the continuity of care based on relationships with a particular medical practitioner. But this relational view is potentially significant for other emerging conceptions of health care – concepts of 'health literacy' and negotiated decision-making (Sihota and Lennard, 2004) are more likely to flourish if lodged in such relationships.

Across both of the quotations above we can see how the normative ideal of a personalised relationship based on reciprocal ways of knowing the other is established through contrasts with the idea of being a 'customer' or of 'going shopping'.

> I mean, for someone in my situation it is very, very important to have that rapport with the GP … I've had the carpet fitted this week and when I rang up a couple of companies to come in and quote for it they were just looking at doing a job for me, I was a customer for a particular item. Which you can't say with the doctor because it is not for one particular item, it's for a very widespread number of items and so as a consequence of which it's a quite different relationship than the one where you're a customer and you are going to buy something or you want a service from them. But it's generally a one off thing, you might be repeating it later, but it's generally a one off thing. (Newtown health user interview 02)

Not only is the relationship more personal and is associated with a longer term investment, but the nature of the 'commodity' – health – is clearly very different from other commodities, and the nature of the transactions different from those in the marketplace. This is not particularly surprising – what is interesting, though, is the clarity and sophistication of the analysis on the part of 'lay' users, most of whom were well able to talk about the difference between health care relationships and those of the marketplace.

This view of the patient – and the doctor-patient relationship – interrupts the attempt to construct health users as consumers. In recent policy discourse, 'patient' is understood as an 'old' term, reflecting the architecture of power and dependency; while 'consumer' reflects the transfer of power (through choice) to the user. This old/new distinction is characteristic of New Labour accounts of modernisation (as is the discussion here of choice and equity, see also Clarke et al., 2005):

> It is often said that choice and equity are in some way in opposition. I don't accept that argument. Consumers act individually but the effect of their actions is communal. The cumulative effect of individual choices increases choice for others. In this sense choice widely available is not inimical to equity, it is a driver for change for everyone. So often in state provision of services universal provision meant the equity of the mediocre. That might have been acceptable to those *lying down patients of the past but it will not do for the standing up consumers of the future*. What we aspire to is the equity of excellence and choice is a necessary, though not sufficient, part of that transformation. (Cayton, 2003; emphasis added)

This conception of change and the implications of its model of consumer choice was a focus for concern for many of our interviewees. They located their own experiences and expectations in the context of reflections about the policy discourse of consumerism:

> I know 'consumer' and 'customer' imply choice and that is what we are supposed to want. I would consider it an acceptable achievement if everyone would have what was best in the matter of treatment as of right. (Newtown health user questionnaire 23)

> I don't quite know what choice is about, but if it's about getting the best treatment, to give you the best chance, I don't think that should be choice, I think that should be a *fait accompli*. (Newtown health user interview 05)

Here we clearly have 'standing up' patients but they may be standing up for something rather different from that envisaged by government. We suspect that these reactions mark a political problem: the relationships, identifications and desires that people in our study give voice to seem to exist in angular and uncomfortable alignments with government discourse and policy prescription. These 'standing up patients' fit neither the 'old' nor the 'new' model on offer in government discourse – their orientations cannot be understood in terms of satisfaction with an old model of dependency or passivity (Newman and Vidler, 2006b). They are assertive about their own experience and the system as a whole. Some operate as 'experts of their own condition', understanding the 'interdependency' of their relationship to public services. Finally, they have both desires for improvement and views about what such improvement might look like and how it might – and might not – be achieved.

Public provision and private desire

These positive orientations to public health care and the doctor-patient relationship should not be read as evidence of either contentment or passivity. There was a consistently strong desire for better health care. Some respondents appreciated the kinds of facilities that they had experienced in contacts with the private sector:

> I've been to private doctors, and my private doctor, the way they treated you and the way my current doctor treats, is time. They sit with you, they understand you, whereas they talk to you a lot more and they give you a lot more options. They spend more time with you, it's just time. Whereas an NHS doctor wants to get you out and get the next patient in as quickly as possible... If I am in the private sector, if I am in PPP or whatever, if I'm sick they say well come in now, whereas if I phone my GP they give me a date. If you are ill and you have PPP they book you in the next day, whereas here you have to be on the waiting list. If you go into a PPP hospital, when I worked in the private sector we used to have PPP, and you walk into a hospital and you think oh my god, it's a bloody hotel. It is beautiful, it is neat, the doctors treat you with courtesy, the nurses treat you with courtesy, you don't sit around reading 1945 *Home and Country*, or whatever magazine. You know you are treated just like that. The services might not be better. It might be the same doctor that is treating you in the NHS that is treating you privately but again it is just the environment, the courteousness, the response you get. You say can I have a glass of water, they get you a glass of cold water. They treat you nicely. You don't get that on the NHS but again that is probably not the NHS's fault because they have a lot to deal with. (Newtown health user interview 01)

> Yeah, the fabulous thing about private, I suppose, the doctor has a long time, or however much time you need to talk to you about your problem. I've found that they discuss, they are more willing to discuss what the problem is, and to consider various options. And I've also found they are much more willing to answer questions. I have found that a lot better ... X Clinic is of course very clean. I have been there as a day patient and the room was – the bathroom was absolutely immaculate, you don't have to take your own cleaning stuff and that sort of thing ... You may not get any better treatment, I'm sure you don't, because you know the NHS standards of treatment are absolutely excellent, but ... it's not stressful in any shape or form. (Newtown health user interview 06)

We can see the sense of appreciation for the kinds of facilities available in private hospitals, and for the time and attention received from medical practitioners in the private sector. These factors are at least as strong – if not stronger – than the waiting list issue around which the 'choice' agenda has been constructed. The critical element identified above was the time and attention in the consultation process, but after that it seemed to be the little things that stuck in people's memories and that symbolised the virtues of private treatment: the 'immaculate bathroom', the 'cold glass of water', being treated 'with courtesy', not having to 'sit around reading 1945 *Home and Country*', and so on.

In spite of such sentiments, even among respondents who regularly used the private sector there was a strong public identification with the NHS. This is present in the final comments at the end of each of the quotations above: the idea that it's not the NHS's fault that such longings cannot be realised 'because they have a lot to deal with', or that such longings are only superficial because 'you know the NHS's standards of treatment are excellent'. This latter idea came through strongly in the focus groups we held in each town:

> The private sector can deliver a television in a room and decent meals, maybe. I don't believe it delivers better health services. A consultant or a surgeon who is doing operations at the end of an NHS day and rushing into the X Clinic to do hip operations at 10 o clock at night is not giving the same service as he is during the day. You can hear horror stories about private health much more than you can about the NHS. (Newtown health focus group)

> [T]hey don't have the same medical cover in a private hospital. If anything goes wrong, where do they have to go? They have to come back into the NHS for A&E or intensive care. You know, it's all very nice if you have got something mild wrong with you and you go in and you have a nice environment and everything else. But if you want to have doctors who know what they are doing, have someone on call twenty four hours a day. People have the wrong perspective about private hospitals. Who do you think provides medical care in private hospital? It is the NHS doctors ... . People have got to wake up to the idea that they do not get better clinical care in a private hospital ... People would be horrified at the lack of clinical care in a private hospital – the drug errors, etc. that go on in a private hospital. They would be horrified. (Oldtown health focus group)

And we found a deep attachment to the idea of the NHS and an antipathy to a more privatised health model which would produce greater inequalities:

> Respondent 1:   I do think it really matters who provides the service because if we are going to have a society where people have equal access, it can't happen while we have this stupid thing about it doesn't matter who delivers the service. It is absolutely essential that the public service can provide the best quality service, ...
>
> Respondent 2:   In the end the private sector has to make money, that is what they are there for. And the NHS doesn't. And that is why I am uneasy. And I am uneasy that they are pushing us towards an American model where you will either be in and OK or out and very poor and get the basics, with a huge swathe in the middle. And if you've got a condition that knocks you out of health insurance – I just don't want to go the American way. (Newtown health focus group)

These are ways of asserting the value of the *publicness* of health, also evident in the numbers of respondents who ticked 'member of the public' or 'member of the community' in the questionnaires (see above). It involves a commitment that transcends problems arising in people's actual experiences of using the NHS. As a result we may need to think that the NHS is always a double entity – both a specific assemblage of organisations, people and practices and an idea, an ideal or a representation (see Sharma and Gupta, 2006). Debates about the NHS move – often implicitly – between these two dimensions. For our respondents, while specific experiences (either public disappointments or private pleasures) may be problematic, the idea of the publicness of the NHS dominates their concerns about the future. The idea(l) of a collective, inclusive, public resource commands their attention in ways that consumerist choice cannot.

Coming to terms?

Such complex and subtle reflections on identifications with publicness raise analytic questions that outrun the policy and academic debates around consumerism, choice and the reform of public services. We are only just starting to come to terms with these questions. 'Terms' is, of course, the key word. In these reflections, we encounter identifications, rather than identities: ways of representing imagined or desired forms of attachment and belonging to domains, institutions, practices and people. Each term – each name – is itself the subject of different inflections and interpretations: the patient, for example, is not a singular mode of being. These terms voice desires and anxieties, as well as making sense of experiences. These people are reflexive subjects – capable of reasoning about their own experience, its relationship to others, the nature of the institution, political discourse and the implications of bringing such elements together.

At the same time, the identifications being explored and recounted are multiple and mobile. They may evoke deep commitments while being contingently deployed. We have been struck by the capacity of people to engage in complex forms of what we have called 'relational reasoning' about public services (Clarke, forthcoming b; see also Malpass et al., 2006). This suggests that the dominant binary categorisations of people's relationship to, and view of, public services (citizen-consumer; active-passive; patient-expert patient) may miss the multiplicity and mobility with which people understand these relationships. In this final extract, one respondent picks her way through the different relationships by which she and the NHS are connected (and the identifications through which she recognises them):

> With the health service as a national health service, it's more than, I feel it's more than just the services that you consume. I mean I am concerned with it more on the whole than just being consumers. So even if I wasn't attending the

hospital or seeing my GP regularly, OK I'd still register with a GP, so from that point yes I would be a consumer, but it's not … If I was 100 per cent healthy and not using, consuming the services, I would still feel a relationship to the health service because I pay for it, it is not Tony Blair's or whoever's money, it's our money, we paid for it, it's the nation's, the *national* health service. And I do consider that when I cast my vote. So even if I wasn't actually in need of the service it still does affect me and I still would consider that at election time. So I feel it's more than just a direct consumer because you are paying for a national service for everyone's benefit. Whether you actually need to consume that service or not, is not the primary consideration. So it's wider than just being considered a consumer, I feel. More of a citizen than a consumer. (Newtown health user interview 03)

The implications for the politics, policy and practice of public services of such mobile, reflexive and relational reasoning are significant; so are the potential consequences for social analysis. We take up some of these wider implications in the final chapter. But in this chapter we have seen how the 'terms' in use to describe the relationships people have to public services are in flux. Their fluidity and contested character reflect the turbulent combination of changing publics and changing public services. It is clear that both providers and users of services are engaged in 'making up meanings' to express their experiences and expectations, and their ambitions and anxieties. It is also clear that the 'consumer' has failed to capture popular and organisational imaginations. It commands little enthusiasm and, indeed, appeared largely as a figure *against* which people constructed their desired relationships. In these reflections, the 'consumer' seemed to speak of a banal or everyday character of 'shopping' that was some distance from the 'heroic' consumer (Hilton, 2006). Its commercial and impersonal character provided a discursive foundation from which people elaborated a model of how public services might be both public and personal.

8

Beyond the Citizen-Consumer

Our exploration of New Labour's citizen-consumers has raised a variety of different issues and arguments. In this conclusion, we look back across four sets of concerns. We begin with the identifications and relationships that people perceive as important in the provision of public services. We have already indicated the lack of fit between public responses and the consumer centred imagery of New Labour. In this chapter:

- we reflect further on the implications of public distance from the figure of the citizen-consumer;
- we look at the links between the public and the organisations that provide public services;
- we ask what is at stake in the encounters between changing publics and changing public services?
- we consider the problems of analysing New Labour as a political and governmental project;
- finally, we return to the problems of theorising the rise (and limitations) of the figure of the citizen-consumer.

In the process, we consider some of the strengths and limitations of the three dominant perspectives discussed in Chapter 1: the political economy of neo-liberalism; a governmentality perspective on advanced liberalism; and a sociology of reflexive modernity. We suggest that analysing a new formation like that of the citizen-consumer requires a more mobile approach to theorising than is provided by these approaches.

Relational reasoning: the problem of public doubt

It is a significant finding that people do not see themselves as consumers or customers of public services, but our study also makes visible the ways in which they articulate complex identifications to such services. As Chapter 7 showed, these are, in Giddens' terms, 'reflexive subjects', able to engage in complex reasoning about their relationships to institutional arrangements, their own needs and political/policy discourses. They are not the passive victims of ideological domination, aligning themselves unproblematically with 'market populism' (Frank, 2001) and its extension to public services. Nor are they apparently subject to the discursive logics of advanced liberalism, failing to recognise themselves as consuming subjects, and actively articulating alternative conceptions of the relationships between publics and public services. This is difficult ground for social analysis. It would clearly be wrong to ignore the dominance of certain ideologies or discourses in specific social and historical circumstances. Indeed, we have tried to address the ways in which New Labour connected national and global discourses of modernisation through the repertoire of competition, choice and consumerism. But marking the public dominance of certain discourses – their capacity to organise mediated political framings – is not the same as assessing their popular reach or embeddedness.

There are different sorts of analytical resources that might help with this issue. Here we begin to sketch an account of this process of relational reasoning that draws on Antonio Gramsci's conception of 'common- sense' as a heterogeneous field of ideas – a field with which specific political and ideological strategies attempt to construct connections. This Gramscian view is different from more sociological conceptions of common-sense as the realm of everyday knowledge colonised by dominant understandings. Gramsci was insistent about its multiplicity and the implications for the possibilities of political work and engagement:

> The starting point of critical elaboration is the consciousness of what one really is, and is 'knowing thyself' as a product of the historical process to date which has deposited in you an infinity of traces without leaving an inventory... Moreover, common sense is a collective noun, like religion: there is not just one common sense, for that too is a product of history and a part of the historical process. (1971: 324–5)

Ideological or discursive work attempts to articulate selected elements from the stock of popular or common-sense ones – and, of course, to disarticulate or de-mobilise other elements less favourable to the would-be dominant way of thinking. Gramsci's discussion of common-sense was allied with a conception of everyday or practical philosophising, implying that people were actively engaged in the work of representing themselves and their conditions. This combination – heterogeneous 'traces' of discourses and practical philosophising – points towards the sorts of relational reasoning about public services that we explored in Chapter 7. People drew on a variety of discursive resources as the basis for conceptualising their actual and desired relationships to public services. The persistence of such resources and their perceived relevance provided a strong basis for constructing a sceptical distance from consumerist reforms and their implied relationships.

In particular, collective or solidaristic conceptions of the public remain powerful organising principles for thinking about relationships with public services. Clearly, these imply different bases or locations of solidarity – some imply a national public, others a more local collectivity. While our study was not designed to draw out the different forms of solidarity and exclusion that may be at stake in conceptions of the public, we can see their traces. Collective attachments to local or national bodies expressed through 'membership' seemed a more desirable or meaningful form of attachment than the formal status of citizen. Membership seemed to be derived from different types of connection:

- entitlement through material contributions (being a tax payer);
- location (especially in the 'local community');
- reciprocal obligation (to other members); and
- identity (a localised, nationalised, racialised or ethnicised sense of belonging).

At present there are intense debates about the relationship between solidarity and diversity that are seen as challenging the collectivist basis of welfare states and public services more generally (e.g., Alesina and Glaeser, 2004; Goodhart, 2004; and the discussion in Taylor-Gooby, 2005). Discourses of membership are typically structured around dynamics of inclusion and exclusion in which the different principles of connection listed above may conflict, merge and overlap. Although localised, nationalised, racialised and ethnicised identities may be represented as essentially connected, they do not necessarily correspond: for example, local-ness is not necessarily marked as ethnically uniform. While some versions of the Public and the Community are saturated with racialised discourses of inclusion and exclusion, others lean towards more expansively civic discourses of solidarity articulated around both place (which might be local, national or transnational) and the public realm. In such versions, concern for the needs and rights of others was explicitly set against consumerist/individualist orientations. Similarly, conceptions of reciprocal obligations to other members also articulate versions of solidarity. Given contemporary debates about the presumed tension between diversity and solidarity, it is increasingly important to grasp the different versions of identification and belonging that may be at stake in conceptions of membership, rather than assuming that inclusion/exclusion always operates through nationalist or racialised registers.

Our study demonstrated strong attachments to the 'local', sometimes imagined as places of living, sometimes as networks of relationships and sometimes as sites of service provision (though such 'sites' are not spatially aligned). Community has become an increasingly significant focus of governance arrangements in the UK, reflected in the decentralisation of public services and the increasing expectations of participation, consultation and involvement of communities and neighbourhoods. There is a significant overlap here between governmental and popular orientations, since community persists as the site of potent popular identifications and desires – for attachment, belonging, order and security, at least. It remains a profoundly unstable term – conceptually, socially and governmentally (Clarke, 2002). Our respondents draw on traces of all of these larger discourses about community, publicness and nation: models of what Morris (1998) called 'legitimate membership of the welfare community'. They put them to work in complex reasoning about experiences and expectations of public services. They also use them to provide a standpoint for critical reasoning about government programmes and proposals. Focus groups and interviews clearly provide a setting that evokes this sort of relational reasoning. They provide a sort of public setting in which people act, as our colleague Clive Barnett has suggested, as 'little Habermasians', performing and producing the 'public realm' in their speech. We wonder if they might also be seen as 'little Bahktinians', given Mikhail Bahktin's emphasis on dialogic relationships and the multiplicity of 'voices' that could be in play (Bahktin, 1981). Dorothy Holland and Jean Lave (2001) have taken up this Bahktinian view of dialogic subjects, arguing that people are not just addressed or summoned by dominant discourses – but also 'answer back'. Our study supports this conception of subjects and underlines Holland and Lave's view of the analytical and political importance of the potential distance it implies.

As such, our respondents are 'subjects of doubt' (Clarke, 2004a). They reflect upon the dominant discourse, its interpellations and the subject positions it offers. They reason about different sorts of identifications and the relationships they imply. They make choices about what terms evoke their desired personal and political subject positions. They suggest that the practice of scepticism is a popular – rather than an academic – commonplace. The extracts in Chapter 7 showed people who know that they are being spoken to, and are reluctant to acquiesce. Listen to the complex reflexivity at play in this sentence: 'I know "consumer" and "customer" imply choice and that is what we are supposed to want'... There speaks a person who hears the process of subjection ('that is what we are supposed to want'), recognises its political-cultural character, and goes on to offer an alternative account of 'what we want': as a 'matter of right'. These are subjects who require an analysis that is attentive to the breaks and disjunctures in the circulation of discourses, rather than assuming their effectivity (see also Marston, 2004).

Hope and experience: using and providing public services

So far, we have mostly dealt with the theoretical implications of this complex 'public'. But its orientations and forms of reasoning also have implications for the policy and practice of public service provision. If there is a consistent thread in our respondents' desires, it was the hope that they would encounter 'better public services'. They shared this ambition with staff and managers in services – all of whom were committed to improvement. It was a view also shared by governments whose reform agenda was fundamentally committed to improving standards and quality. When specified in more detail, however, this ambition looks a little less unifying. We want to identify three focal points of instability that were intensified by New Labour's approach to modernisation. It is important to stress that these were not newly created by modernisation – on the contrary, they have been long running themes in the relationships between public services and the public. But our study suggests that they became more troubling during New Labour's rule. The first concerns questions of governance, the second is centred on resources, while the third returns us to the 'knowledge/power knot'.

We begin with the banal observation that 'consumerism' was not the only reform imperative in New Labour's modernisation of public services. It co-existed in more or less uncomfortable ways with other imperatives – all of which contain implicit models of governance (Newman, 2001). Most of the managers of services in the study were concerned about how the drive towards consumerism fitted with other changes they were expected to put into place. The dominant theme here was about 'performance': achieving centrally established targets that defined organisational success. Targets were also associated with a distinctively unstable dynamic of centralisation and decentralisation. Considerable governmental enthusiasm for the decentralisation of provision (and consultative/participative decision-making) to localities, communities and neighbourhoods co-existed with supposedly efficiency-producing scaling up of organisational units in services (the merger of police forces and Primary Care Trusts to create larger units were both proposed during 2005–6). Meanwhile, neither the governmental centre nor its agents (such as the evaluation and scrutiny organisations) found it possible to give up 'command and control' orientations to service providing organisations. This mixture of vertical and horizontal relationships (which include forms of competition, contracting and collaboration or partnership working) resembles what Bode has called 'disorganised governance' (Bode, forthcoming; see also Clarke, 2006b; Newman, 2006).

Consumerism was important to New Labour's programme of reform. It provided a framing populist discourse that articulated the 'consumer interest' against the power and interests of 'producers'. It also became enacted in a set of mechanisms: the means by which people could express 'choice' such as new financial arrangements ('money following the patient' in the NHS, for example) and new audit and scrutiny processes (embodying the 'virtual consumer', Miller, 2005). But it was pursued alongside the other governance innovations noted above. The combination had the effect of keeping 'producers' off balance. Receiving mixed messages, their new autonomy framed by new constraints, and trying to work out their own relationships with changing publics, staff and managers clearly felt under considerable strain as they tried to create 'improved public services' in less than helpful circumstances.

A critical aspect of these difficult circumstances centred on the question of resources. It is perhaps more accurate to say that the question of resources condensed a variety of tensions in service providing organisations. In the first place, the discourse of resources denoted the persistent public sector concern with managing the relationship between resources and demand which almost always implies the challenge of managing demand by setting priorities, creating hierarchies of need and limiting eligibility. All three services that we studied had grappled with this problem and saw it as being changed by the consumerist orientation of New Labour reforms. They recognised – with both enthusiasm and anxiety – the disruptive effect of consumerism. They saw it as challenging established organisational and occupational processes for managing the relationship between demand and resources. Both choice and voice mechanisms created new pressures that required organisations to find new ways of accommodating a more assertive or insistent set of publics (while worrying about how to serve those who were not assertive or insistent).

The discourse centred on 'resources' connected two further problems. First, it linked to concerns about the troubled 'public service ethos' and 'equity/equality'. While many staff and managers saw the need and opportunity to improve public services, they expressed considerable anxiety about how to ensure that a consumerist orientation did not (further) marginalise or exclude the poor, the vulnerable and the inarticulate. Choice driven models seemed to threaten public service principles about equity or serving the 'most needy'. Secondly, the shifting of the problem of managing resources and demand into a consumerist framing implied the expansion of particular sorts of labour in the organisation. This might be called the 'emotional labour' of expectation management. Managers and staff saw a growing task of constructing the 'reasonable' and 'responsible' consumer or community who could appreciate the conditions, constraints and 'tough choices' faced by provider organisations.

This process of 'expectation management' intersected in powerful ways with the tangles of what we have called the knowledge/power knot. In many ways, it is clear that the deference systems that supported the claim that 'professionals know best' have changed substantially. Professional scandals, a more sceptical public realm, alternative sources of information and, especially, an insistence on the value and power of forms of 'lay' knowledge have combined to unsettle the established formations of knowledge and power that generated expertise-legitimated authority. This unsettling has created new tangles in the knot at the point where changing publics meet changing public services. People using public services want – and expect – expertise on which they can rely. They would not be approaching public services if they could 'do it themselves': illness or other forms of vulnerability lead them to seek assistance and support from public services. In some cases, particularly in relation to policing, they look for the exercise of authority. Nevertheless, the people in this study were also concerned by the apparently arbitrary exercise of authority in their encounters with public services. Authority that was exercised in disengaged, impersonal and dismissive ways created a sense of disempowerment and an antagonistic distance. This is hardly a new discovery – it runs through the history of public services in an oscillation between services providing what people need and being experienced as a power standing over people.

This knowledge/power knot has been the focus of considerable innovation, experiment and attempts at realignment. From the expert patient initiative to direct payments in social care; from new practices of consultation and participation to customer care training; from 'user driven design' to the 'virtual consumer' imagined in audit and scrutiny processes – the forms of relationship between publics and public services have been a consistent focus of reinvention. Nevertheless, they remain unresolved. This is not surprising in at least two senses. On the one hand, people's expectations and demands are contextual and relationally constituted: the ways in which they hope to be treated are multiple and mobile. Being 'an expert of one's own condition' is not necessarily a universal position. People may wish to be vulnerable and dependent in some circumstances without being rendered passive or incompetent. On the other hand, organisations and occupations certainly find it difficult to give up power and the associated belief that there are things about which they 'know best'.

Our study suggests some possible tendencies for realignment that, rather strangely, centre on two other New Labour 'keywords': respect and partnership. New Labour's 'Respect' agenda was primarily addressed to issues of public conduct, aiming to regulate anti-social behaviour and promote civility in public spaces. It was not directed to relationships between government, public services and the public. It did, however, emerge as a consistent theme among people who used the services. It centred on how they felt they were perceived, addressed and treated in the service encounter. Perceived indifference, impersonality, inattentiveness or rudeness constituted a lack of respect: they felt they were not 'being taken seriously' as needs or rights bearing individuals. This desire for 'respect' was not the same as an expectation that all the needs or wants would be met. People knew that they operated in a milieu of competing priorities and limited resources, and they understood that not all conditions (from being a crime victim to having a chronic illness) could be remedied. But 'outcomes' are different from 'processes' and respect identified a key processual and relational dimension that people valued highly in public services. This is close to Sennett's conception of respect (in welfare policy and practice) meaning treating people as 'competent to participate in the terms of their own dependency' (2003: 178).

This conception of respect was closely linked to popular orientations to partnership. Again, this was different from New Labour's 'flagship' model of partnerships as combinations of public and private sector organisations (such as the Private Finance Initiative, for example). People talked of partnership as marking a negotiated practice in which they were active participants engaged with 'professionals' in deciding on courses of action and treatment. Most people did believe that there were things that professionals 'knew best' and wanted to have access to, and make use of, such expertise. But their ideal was to have such knowledge put to work in their service, involving a negotiation between personal or experiential expertise on the one hand, and professional expertise on the other. There are two more general points to make about the respect and partnership orientation. The first is that it clearly requires investments of time and resources on the part of public service organisations and their staff. Dealing with people with respect, or practising negotiation and partnership, clearly require more effort, energy and emotional labour than does efficient 'people processing' (but such people processing is only ever efficient from the perspective of a managerialised organisational calculus). Nevertheless, such investment of time and resources might deliver a variety of public goods ranging from perceived customer satisfaction through to deepened attachments to public services and their 'publicness'. The second general point is that hardly anyone thought that the consumer/choice direction of New Labour's reforms captured these concerns or promised to deliver the experiences that people (as staff, managers and users) wanted. Indeed, many thought that the consumerist imperative (especially when linked to other models of efficiency and performance evaluation) would undermine such possibilities.

New Labour, neo-liberalism and more

In this context, how can we make sense of New Labour's persistence with the citizen-consumer model of public service reform? In these concluding comments we want to make three linked arguments. The first concerns New Labour as a political project, constructing a 'modern nation' in the 'modern world'. The second concerns New Labour as a governmental project, reconstructing the apparatuses, policies and practices of governing the social into new assemblages. The third addresses the contradictions and limitations of New Labour's rule.

Turning first to New Labour as a political project, the conjunctural analysis that we introduced in Chapter 2 pointed to the importance of a 'politics of articulation' rather than treating New Labour as a singular political or ideological programme. New Labour's neo-liberalism is an uncomfortable and strained construction rather than an essential political character. New Labour initially worked to distinguish itself from the vulgar marketisation of the preceding Conservative governments, insisting on the importance of the 'social' and the 'public'. Its programme and its discursive repertoire has drawn on many currents and movements, including social and user movements as well as older Labourist or social democratic conceptions of equality and progress. We want to underline the heterogeneity of social forces, trends and discursive resources with which New Labour is engaged. Hall's concept of articulation as 'trans-formism' points to critical processes by which alternative discourses are reworked into subordinated positions in relation to dominant neo-liberalism (Hall, 2003). We think the analysis needs to be developed in two particu-lar ways. First, there was a diversity of alternative discourses on which New Labour had to perform political discursive work. New Labour mobilised some of them, transforming them into subordinate and support-ing roles (for example, the transformational work performed on the dis-courses and politics of difference and diversity). It aimed to de-mobilise others, identifying them as 'old fashioned' or out of synchrony with the 'modern world' (including state-centric conceptions of public service and equality, for example). Second, the outcome of this transformative politi-cal work was never a singular or stable neo-liberalism. New Labour's neo-liberalism is modulated by the need to address 'equity', the concern to promote a traditionalist conception of the social (the promotion of civil-ity, responsibility and authority), the difficult and shifting encounter with 'multi-culturalism' and more. New Labour was multi-vocal, drawing on and accommodating different social and political discourses (Steinberg and Johnson, 2004a).

We think this may be important. There is a temptation to pick out the true or essential New Labour (which usually turns out to be neo-liberal). The alternative is to look for a paradoxical, contradictory or hybridised conjunction of two different discourses or positions. We think this view of hybridity in New Labour is problematic since this is exactly what New Labour always identified as its own practice – the 'Third Way' was announced and celebrated as a route between (apparently) contradictory positions or principles. It was, after all, New Labour – not us – who hyphenated the 'citizen-consumer' as a discursive figure. The view of hybridity also tends towards a binary view of New Labour's composite discourse (neo-liberalism plus X). In contrast, we think it matters to pay attention to the heterogeneity of contending forces and discourses with which New Labour engaged – and on which it drew selectively. This echoes our argument in the first part of this conclusion about the selective mobilisation and de-mobilisation in the encounters between political strategies and 'common sense'. This does not mean giving up on ques-tions of the dominating principles or the attention to the work of trans-formism through which alternative discourses are recoded as if they are in support of the dominant. But it does imply combining these concerns with a concern for how the dominant might itself become modified in the encounters with heterogeneous others.

This leads to questions about New Labour as a governmental project. Much recent scholarship has explored the complex changes in modes, sites and practices of governing, exploring ways in which they might be understood as framed by a neo-liberal or advanced liberal governmentality (see, for example, Brown, 2006; Hartmann, 2005; Larner, 2000; Larner and

Walters, 2004; McDonald and Marston, 2006; Rose, 1999). This approach makes neo-liberalism mean something different from a class project directed to some combination of privatisation, deregulation, marketisation and the construction of the flexibilities desired by capital. This Foucauldian perspective has certainly been more attentive to the proliferation of diverse forms of governing – both beyond the state and in the recomposition of the states themselves. Starting from this point, we can see New Labour as part of a wider remaking of both the mentalities and technologies of governing. The conception of people as enterprising and consuming subjects; the shifting of governance agencies and practices beyond the state; the dispersal or disaggregation of existing governmental institutions and forms of authority; the reinvention of community as a site, mode and object of governing – all look like distinctive and innovative approaches to the challenges of governing peoples, publics and populations (see, for example, Chatterjee, 2003; Du Gay, 1996; Hansen and Salskov-Iversen, forthcoming). In our more specific context, we can read the transformation of the citizen into the consumer as the practice of a shifting mode of governance that involves the simultaneous remaking of subjects (citizens to consumers), sites (from state institutions to plural and competing agencies) and practices (from bureau-professionally structured delivery to choice).

This Foucauldian perspective has both appeal and limitations in the context of analysing New Labour. As Hartmann argues, it allows a way of analysing situations in which something other than the 'withdrawal of the state' has been taking place. Rather than the proclaimed 'end of welfare', she points to the ways in which public expenditures and authority has been invested in trying to produce the flexible and entrepreneurial would-be workers sought by employers (Hartmann, 2005; see also Goode and Maskovsky, 2001; Clarke, 2004b). We might see the ferment of innovation around choice and voice, including the multiplying varieties of consultation, involvement and participation, as part of this remaking of governmentality towards governing without or beyond the state. But in the context of thinking about New Labour as a governmental project (or as located within the wider transition to neo- or advanced liberal governmentality), we think this perspective needs qualifying. How do we theorise the heterogeneity of governmental modes, sites and practices? There is a tendency to read contemporary changes in a rather 'epochal' way: they are attributed a neo/advanced liberal character by virtue of taking place in a neo/advanced liberal period. In contrast, Larner argues for a view of 'contemporary forms of rule' that sees them as 'composite, plural and multi-form' (2000: 20).

At the same time, some Foucauldian analyses treat liberal governmentalities as modes of governing through self-governance, contrasting this with 'coercion'. The inclusion of the police in our study requires us to think about this distinction as itself the site of combined modes of governing. The expansion of policing and linked 'criminalising' practices in the contemporary period suggest that coercive power – enacted by state agencies – needs attention. Some analysts have suggested that 'a culture of control' is the dominant form of social governance (Garland, 2001; see also Stenson, 2000). Certainly, this is not a process in which policing has become 'de-statalised' (moved outside the state), despite the growth of para-professional roles and private security providers (Crawford, forthcoming). Nevertheless, there are changing modes of governance at stake in policing as 'communities' become participants and partners in the construction of 'community safety' (Hughes and Edwards, 2002).

We think attention to New Labour's heterogeneity is important. The multiple strategies, modes of governance, combined and contradictory practices suggest that it may be less than coherent or unified. In part, this reflects the 'innovative' character of governing – the search to find ways of making the world conform to imagined conceptions of how it should work. But this heterogeneity also arises at the intersection of the governmental and the political (in its narrower sense). New Labour may be engaged in a wider process of shifting or emergent governmentalities, but it is also a political agent: attempting to rule, and trying to stay popular in general and specific terms (involving both wider public opinion and those groups or interests that it sees as 'key stakeholders' and 'opinion formers'). If we examine the intersections of the governmental and the political, some peculiar paradoxes come to light. One is the 'hyperactivity' of political/policy innovation in an era where demands that 'something must be done' continue to be addressed to the government, even as neoliberal governmentality centres on 'governing at a distance' through 'self-governing subjects'. A second is the associated temptation for 'hands on' policy direction (at least in some areas) rather than a 'hands off' approach to devolved practices. A third is the oscillation between a commitment to 'self-governance' (autonomous, choice-making individuals) and a recurrent moral authoritarianism (intervening on the growing numbers of people seen to be 'behaving badly'). Our study has traced only part of this heterogeneity of modes and practices of governing. We think they are certainly 'composite, plural and multi-form' (see also Clarke, 2005a). They pose the problem of how we can think of this as field of strategies, technologies and practices of governing that has no essential coherence, but is organised or articulated as a 'unity in difference'.

Before leaving New Labour, we want to return to the question of its distinction between New and Old that has been a central feature of its political discourse (Clarke and Newman, 1998; 2004; Finlayson, 2003a; Steinberg and Johnson, 2004b). As we indicated in Chapter 7, it has a particular connection with the issues raised in our study. It enables a situation in which the views of our respondents are already 'out of time'. Bundled up in this question of being 'out of time' are a number of different issues. Are the people we have interviewed 'older' or the products of a social democratic or collectivist generation? Are we encountering the 'legacy effect' of older ideas in a period of transition? If we went back two years later, would we discover that people had changed their identifications? At one level, these are all reasonable questions to ask about the results of a small piece of social investigation. They reflect limitations of the data, its mode of collection and its timing. And yet, there is something about the frequency and intensity with which these questions are posed – particularly in political and policy settings – that suggests 'time' may be doing important discursive work here. A particular sort of time is being told.

The time at stake in these comments is constructed through characteristic temporal imaginaries that seem to play a potent role in New Labour and neo-liberal discourses (Clarke, forthcoming c). Distinctions between old and new, or between traditional and modern, work on constructing a flow of time between Past and Future. In these distinctions, the Past appears as the location of our troubles, mistakes and misfortunes. In contrast, the Future holds out the promise of overcoming such conditions. In the present, the work of political discourse is to distribute people, orientations and political imaginaries to either the Past or the Future. Strange collectivist orientations, conceptions of publics, communities and categories of membership are – in this view – merely residual. They are the left-overs of older formations: the detritus of collectivism, welfarism or social democracy, and such detritus will inexorably be washed away by the river of time. We do not want to argue against the possibilities of historical change, but there is something significant here about the ways that political projects deploy 'residualising' discourses: telling the time in ways that locate critics, refusals and alternative imaginaries as belonging to the past. This is a recurrent motif in New Labour discourse – indeed, time is inscribed into its very title. Nevertheless, we have been struck by a different 'temporal' framing in our interviews and focus group discussions. There is a complete absence of nostalgia as a framing device: people are committed to seeing public services improve, rather than wishing to get back to some imagined 'golden age' of public services. This is a different way of 'telling the time': one that is future oriented and committed to a view of progress, but does not see how the desired progress will be delivered by current government policy. In the final section of the conclusion, we will return to these practices of residualisation as part of how we might think conjuncturally about the present.

The elusive citizen-consumer: making sense of the missing subject

In Chapter 1, we talked about three significant theoretical approaches that might provide the analytical framework for examining the 'citizen-consumer'. At that point, we also raised some doubts and reservations about their capacity to address the specific features of this political and governmental project as anything more than an example or illustration of larger trends or tendencies. Political economy approaches located the spread of the consumer in the rise of neo-liberalism and its valorisation of markets over states. Foucauldian approaches centred on governmentality treated the consumer as marking the shift from expansive liberal to neo- or advanced liberal governmentality: an embodiment of the self-managing subject governed 'at a distance'. Finally, sociologies of modernity treated the citizen-consumer as exemplifying the place of reflexive subjects and the salience of choice as features of late or reflexive modernity.

We remain convinced that these approaches illuminate different aspects of both the general turn to consumerism and its connections to the reform of public services in the UK. Political economy approaches make visible the remaking of the relations between capital and the state in a period of corporate or neo-liberal globalisation. They point to the changing terms of the national and international settlements between labour and capital associated with what has variously been termed welfare capitalism, the Keynesian welfare state or Atlantic Fordism (e.g., Esping-Andersen, 1990; Jessop, 2002). Finally, they focus our attention on dynamics of marketisation and, especially, privatisation in the new 'mixed economy' of publics services in which 'private providers' have become favoured partners in public-private partnerships and in smaller contracting arrangements (Farnsworth, 2004; Pollock, 2004).

Foucauldian approaches offer a way of escaping from the state/market binary that dominates much political economy (as well as their centering of class forces as the dominant, if not exclusive, forms of agency). The view through governmentality is concerned with dispersed forms of power and authority and with a more complex view of the 'social' as both the object and the product of different governmental technologies and strategies. So, Foucauldian studies have captured the multiple sites and subjects of governance – the enrolment of communities, consumers, enterprising and prudential selves and 'active' citizens as subjects of 'governing at a distance' (e.g., Larner, 1997, 2000; O'Malley, 2005; Rose, 1999). This sense of the proliferation of governmental strategies and subjects offers a reading of 'individuation' that contrasts with more sociological analyses such as Beck and Beck-Gersheim (2002) and Giddens (1991).

But these sociological approaches to modernity make other dynamics visible – in particular the rise of a 'democratic' (or perhaps demotic) sensibility in 'reflexive modernity' that infuses personal, public and political relations. This tendency is based in the condition of reflexivity (people as reasoning and choice formulating subjects) and infuses interpersonal relationships (including the 'democratic family') and people's engagement with public institutions (from corporations to government agencies). It is also visible in the shifting engagement with politics, away from established or institutionalised party politics to more social or environmental movement based engagements (or a 'sub-politics' of life choice issues). For us, this perspective gives a particular visibility to our 'reasoning' subjects (the 'little Habermasians' or 'Bahktinians' discussed earlier). It also touches on something about a widespread scepticism in relation to forms and sources of authority. We can see here the elaboration of a certain distance between popular opinion and the announcements of authoritative voices – political, commercial and professional. Such sceptical subjects both feature centrally in our study and look like a major issue for the future development of the politics and policies around public services (Clarke, 2005c).

These three perspectives create different 'visibilities': they bring different processes, relationships and actors into view. It would be convenient to see progress as the result of aggregating them – seeing more and more things. Our earlier arguments about heterogeneity suggest there is some merit in this since the focused visibility of each perspective tends to discount some things as not the main, real or essential concern. But adding them together does not guarantee attention to heterogeneity (only three views) and ignores the problems of theoretical and other incompatibilities. These are not perspectives inclined to peaceful co-existence. However, rather than pursue questions of theoretical differentiation between them, we want instead to reflect on some shared inclinations that we think limit their engagement with the specific cluster of politics, discourses, apparatuses and practices in which New Labour's citizen-consumers were located. For each perspective, this figure – the hyphenated citizen-consumer – functions as an example, illustration or embodiment of the wider tendency: the realignment of state and market; the shift in governmentality; the emergence of reflexive modernity's individualism. The more specific conditions, dynamics, processes and consequences tend to disappear in such 'epochal' accounts of dominant trends.

Some time ago, Raymond Williams drew an important distinction between epochal analysis and 'authentic historical analysis' that remains relevant. 'Epochal analysis' concentrated only on a 'selected and abstracted dominant system' while in doing 'authentic historical analysis' it was 'necessary at every point to recognize the complex interrelations between movements and tendencies both within and beyond a specific and effective dominance' (1977: 121). He went on to suggest that in a specific historical moment it might be useful to organise the multiple – or heterogeneous – movements and tendencies in play by distinguishing between the dominant (itself *containing* different movements and tendencies), the 'residual' (older ideas and institutionalisations that have resisted transformation and persist as active forces in the present) and the 'emergent' (new movements, forces and ways of thinking). The political-cultural work of the dominant tendency involves trying to maintain its own internal coherence; trying to displace the 'residual' elements (undermining their persistence or apparent relevance to the present); and trying to co-opt elements of the emergent and residual ('transforming' them in ways that apparently support the dominant). In this way the dominant forces can represent themselves as the path to the future that is simultaneously coherent, necessary and inevitable. In Gramsci's terms, political forces (in his terms 'opposition' forces) 'seek to demonstrate that the necessary and sufficient conditions already exist to make possible, and hence imperative, the accomplishment of certain historical tasks' (1971: 178). New Labour and other neo-liberal inflected populist politics have certainly represented themselves as 'oppositional' – posing the necessity of transforming out-moded ways of life to become part of the modern world (see also Andrews, 2006, on Berlusconi's 'postmodern populism' and Frank, 2001, on 'market populism').

This 'authentic historical analysis' might also be described as conjunc-tural analysis (see also Grossberg, 2006; Hall, 1996) which focuses on the movements and tendencies at stake in a particular conjunction of time and space – each of which may be trying to construct a path to the future (or a model of the 'modern world'). We need to beware of being over-literal about the conjunction of time and space: the analysis of New Labour's citizen-consumers is not just a matter of those things that went on in the UK during a decade of New Labour rule (1997–2006: the time of writing). Like other nations, Britain is a transnationally constituted place, traversed by relations, processes and flows that both connect it and dif-ferentiate from elsewhere. In the context of New Labour, there are power-ful connections that link Britain to the 'modern world' – to both the real and the imagined 'geographies of globalisation' (Cameron and Palan, 2004); to the ideas and institutions of 'Europe' (Balibar, 2002; Clarke, 2005d; Fink et al., 2001;); to the economic, political, cultural and espe-cially policy relations to 'America'; and to 'Empire' and its postcolonial presences (Gilroy, 2005). Time, too, is not singular: the conjuncture con-tains both long running and immediate movements and tendencies – ideas and institutions about publicness forged in nineteenth century struggles exist conterminously with much more recent voicings of social movements, think-tanks and policy networks.

As we argued in Chapter 2, we see conjunctural analysis as a way of framing our study of citizen-consumers, not because it identifies the dominant trend or tendency, but precisely because it requires attention to the multiplicity of movements and tendencies; how they are mobilised, de-mobilised and articulated into an attempt at dominance in a specific political and governmental project. In the previous section, we have tried to show how attention to heterogeneity in thinking about New Labour is of critical importance. It allows us to see the multiple movements, tendencies and currents that formed the conditions of New Labour – and formed the conjuncture which New Labour tried to organise and direct in certain ways.

There are important links between this view of conjunctures as multiple or heterogeneous and our discovery of the missing citizen-consumer. The three major theories with which we began have tended to assume that the subjects implied in the dominant trends materialise in practice. This may be particularly visible in Foucauldian studies because of their explicit concern with subjects. So, the unemployed become 'job seekers'; 'commu-nities' spring into being when summoned; teenagers become 'active, responsible decision-makers' about sex; and citizens become consumers (or, more uncomfortably, citizen-consumers). But it is true for the other two positions, too. Political economy thinks that citizens will be transformed into individual consumers who behave like the consumers of neo-classical economic textbooks. Sociologists of modernity (both optimists and pessimists) point to the decline of 'traditional' solidarities and the rise of more reflexive, individuated and consumption centred ways of being. There are both analytical and political problems about such assumptions that persistently short-circuit the empirical question of whether any of these new subjects actually materialise and deliver their performances.

Our study suggests that people (staff, managers and users of public services) have a complicatedly sceptical relationship to New Labour's view of consumer choice as a means of reforming public services. People using the services do not have any strong inclination towards the identifications offered by terms like consumer and customer. Indeed, they have complex and reflexive accounts of why they do not understand their relationships to public services in such terms: they are *dialogic* subjects. They understand the dominant discourse and understand how they are spoken for within it. But they draw on a variety of 'residual and emergent' discursive resources to distance themselves from it, from the identifications that it offers them and from the model of the future that it offers. We think this dialogic mode cannot be captured in a simple domination/resistance model for two reasons. The first is the heterogeneity of the political, cultural and discursive resources on which people draw in articulating their distance from the dominant discourse. In Gramscian terms, they make use of the diversity of 'traces' within contemporary common-sense – including some of the traces that are voiced differently within the dominant discourse (ideas of fairness and equity, for example). Secondly, 'resistance' implies an active state or set of practices. While many of our subjects in this study are resistant to New Labour's model of consumer centred choice, this describes something closer to an immunological condition rather than a mobilised or mobilising set of practices. It might best be described as a condition of 'passive dissent', lacking processes of activation and mobilisation.

This condition of passive dissent could be described as either a problem for, or an achievement of, New Labour as a political and governmental project. It marks a degree of 'sceptical distance' from the project: a set of doubts about whether New Labour can, or even wants to, deliver in relation to public desires. This view would emphasise the 'dissent' part of passive dissent – pointing to a failure to engage and mobilise sections of the public. The alternative view would place rather more stress on the 'passive' term, seeing New Labour as having successfully de-mobilised potential sources and resources of opposition. The sense of passivity has something to do with feeling disconnected from New Labour, from 'politics', and from the dominant consensus (since all the main parties have become enthusiasts for choice in public services). Passive dissent may not be a distinctive condition associated with New Labour's public service reforms – it might be a more widespread relationship between substantial sections of the public and the political process.

In the end, we think an analysis centred on the politics and practices of articulation provides the sort of mobile theorising needed to address the multiple sites, discourses and practices that we have been addressing in this book (Hall, 1996; Slack, 1996; see also Clarke, 2004b). Articulation offers a way of thinking about how specific conceptions, understandings and discursive positions or 'traces' are brought to voice. Articulation also defines the attempt to bring the people or social forces attached to such voicings into a popular bloc. The political discourses with which we began in Chapter 2 involved the work of articulation to create an apparently coherent narrative of public service modernisation in a 'consumer culture'. As we have seen subsequently, articulation is also the practice through which 'transformism' is conducted – the simultaneous work of subordinating and re-inflecting alternative positions. We might also note that articulation also includes 'dis-articulation' – the denial of voice or de-mobilisation of alternatives (particularly the process of ascribing them to the past).

Articulation also provides a way of thinking about the construction or composition of the assemblages of policies, people and practices that form the institutional settings of public services. As Sharma and Gupta (2006) have argued, treating states as assemblages can help us to escape the overly monolithic, integrated or unitary conceptions of states that have dominated much of social science thinking. We see this approach as equally relevant to 'sub-state' institutions and dispersed agencies. The three services on which we have focused here are constituted out of complex – and changing – places, scales, forms of management and occupational groups, cultures and practices. To the extent that they form apparently coherent systems, institutions and organisations, this is the outcome of the work of articulation needed to construct a 'unity of difference' (Clarke, 2004b).

Finally, we think that the politics of articulation alerts us to the continuing and contested practices of dis-articulation and re-articulation across a number of sites. In this book, we have focused on two such sites: the institutional world of public services and popular understandings of the public's relationships to such services. In the former, we explored the ways in which New Labour's consumerist discourse was inflected and re-articulated through encounters with organisational, occupational and service discourses in ways that challenged, adapted, redirected and even reaffirmed the original New Labour political and policy conceptions of public services. In the latter, we saw how the consumer identification and the Choice agenda were subject to critical engagements, ranging from the articulation of 'residual' discourses of the publicness of public services to emergent conceptions of service relationships built around respect and partnership. This concept of articulation provides an orientation to analysis and investigation rather than an epochal narrative of the dominant causes, directions and consequences of change. For that reason, we find it a more flexible, mobile and productive way of engaging with the sorts of sites, practices and relationships that concern us here.

Changing publics and changing public services: the end of the citizen-consumer?

The study on which this book is based was inspired by New Labour's distinctive deployment of the citizen-consumer and the way in which this figure provided a key anchoring point for narrating the modernisation and reform of public services. We saw it as a distinctive way of addressing – and directing – the changing relationships between publics and public services. As we write this book (March 2006) we wonder if we have seen the end of the citizen-consumer, at least in these fields of public services. The term persists as a focus of controversy and negotiation in relation to broadcasting regulation (Hesmondhalgh, 2005; Livingstone, et al., 2006). But we have heard rather less of the consumer and the citizen-consumer in the continuing reform of health and social care services (and, as we have indicated, they were always less of a presence in policing). We would, of course, like to think that this demonstrates the 'policy impact' of research such as ours. But we remain sceptical, seeing instead an embedding of the principle of Choice at the core of proposals for education, health and social care. These developments may no longer require the figure of the citizen-consumer, nor the narrative of the shift to a consumer society, but they emphatically pursue the consumer centred model of market choice. They are addressed to the same conception of a new public: diverse, assertive and with expectations honed in the market-place (see, for example, Taylor, 2006).

Does the disappearance of the name matter? At one level, it does. It indicates a political calculation about the term's limited impact and appeal. Governments are also reflexive subjects, engaged in complex reasoning about how to position and identify themselves – and us. The figure of the citizen-consumer performed a certain sort of discursive work for New Labour, constructing a set of alignments between the public, the idea of the market and the provision on public services. It blurred certain sorts of boundaries, created new pressures on public service providers and, above all, created the space for the extension of the principle of Choice (and its multiple mechanisms). But this brings us to the point where we also need to say 'no, it does not matter'. It may be that the creation of new mechanisms, relationships and practices of governance are more significant than the words. In health and social care, people will be increasingly required to make choices, just as parents must 'choose' secondary schools for their children. As in education, the choices will turn out to be conditional, complicated by their institutional contexts and without any guarantee that your choice will come true. In the process, more dispersed, fragmented and quasi-competitive systems of public provision will be mirrored in more particularised relationships between publics and providers – with a potential diminution or thinning of wider senses of publicness as attachment, ownership and belonging (Clarke, forthcoming b; Newman, 2005a, 2005 c; see also Cooper, 1998).

Like our respondents, we do not approach this set of changes from the point of view of nostalgia. The changing relationship between publics and public services was not the result of singular sets of forces – whether global neo-liberalism or the Thatcher-Major-Blair lineage in British politics. These have certainly played key roles but the Fordist/Keynesian/welfarist model of public services in Britain was the focus of other challenges arising from the contentiously changing publics to which they were addressed. We have tried to indicate how the terms 'diversity' and 'equity' offer co-opted voicings of these changes and challenges in New Labour discourse. We want to end by insisting on the importance of analysing the changing relationships between publics and public services in ways that pay attention to these heterogeneous politics. 'Changing publics' precede changing relationships: indeed it was those contentious publics that first insisted on the importance of changing both the relationships, and the form and content, of services. We suspect that the problem of the relationship between publics and public services is not going to go away, even if the figure of the citizen-consumer does. Too much is at stake – and is wrapped up in politically unstable formations of persistent desires for the publicness of public services, continuing doubts and scepticism about politics and governmental reform programmes, and emergent understandings of new relationships between people and services. The thin conceptions of diversity and equity managed through Choice do not look like the foundations for a viable and sustainable solution.

Appendix: The Project

Creating Citizen-Consumers: Changing Relationships and Identifications was funded by the ESRC/AHRB Cultures of Consumption programme and ran from April 2003–May 2005 (grant number: RES-143-25-0008). The project team was John Clarke, Janet Newman, Nick Smith, Elizabeth Vidler and Louise Westmarland, all based in the Faculty of Social Sciences at The Open University, UK.

We studied three public services: health, policing and social care. These were selected to exemplify different forms of relationship with publics and a variety of institutions reform trajectories. We examined all government policy and guidance texts, together with as many official speeches and political documents as we could access, to trace the trajectory of consumerist discourse in general and in the specific services selected.

The service-centred elements of the study were carried out in two places (Newtown and Oldtown). Both of these were urban settings in England and were chosen to explore whether different urban social formations and political cultures had implications for the installation and appeal of consumerist orientation in services and their users. Newtown, as it name suggests, is a relatively recent planned development in the South East which has a short history of service provision in terms of local authority social care and the organisation of health care through the local Primary Care Trust (PCT). Policing of the area is part of a larger Force. Oldtown, by contrast, is an old industrialised urban area, part of a larger conurbation in the North West. It has a long history of service provision, though both social services and the PCT were conscious of trying to break institutional legacies of the past. Again, policing was organised as part of a larger Force.

We distributed 600 questionnaires to users and front-line staff: 50 to users and 50 to staff in each service in each location (a sample questionnaire can be found below). 106 questionnaires were returned from users and 168 from staff (a 46 per cent return rate). These questionnaires tested orientations to the four aspects of consumerism discussed in the book: Challenge, Choice, Inequality and Responsibility. Results from the questionnaires were mapped on positive and negative axes to produce the weighted figures in Chapter 4. The questionnaire also included a multiple choice question of identifications, accompanied by a space for open comments on the identifications and their significance.

We conducted 24 interviews with managers; 23 with staff; 10 with users and held 6 user focus groups. Interviews with managers took place in their offices at the services and explored their perceptions of the conditions and impacts of consumerism on the service. Managers were selected for interview following first contacts with the most senior person responsible for the service in the area, and further interviewees were identified during the course of interviews.

Staff and user contacts were the result of responses to the questionnaires which included a reply form expressing willingness to be interviewed. Interviews with staff and users were held in a variety of settings after negotiation with the interviewee. As with managers, interviews were semi-structured, exploring issues from the questionnaire and further questions about identifications and relationships with public services. Focus groups with people who used services were held for all three services in both settings. They used a set of 'scenarios' as starting points for discussion and also explored identifications and relationships. All interviews and focus groups were tape recorded and transcribed for analysis (and were coded for processing through Atlas software).

Sample questionnaire

Creating Citizen-Consumers Questionnaire: Social Care (users)

Listed below are a series of statements. Please indicate below how far you agree or disagree with each. Your reply will be anonymous, so please answer as honestly as you can.

For each question, please CIRCLE the number which most closely corresponds to your view.

Use the following scale:

Strongly Disagree	Disagree	Neither Agree Nor Disagree	Agree	Strongly Agree
1	2	3	4	5

Please return your questionnaire in the reply paid envelope within ten days of receiving it.

1   I feel confident expressing what I want from Social Services.

Strongly Disagree				Strongly Agree
1	2	3	4	5

2   In general I trust social workers to know what is the best care package for me.

Strongly   Strongly
Disagree   Agree

1   2   3   4   5

3   I am quite happy to challenge the decisions of social workers.

Strongly   Strongly
Disagree   Agree

1   2   3   4   5

Strongly   Disagree   Neither Agree   Agree   Strongly
Disagree   Nor Disagree   Agree

1   2   3   4   5

4   Social workers do their best and we should give them the benefit of the doubt when things go wrong.

Strongly   Strongly
Disagree   Agree

1   2   3   4   5

5   I think it is everyone's responsibility to stay fit and active.

Strongly   Strongly
Disagree   Agree

1   2   3   4   5

6   The government should do more to look after people.

Strongly   Strongly
Disagree   Agree

1   2   3   4   5

7   It is up to me to make sure I get the support I need.

Strongly Disagree				Strongly Agree
1	2	3	4	5

8   I do not think you can trust ordinary people to know how to stay fit and healthy.

Strongly Disagree				Strongly Agree
1	2	3	4	5

9   At the moment, users do not get enough choices about the care they receive.

Strongly Disagree				Strongly Agree
1	2	3	4	5

Strongly Disagree	Disagree	Neither Agree Nor Disagree	Agree	Strongly Agree
1	2	3	4	5

10   People do not want to make choices about the care they receive.

Strongly Disagree				Strongly Agree
1	2	3	4	5

11   Giving users a say will make social care more responsive to their needs.

Strongly Disagree				Strongly Agree
1	2	3	4	5

12   More choices will make social care more complicated and
     difficult to use.

Strongly   Strongly
Disagree   Agree

     1   2   3   4   5

13   Giving users a greater say will improve social care for all those
     who receive it.

Strongly   Strongly
Disagree   Agree

     1   2   3   4   5

14   Giving users a say with regard to the care they receive means
     those with the skills to work the system will benefit the most.

Strongly   Strongly
Disagree   Agree

     1   2   3   4   5

15   It is about time social care was organised around the needs of
     users, and not those who provide it.

Strongly   Strongly
Disagree   Agree

     1   2   3   4   5

Strongly   Disagree   Neither Agree   Agree   Strongly
Disagree   Nor Disagree   Agree

     1   2   3   4   5

16   Listening to users means concentrating resources on those who
     shout the loudest.

Strongly   Strongly
Disagree   Agree

1   2   3   4   5

17   Which of these words best describes your relationship to Social
     Care (please tick TWO at most)

Consumer	☐	Citizen	☐
Customer	☐	Member of the Public	☐
Service User	☐	Member of the Local Community	☐
Patient	☐		

---

18   Can you explain why these words best fit your view?

If you would be willing to take part in a short interview on this subject
please fill in your contact details on the attached form and return with
your completed questionnaire in the envelope provided. Thank you
very much for your help.

References

Alesina, A. and Glaeser, E. (2004) *Fighting Poverty in the US and Europe*. Oxford, Oxford University Press.

Andrews, G. (1999) 'New Left and New Labour: modernization or a new modernity?', *Soundings*, 13: 14–24.

Andrews, G. (2006) *Not a Normal Country: Italy after Berlusconi*. London, Pluto Press.

Association of Chief Police Officers (ACPO)-Centrex (2006) *Practice Advice on Professionalising the Business of Neighbourhood Policing*. Wyboston (Beds), National Centre for Policing Excellence (Centrex).

Bahktin, M. (1981) *The Dialogic Imagination: Four Essays* (ed. M. Holquist). Austin, University of Texas Press.

Balibar, E. (2002) *We, The People of Europe? Reflections of Transnational Citizenship*. New Jersey, Princeton University Press.

Barnes, M. (1998) 'Whose needs, whose resources?', in M. Langan (ed.), *Welfare: Needs, Rights and Risks*. London: Routledge.

Barnes, M., Newman, J., Knops, A. and Sullivan, H. (2003) 'Constituting "the public" in public participation', *Public Administration*, 81(2): 379–99.

Barnes, M., Newman, J. and Sullivan, H. (2007) *Power, Participation and Political Renewal*. Bristol, The Policy Press.

Barnett, C. (2005) 'The consolations of "neo-liberalism"', *Geoforum*, 36: 7–12.

Barry, N. (1991) 'Understanding the market', in M. Loney et al. (eds), *The State or The Market: Politics and Welfare in Contemporary Britain* (2nd edn). London, Sage.

Bartlett, W., Le Grand, J. and Roberts, J. (eds) (1998) *A Revolution in Social Policy: Quasi-Market Reforms in the 1990s*. Bristol, The Policy Press.

Bauman, Z. (1998) *Work, Consumerism and the New Poor*. Buckingham, Open University Press.

Beck, U. and Beck-Gersheim, E. (2002) *Individualization: Institutionalised Individualism and its Social and Political Consequences*. London, Sage.

Bennett, T., Grossberg, L. and Morris, M. (eds) (2005) *New Keywords*. Oxford, Blackwell.

Benton, T. (2000) 'Reflexive modernization', in G. Browning, A. Halcli and F. Webster (eds), *Understanding Contemporary Society: Theories of the Present*. London, Sage.

Bevir, M. and Trentmann, F. (2006) 'Civic choices: retrieving perspectives on rationality, consumption and citizenship'. Paper presented to conference on *Citizenship and Consumption: Agency, Norms, Mediation and Spaces*, Cambridge, March.

Billig, M. (1995) *Banal Nationalism*. London, Sage.

Blair, T. (1998) *The Third Way*. London, The Fabian Society.

Blair, T. (2001) Speech to public sector workers at the British Library, 16 October, London. www.number-10.gov.uk/output/Page1632.asp

Blair, T. (2002) 'Prime Minister Tony Blair's speech at the Labour Party Conference in Blackpool', *Guardian Unlimited*, 1 October.

Blair, T. (2003a) 'Progress and justice in the 21st century', The Inaugural Fabian Society Annual Lecture, 17 June.http://politics.guardian.co.uk/speeches/story/0,11126,979507,00.html

Blair, T. (2003b) 'Where the Third Way goes from here', Policy Network/Progressive Governance Conference. www.progressive-governance.net

Bode, I. (forthcoming) 'New moral economies of welfare', European Societies, 8.

Bourdieu, P. (1984) Distinction: A Social Critique of the Judgement of Taste. London, Routledge.

Bradley, R. (1998) Public Expectations and Perceptions of Policing. Police Research Series Paper 96. London, The Home Office.

Brewer, J. (2003) 'The error of our ways: historians and the birth of consumer society', Cultures of Consumption Programme Public Lecture, 23 September, London.

Brown, G. (2003) 'A modern agenda for prosperity and social reform', speech at the Social Market Foundation, 3 February, London.

Brown, W. (2006) Edgework: Critical Essays on Knowledge and Politics. Princeton, Princeton University Press.

Byers, S. (2003) 'The former Transport and Local Government Secretary's speech to the Social Market Foundation', Guardian Unlimited, 28 May.

Cabinet Office (2005) Choice and Voice in the Reform of Public Services: Government Response to the PASC Report – Choice, Voice and Public Services. London, Cabinet Office/Office of Public Services Reform (Cm 6630).

Calnan, M., Almond, S. and Smith, N. (2003) 'Ageing and public satisfaction with the health service: an analysis of recent trends, Social Science and Medicine, 57(2): 707–13.

Cameron, A. and Palan, R. (2004) The Imagined Economies of Globalization. London, Sage.

Cayton, H. (2003) 'Trust me, I'm a patient: can healthcare afford the informed consumer?', speech delivered to the Royal College of Physicians, BUPA Health Debate, 2 September, London.

Chakrabarty, D. (2000) Provincializing Europe. Princeton, Princeton University Press.

Chatterjee, P. (2003) The Politics of the Governed. New York, Columbia University Press.

Clarke, J. (1990) 'Pessimism versus populism: the problematic politics of popular culture', in R. Butsch (ed.), For Fun and Profit: The Transformation of Leisure into Consumption. Philadelphia, PA, Temple University Press.

Clarke, J. (1991) New Times and Old Enemies: Essays on Cultural Studies and America. London, HarperCollins.

Clarke, J. (ed.) (1993) A Crisis in Care? London, Sage.

Clarke, J. (1996) 'After social work?', in N. Parton (ed.), Social Theory, Social Change and Social Work. London, Routledge.

Clarke, J. (1997) 'Capturing the customer: consumerism and social welfare', Self, Agency and Society, 1(1): 55–73.

Clarke, J. (1998) 'Consumerism', in G. Hughes (ed.), Imagining Welfare Futures. London, Sage/The Open University.

Clarke, J. (2002) 'Reinventing community? Governing in contested spaces'. Paper presented to the Spacing Social Work – On the Territorialization of the Social conference, University of Bielefeld, November.

Clarke, J. (2004a) 'Subjects of doubt'. Paper presented to Canadian Anthropological Society (CASCA) conference, University of Western Ontario, May.

Clarke, J. (2004b) *Changing Welfare, Changing States: New Directions in Social Policy.* London, Sage.

Clarke, J. (2004c) 'Dissolving the public realm? The logics and limits of neo-liberalism', *Journal of Social Policy*, 33(1): 27–48.

Clarke, J. (2005a) 'New Labour's citizens: activated, empowered, responsibilised, abandoned?', *Critical Social Policy*, 25(4): 447–63.

Clarke, J. (2005b) 'Welfare states as nation states: some conceptual reflections', *Social Policy and Society*, 4(4): 407–15.

Clarke, J. (2005c) 'Performing for the public: doubt, desire and the evaluation of public services', in P. Du Gay (ed.), *The Values of Bureaucracy*. Oxford, Oxford University Press.

Clarke, J. (2005d) 'Reconstituting Europe: governing a European people?', in J. Newman (ed.), *Remaking Governance: peoples, politics and the public sphere.* Bristol, The Policy Press.

Clarke, J. (2006a) 'Consumerism and the remaking of state-citizen relationships', in C. McDonald and G. Marston (eds), *Reframing Social Policy: A Governmental Approach*. Brighton, Edward Elgar Publishing.

Clarke, J. (2006b) 'Disorganizzare il publicco', *La Rivista delle Politiche Sociali*, 2: 107–21.

Clarke, J. (2006c) 'Consumers, clients or citizens? Politics, policy and practice in the reform of social care', *European Societies*, 8(3): 423–42.

Clarke, J. (forthcoming a) 'Unstable encounters: citizens, consumers and public services', *Journal of Consumer Culture*.

Clarke, J. (forthcoming b) 'It's not like shopping: relational reasoning and public services', in M. Bevir and F. Trentmann (eds), *Governance, Citizens and Consumers: Agency and Resistance in Contemporary Politics*. Basingstoke, Palgrave Macmillan.

Clarke, J. (forthcoming c) 'Citizen-consumers and public service reform: at the limits of neo-liberalism?', *Policy Futures in Education*.

Clarke, J. (forthcoming d) 'Subordinating the social? Making sense of post-welfarist capitalisms', *Cultural Studies*.

Clarke, J. and Fink, J. (forthcoming) 'People, places and policies: identity, citizenship and welfare', in W. van Oorschot, B. Pfau-Effinger and M. Opielka (eds), *Culture and Welfare State: Values of Social Policy from a Comparative Perspective.* Brighton, Edward Elgar.

Clarke, J. and Newman, J. (1997) *The Managerial State: Power, Politics and Ideology in the Remaking of Social Welfare*. London, Sage.

Clarke, J. and Newman, J. (1998) 'A modern British people? New Labour and the reconstruction of social welfare'. Paper presented to the *Discourse Analysis and Social Research* Conference, Copenhagen Business School, September.

Clarke, J. and Newman, J. (2004) 'Governing in the modern world', in D. L. Steinberg and R. Johnson (eds), *Blairism and the War of Persuasion: Labour's Passive Revolution*. London, Lawrence and Wishart.

Clarke, J. and Newman, J. (2006) 'The people's choice? Citizens, consumers and public services'. Paper presented to conference on *Citizenship and Consumption: Agency, Norms, Mediation and Spaces*, Cambridge, March.

Clarke, J. and Newman, J. (forthcoming) 'What's in a name? New Labour citizen-consumers and the remaking of public services', *Cultural Studies*.

Clarke, J., Gewirtz, S. and McLaughlin (2000) 'Reinventing the welfare state', in J. Clarke, S. Gewirtz and E. McLaughlin (eds), *New Managerialism, New Welfare?* London, Sage/The Open University.

Clarke, J., Gewirtz, S., Hughes, G. and Humphrey, J. (2000) 'Guarding the public interest? Auditing public services', in J. Clarke, S. Gewirtz and E. McLaughlin (eds), *New Managerialism, New Welfare?* London, Sage/The Open University.

Clarke, J., Smith, N. and Vidler, E. (2005) 'Constructing citizen-consumers: inequalities and instabilities', in M. Powell, K. Clarke and L. Bauld (eds), *Social Policy Review 17*. Bristol, The Policy Press.

Clarke, J., Smith, N. and Vidler, E. (2006) 'The indeterminacy of choice: political, policy and organisational dilemmas', *Social Policy and Society*, 5(3): 1–10.

Cooper, D. (1998) *Governing Out of Order*. London, Rivers Oram Press.

Coulter, A. and Magee, H. (2003) *The European Patient of the Future*. Picker Institute Europe, Open University Press.

Crawford, A. (2006) 'Reassurance policing: feeling is believing', in A. Henry and D. J. Smith (eds), *Transformations in Policing*, Aldershot, Ashgate.

Crawford, A. (forthcoming) 'Networked governance and the post-regulatory state? Steering, rowing and anchoring the provision of policing and security', *Theoretical Criminology*.

Crawford, A. and Lister, S. (2006) 'Additional security patrols in residential areas: notes form the marketplace', *Policing and Society*, 16.

Cruikshank, B. (1999) *The Will to Empower*. Ithaca, NY: Cornell University Press.

Cutler, T. and Waine, B. (1997) *Managing the Welfare State*. Oxford, Berg.

Cutler, T., Waine, B. and Brehony, K. (forthcoming) 'A new epoch of individualisation? Problems with the "personalisation" of public sector services', *Public Administration*.

Dean, M. (1999) *Governmentality: Power and Rule in Modern Society*. London, Sage.

Department of Health (1989a) *Working for Patients*. London, HMSO.

Department of Health (1989b) *Caring for People: Community Care in the Next Decade and Beyond*. London, HMSO.

Department of Health (1998) *Modernising Social Services*. London, The Stationery Office.

Department of Health (2000) *The NHS Plan: A Plan for Investment, A Plan for Reform*. London, The Stationery Office.

Department of Health (2003a) *Fair for All and Personal to You: Choice, Responsiveness and Equity in the NHS and Social Care*. London, The Stationery Office.

Department of Health (2003b) *Building on the Best: Choice, Responsiveness and Equity in the NHS*. London, The Stationery Office.

Department of Health (2005a) *Health Reform in England: Update and Next Steps*. London, The Stationery Office.

Department of Health (2005b) *Independence, Well-being and Choice: Our Vision for the Future of Social Care for Adults in England*. London, The Stationery Office.

DiMaggio, P. and Powell, W. (eds) (1991) *The New Institutionalism in Organization Analysis*. Chicago, IL, University of Chicago Press.

Dowler, K., (2002) 'Media influence on citizen attitudes toward police effectiveness', *Policing and Society*, 12(3): 227–38.

Driver, S. and Martell, L. (1998) *New Labour: Politics after Thatcher*. Cambridge, Polity Press.

Du Gay, P. (1996) *Consumption and Identity at Work*. London, Sage.

Du Gay, P. (2000) *In Praise of Bureaucracy: Weber/Organization/Ethics*. London, Sage.

Du Gay, P. (ed.) (2005) *The Values of Bureaucracy*. Oxford, Oxford University Press.

Dunleavy, P. (1991) *Democracy, Bureaucracy and Public Choice*. London, Harvester Wheatsheaf.

Dwyer, P. (1998) 'Conditional citizens? Welfare rights and responsibilities in the late 1990s', *Critical Social Policy*, 18(4): 493–518.

Edwards, T. (2000) *Contradictions of Consumption: Concepts, Practices and Politics in Consumer Society*. London, Sage.

Esping-Andersen, G. (1990) *Three Worlds of Welfare Capitalism*. Cambridge, Polity Press.

Evett, J. (2003) 'The sociological analysis of professionalism: occupational change in the modern world', *International Sociology*, 18(2): 395–415.

Exworthy, M. and Halford, S. (eds) (1999) *Professionals and the New Managerialism in the Public Sector*. Buckingham, Open University Press.

Farnsworth, K. (2004) *Corporate Power and Social Policy in a Global Economy*. Bristol, The Policy Press.

Featherstone, M. (1991) *Consumer Culture and Postmodernism*. London, Sage.

Ferguson, I., Lavalette, M. and Mooney, G. (2002) *Rethinking Welfare States*. London, Sage.

Fergusson, R. (1998) 'Choice, selection and the social construction of difference: restructuring schooling', in G. Hughes and G. Lewis (eds), *Unsettling Welfare: The Reconstruction of Social Policy*. London, Sage/The Open University.

Ferlie, E., Pettigrew, A., Ahshburner, L. and Fitzgerald, L. (1996) *The New Public Management in Action*. Oxford, Oxford University Press.

Fink, J., Lewis, G. and Clarke, J. (eds) (2001) *Rethinking European Welfare*. London, Sage/The Open University.

Finlayson, A. (2003a) *Making Sense of New Labour*. London, Lawrence and Wishart.

Finlayson, A. (2003b) 'Public choice theory: enemy of democracy', *Soundings*, 24(Autumn): 25–40.

Fischer, F. (2003) *Reframing Public Policy: Discursive Politics and Deliberative Practices*. Oxford, Oxford University Press.

Fitzpatrick, T. (1998) 'The rise of market collectivism', in E. Brunsdon, H. Dean and R. Woods (eds), *Social Policy Review 10*. London, Social Policy Association.

Flynn, N. (1997) *Public Sector Management*. Hemel Hempstead, Prentice-Hall/Harvester Wheatsheaf.

Forrest, R. and Murie, A. (1991) *Selling the Welfare State: The Privatisation of Welfare Housing*. London, Routledge.

Foucault, M. (1977) *Discipline and Punish: The Birth of the Prison*. London, Allen Lane.

Foucault, M. (1979) *The History of Sexuality, Volume 1: An Introduction*. London, Allen Lane.

Frank, T. (2001) *One Market Under God: Extreme Capitalism, Market Populism and the End of Economic Democracy*. New York, Anchor Books.

Fraser, N. (1997) *Justice Interruptus: Critical Reflections of the 'Postsocialist' Condition*. New York, Routledge.

Gabriel, Y. and Lang, T. (1995) *The Unmanageable Consumer: Contemporary Consumption and its Fragmentations*. London, Sage.

Garland, D. (2001) *The Culture of Control: Crime and Social Order in Contemporary Society*. Chicago, IL, University of Chicago Press.

Gewirtz, S. (2002) *The Managerial School*. London, Routledge.

Gewirtz, S., Ball, S. and Bowe, R. (1995) *Markets, Choice and Equity in Education*. Buckingham, Open University Press.

Giddens, A. (1991) *Modernity and Self Identity*. Oxford, Basil Blackwell.

Giddens, A. (1994) *Beyond Left and Right*. Cambridge, Polity Press.

Giddens, A. (1998) *The Third Way: The Renewal of Social Democracy*. Cambridge, Polity Press.

Giddens, A., Beck, U. and Lash, S. (1994) *Reflexive Modernization*. Cambridge, Polity Press

Gilroy, P. (2005) *Postcolonial Melancholia*. New York, Columbia University Press.

Glendinning, C., Powell, M. and Rummery, K. (eds) (2002) *Partnerships, New Labour and the Governance of Welfare*. Bristol, The Policy Press.

Goldstein, H. (2005) 'Improving policing: a problem-oriented approach', in T. Newburn (ed.), *Policing: Key Readings*. Cullompton, Willan.

Goode, J. and Maskovsky, J. (eds) (2001) *The New Poverty Studies: the Ethnography of Power, Politics and Impoverished People in the United States*. New York, New York University Press.

Goode, J., Greatbatch, D., O'cathain, A., Luff, D., Hanlon, G. and Strangleman, T. (2004) 'Risk and the responsible health consumer: the problematics of entitlement among callers to NHS Direct', *Critical Social Policy*, 24(2): 210–32.

Goodhart, D. (2004) 'Is Britain too diverse?', *Prospect*, February.

Gramsci, A. (1971) *Selections from the Prison Notebooks*. London, Lawrence and Wishart.

Greener, I. (2002) 'Agency, theory and social policy', *Critical Social Policy*, 22(4): 688–705.

Greener, I. (2003) 'Who choosing what? The evolution and impact of "choice" in the NHS, and its importance for New Labour', in C. Bochel, N. Ellison M. and Powell (eds), *Social Policy Review*, 15: 49–68. Bristol, The Policy Press.

Grossberg, L. (2006) 'Does cultural studies have futures? Should it? (or what's the matter with New York?): cultural studies: contexts and conjunctures', *Cultural Studies*, 20(1): 1–32.

Hall, S. (1989) *The Hard Road to Renewal: Thatcherism and the Crisis of the Left*. London, Verso.

Hall, S. (1996) 'Gramsci's relevance for the study of race and ethnicity', in D. Morley and K-H. Chen (eds), *Stuart Hall: Critical Dialogues in Cultural Studies*. London, Routledge.

Hall, S. (2003) 'New Labour's double shuffle', *Soundings*, 24: 10–24.

Hansen, H.K. and Salskov-Iversen, D. (eds) (forthcoming) *Critical Perspectives on Private Authority in Global Politics*. Basingstoke, Palgrave Macmillan.

Hartmann, Y. (2005) 'In bed with the enemy: some ideas on the connections between neoliberalism and the welfare state', *Current Sociology*, 53(1): 57–73.

Harvey, D. (2005) *A Brief History of Neoliberalism*. Oxford, Oxford University Press.

Her Majesty's Inspectorate of Constabulary (HMIC) (2002) *Open All Hours*. London, Home Office.

Hesmondhalgh, D. (2005) 'Media and cultural policy as public policy: the case of the British Labour government', *International Journal of Cultural Policy*, 11(1): 95–115.

Heward, T. (1994) 'Retailing the police: corporate identity and the Met', in R. Keat, N. Whiteley and N. Abercrombie (eds), *The Authority of the Consumer*. London: Routledge.

Hilton, M. (2003) *Consumerism in Twentieth Century Britain: The Search for a Historical Movement*. Cambridge, Cambridge University Press.

Hilton, M. (2006) 'The banality of consumption'. Paper presented to conference on *Citizenship and Consumption: Agency, Norms, Mediation and Spaces*, Cambridge, March.

Hirschmann, A. (1970) *Exit, Voice and Loyalty: Responses to Decline in Firms, Organizations and States*. Cambridge, MA, Cambridge University Press.

Holland, D. and Lave, J. (2001) 'History in person: an introduction', in D. Holland and J. Lave (eds), *History in Person: Enduring Struggles, Contentious Practices, Intimate Identities*. Santa Fe, School of American Research; Oxford, James Currey Ltd.

Home Office (2001) *Policing a New Century: A Blueprint for Reform*. London, The Home Office.

Home Office (2003) *Policing: Building Safer Communities Together*. London, Home Office.

Home Office (2004) *Confident Communities in a Secure Britain: The Home Office Strategic Plan 2004–08* (Cm 6287). London, The Home Office.

Home Office (2005) *The National Policing Plan 2005–08*. London, The Home Office

Huber, E. and Stephens, J.D. (2001) *Development and Crisis of the Welfare State: Parties and Policies in Global Markets*. Chicago, IL, University of Chicago Press.

Hughes, G. (ed.) (1998) *Imagining Welfare Futures*. London, Routledge/The Open University.

Hughes, G. and Edwards, A. (eds) (2002) *Crime Control and Community: The New Politics of Public Safety*. Collumpton, Willan.

Innes, M. (2003) *Understanding Social Control. Deviance, Crime and Social Order*. Buckingham, Open University Press.

Innes, M. (2005) 'Why "soft" policing is hard: on the curious development of reassurance policing, how it became neighbourhood policing and what this signifies about the politics of police reform', *Journal of Community & Applied Social Psychology*, 15: 156–69.

Isin, E. (2002) *Being Political: Genealogies of Citizenship*. Minneapolis, MN, University of Minnesota Press.

Jessop, B. (2000) 'From the KWNS to the SWPR', in G. Lewis, S. Gewirtz and J. Clarke (eds), *Rethinking Social Policy*. London, Sage/The Open University.

Jessop, B. (2002) *The Future of the Capitalist State*. Cambridge, Polity Press.

Johnson, N. (ed.) (1995) *Private Markets in Health and Welfare: An International Perspective*. Oxford, Berg.

Johnson, T. (1973) *Professions and Power*. London, Macmillan.

Johnston, L. (1993) 'Privatisation and protection: spatial and sectoral ideologies in British policing and crime prevention', *Modern Law Review*, 56(6): 220–36.

Johnston, L. (2000) *Policing Britain*. Harlow, Longman

Jones, A. and Williams, L. (2005) *Public Services and ICT. Why ICT? The Role of ICT in Public Services*. London, The Work Foundation.

Keat, R., Whiteley, N. and Abercrombie, N. (eds) (1994) *The Authority of the Consumer*. London: Routledge.

Kingfisher, C. (ed.) (2002) *Western Welfare in Decline: Globalization and Women's Poverty*. Philadelphia, University of Pennsylvania Press.

Kirkpatrick, I., Ackroyd, S. and Walker, R. (2004) *The New Managerialism and Public Service Professionals*. Basingstoke, Palgrave Macmillan.

Langan, M. (ed.) (1998) *Welfare: Needs, Rights and Risks*. London, Routledge/The Open University.

Langan, M. (2000) 'Social services: managing the third way', in J. Clarke, S. Gewirtz and E. McLaughlin (eds) *New Welfare, New Managerialism?* London, Sage/The Open University.

Larner, W. (1997) 'Market governance and the consumer', *Economy and Society*, 26(3): 373–99.

Larner, W. (2000) 'Neo-liberalism: policy, ideology, governmentality', *Studies in Political Economy*, 63: 5–25.

Larner, W. and Walters, W. (eds) (2004) *Global Governmentality*. London, Routledge.

Le Grand, J. (1982) *The Strategy of Equality: Redistribution and the Social Services*. London, Allen and Unwin.

Leadbeater, C. (2004) *Personalising Participation: A New Script for Public Services*. London, Demos.

Leeson, G., Harper, S. and Levin, S. (2003) *Independent Living in Later Life: Literature Review*. London, Department of Work and Pensions, in-house Report 137.

Leibfried, S. and Zürn, M. (2005) 'The unravelling of the Golden Age nation state', in S. Leibfried and M. Zürn (eds), *Transformations of the State*. Cambridge, Cambridge University Press.

Lewis, G. (1998) 'Citizenship', in G. Hughes (ed.), *Imagining Welfare Futures*. London, Sage/The Open University.

Lewis, G. (2000) *'Race', Gender, Welfare: Encounters in a Postcolonial Society*. Cambridge, Polity.

Lister, R. (2002) 'The responsible citizen: creating a new British welfare contract', in C. Kingfisher (ed.), *Western Welfare in Decline*. Minneapolis, University of Minnesota Press.

Lister, R. (2003) *Citizenship: Feminist Perspectives* (2nd edn). Basingstoke, Palgrave.

Livingstone, S., Lunt, P. and Miller, L. (2006) *Citizens and Consumers: Discursive Debates During and After the Communications Act 2003*. Social Contexts and Responses to Risk (SCARR) Working Paper 2006/10.

Loader, I. (1999) 'Consumer culture and the commodification of policing and security', *Sociology*, 33(2): 373–92.

Lury, C. (1996) *Consumer Culture*. Cambridge, Polity Press.

Lyotard, J-F. (1984) *The Postmodern Condition: A Report on Knowledge*. Minneapolis: University of Minnesota Press.

Maclachlan, P. and Trentmann, F. (2004) 'Civilising markets: traditions of consumer politics in twentieth century Britain, Japan and the United States', in M. Bevir and F. Trentmann (eds), *Markets in Historical Contexts*. Cambridge, Cambridge University Press.

Macpherson, C.B. (1962) *The Political Theory of Possessive Individualism*. Oxford, Oxford University Press.

Malpass, A., Barnett, C., Clarke, N. and Cloke, P. (2006) 'Problematizing choice: responsible subjects and citizenly consumers'. Paper presented to conference on *Citizenship and Consumption: Agency, Norms, Mediation and Spaces*, Cambridge, March.

March, J. and Olsen, J. (1989) *Rediscovering Institutions: The Organisational Basis of Politics*. New York: Free Press.

Marquand, D. (2004) *The Decline of the Public*. Cambridge, Polity Press.

Marston, G. (2004) *Social Policy and Discourse Analysis*. Aldershot, Ashgate Publishing.

Massey, D. (1999) 'Imagining globalisation: power-geometries of time–space', in A. Brah, M. Hickman and M. Mac an Ghaill (eds), *Global Futures: Migration, Environment and Globalization*. Basingstoke, Macmillan.

Massey, D. (2005) *For Space*. London, Sage.

McDonald, C. and Marston, G. (eds) (2006) *Reframing Social Policy: A Governmental Approach*. Brighton, Edward Elgar Publishing.

Milburn, A. (2001) *Reforming Public Services: Reconciling Equity with Choice*. London, Fabian Society Health Policy Forum, Fabian Society.

Milburn, A. (2002a) *Speech to the Annual Social Services Conference*, 16 October, Cardiff.

Milburn, A. (2002b) *Redefining the National Health Service*, New Health Network, 14 January.

Miliband, D. (2000) 'This is the modern world', *Fabian Review*, 111(4): 11–13.

Miller, D. (1998) *A Theory of Shopping*. Cambridge, Polity Press.

Miller, D. (2005) 'What is best "value"? Bureaucracy, virtualism and local governance', in P. Du Gay (ed.), *The Values of Bureaucracy*. Oxford, Oxford University Press.

Ministers of State for Department of Health, Local and Regional Government, and School Standards (2004) *The Case for User Choice in Public Services*. A Joint Memorandum to the Public Administration Select Committee Inquiry into Choice, Voice and Public Services.

Mintzberg, F. (1983) *Structure in Fives: Designing Organisational Effectiveness*. London, Prentice-Hall.

MORI (2002) *Public Service Reform: Understanding and Measuring Customer Satisfaction: A MORI Review for the Office of Public Services Reform*, London.

Morris, L. (1998) 'Legitimate membership of the welfare community', in M. Langan (ed.), *Welfare: Needs, Rights and Risks*. London, Routledge/The Open University.

Mort, F. (1996) *Cultures of Consumption: Masculinities and Social Space in Late Twentieth-Century Britain*. London, Routledge.

National Consumer Council (2004) *Making Public Services Personal: A New Compact for Public Services* (The report of the Independent Policy Commission on Public Services). London, National Consumer Council.

Needham, C. (2003) *Citizen-Consumers: New Labour's Marketplace Democracy*. London, The Catalyst Forum.

Newburn, T. (2003) 'Doing policing', in T. Newburn (ed.), *Handbook of Policing*. Cullompton, Willan.

Newman, J. (2001) *Modernising Governance: New Labour, Policy and Society*. London, Sage.

Newman, J. (2004) 'Through thick or thin? The problem of "the social" in societal governance'. Paper presented to the *Contemporary Governance and the Question of the Social* Conference, University of Alberta, 11–13 June.

Newman, J. (2005a) *Going Public*. Inaugural lecture, The Open University, May.

Newman, J. (2005b) 'Enter the transformational leader', *Sociology*, 39(4): 717–34.

Newman, J. (ed.) (2005c) *Remaking Governance: Peoples, Politics and the Public Sphere*. Bristol, The Policy Press.

Newman, J. (2006) 'Rowing, steering or out of control? The dilemmas of governance in neo-liberal times'. Paper to the Scientific Council for Government (WRR), The Hague, 23 February.

Newman, J. (forthcoming) 'Governance as cultural practice: texts, talk and the struggle for meaning', in M. Bevir and F. Trentmann (eds), *Governance, Citizens and Consumers: Agency and Resistance in Contemporary Politics*. Basingstoke, Palgrave.

Newman, J. and Vidler, E. (2006a) 'Discriminating customers, responsible patients, empowered users: consumerism and the modernisation of health care', *Journal of Social Policy*, 35(2): 193–209.

Newman, J. and Vidler, E. (2006b) 'More than a matter of choice? Consumerism and the modernisation of health care', in L. Bauld, K. Clarke and T. Maltby (eds) *Social Policy Review 18*. Bristol, The Policy Press.

Niskanen, W.A. (1971) *Bureaucracy and Representative Government*. New York, Aldine-Atherton.

O'Malley, P. (2005) *Risk, Uncertainty and Government*. London, The Glasshouse Press.

Office of Public Services Reform (2002) *Reforming our Services: Principles into Practice*. London, Office of Public Services Reform.

Pateman, C. (1988) *The Sexual Contract*. Stanford, CA, Stanford University Press.

Peterson, A., Barns, I., Dudley, J. and Harris, P. (1999) *Post-Structuralism, Citizenship and Social Policy*. London, Routledge.

Pollitt, C. (1993) *Managerialism and the Public Services* (2nd edn). Oxford, Basil Blackwell.

Pollitt, C. (1994) 'The Citizen's Charter: a preliminary analysis', *Public Money and Management*, April–June: 9–14.

Pollitt, C., Birchall, J. and Putnam, K. (1998) *Decentralising Public Service Management*. Basingstoke, Macmillan.

Pollock, A. (2004) *NHS plc: The Privatisation of our Health Care*. London, Verso.

Pryke, M. (1998) 'Thinking social policy into social housing', in G. Hughes and G. Lewis (eds), *Unsettling Welfare: The Reconstruction of Social Policy*. London, Sage/The Open University.

Public Administration Select Committee (2005) *Choice, Voice and Public Services*. Fourth Report of Session 2004–5, vol. 1. London, House of Commons (HC 49-1).

Rose, N. (1999) *Powers of Freedom*. Cambridge, Polity Press.

Rose, N. (2000) 'Governing cities, governing citizens', in E. Isin (ed.), *Democracy, Citizenship and the Global City*. London, Routledge.

Secretary of State for Health (2004) *Choosing Health: Making Healthier Choices Easier*. London, The Stationery Office.

Secretary of State for Health (2006) *Our Health, Our Care, Our Say: A New Direction for Community Services* (Cm 6737). London, The Stationery Office.

Secretary of State for Social Security and Minister for Welfare Reform (1998) *New Ambitions for Our Country: A New Contract for Welfare* (Cm 3805). London, The Stationery Office.

Sennett, R. (2003) *Respect: The Formation of Character in an Age of Inequality*. London, Penguin.

Sharma, A. and Gupta, A. (2006) 'Rethinking theories of the state in an age of globalization', in A. Sharma and A. Gupta (eds), *The Anthropology of the State: A Reader*. Oxford, Blackwell Publishing.

Sihota, S. and Lennard, L. (2004) *Health Literacy: Being Able to Make the Most of Health*. London, National Consumer Council.

Slack, J. (1996) 'The theory and method of articulation in cultural studies', in D. Morley and K-H. Chen (eds), *Stuart Hall: Critical Dialogues in Cultural Studies*. London, Routledge.

Smith, D. (2005) *Institutional Ethnography: A Sociology for People*. Lanham and Oxford, Altamira Press.

Social Care Institute for Excellence (2004) *Has Service User Participation made a Difference to Social Care Services?* London, Social Care Institute for Excellence, Position Paper no. 3.

Social Services Inspectorate (2000) *Modern Social Services: A Commitment to People. The 9th Annual Report of the Chief Inspector of the Social Services Inspectorate, 1999/2000*. London, Social Services Inspectorate.

Social Services Inspectorate (2002) *Modern Social Services: A Commitment to Reform. The 11th Annual Report of the Chief Inspector of Social Services, 2001/2002*. London, Social Services Inspectorate.

Social Services Inspectorate (2003) *Modern Social Services: A Commitment to the Future. The 12th Annual Report of the Chief Inspector of the Social Services Inspectorate, 2002/2003*. London, Social Services Inspectorate.

Steinberg, D. and Johnson, R. (2004a) 'Blairism and the war of persuasion: Labour's passive revolution', in D.L. Steinberg and R. Johnson (eds), *Blairism and the War of Persuasion: Labour's Passive Revolution*. London, Lawrence and Wishart.

Steinberg, D. and Johnson, R.. (eds) (2004b) *Blairism and the War of Persuasion: Labour's Passive Revolution*. London, Lawrence and Wishart.

Stenson, K. (2000) 'Crime control, social policy and liberalism', in G. Lewis, S. Gewirtz and J. Clarke (eds), *Rethinking Social Policy*. London, Sage/The Open University.

Taylor, C. (2004) *Modern Social Imaginaries*. Durham, NC, Duke University Press.

Taylor, M. (2006) 'Empowerment: a Labour vision for public services', in L. Byrne, J. Purnell and M. Taylor, *Power to the People: Next Steps for New Labour*. London, Progress.

Taylor-Gooby, P. (2005) 'Is the future American? Or, can Left politics preserve European welfare states from erosion through growing "racial" diversity?', *Journal of Social Policy*, 34(4): 661–72.

Taylor-Gooby, P. and Hastie, C. (2003) 'Paying for "world class" services: a British dilemma', *Journal of Social Policy*, 32(2): 271–88.

Tomlinson, A. (ed.) (1990) *Consumption, Identity and Style*. London, Comedia/Routledge.

Tomlinson, S. (2001) *Education in a Post-Welfare Society*. Buckingham, Open University Press.

Trentmann, F. (2001) 'Bread, milk and democracy: consumption and citizenship in twentieth-century Britain', in M. Daunton and M. Hilton (eds), *The Politics of Consumption: Material Culture and Citizenship in Europe and America*. Oxford, Berg.

Trentmann, F. (2006a) 'Knowing consumers – histories, identities, practices: an introduction', in F. Trentmann (ed.), *The Making of the Consumer: Knowledge, Power and Identity in the Modern World*. Oxford, Berg.

Trentmann, F. (ed.) (2006b) *The Making of the Consumer: Knowledge, Power and Identity in the Modern World*. Oxford, Berg.

Vidler, E. and Clarke, J. (2005) 'Creating citizen-consumers: New Labour and the remaking of public services', *Public Policy and Administration*, 20(2): 19–37.

Walklate, S. (2000) 'Trust and the problem of community in the inner city', in T. Hope and R. Sparks (eds), *Crime , Risk and Insecurity*. London, Routledge.

Warner, M. (2002) *Publics and Counterpublics*. New York, Zone Books.

Watson, S. (2000) 'Foucault and the study of social policy', in G. Lewis, S. Gewirtz and J. Clarke (eds), *Rethinking Social Policy*. London, Sage/The Open University.

Wedel, J. (2001) *Collision and Collusion: The Strange Case of Western Aid to Eastern Europe*. New York, Palgrave.

Westmarland, L. (2001) *Gender and Policing: Sex, Power and Police Culture*. Cullompton, Willan.

Westmarland, L. and Smith, N. (2004) 'From scumbags to consumers: customer service and the commodification of policing'. Paper presented at the *British Criminological Society annual conference*, July.

Wetherell, M. and Potter, J. (1992) *Mapping the Language of Racism: Discourse and the Legitimation of Exploitation*. Hemel Hempstead, Harvester Wheatsheaf.

Wetherell, M., Taylor, S. and Yates, S. (eds) (2001) *Discourse Theory and Practice: A Reader*. London, Sage.

Williams, F. (2000) 'Principles of recognition and respect in welfare', in G. Lewis, S. Gewirtz and J. Clarke (eds), *Rethinking Social Policy*. London, Sage/The Open University.

Williams, R. (1976) *Keywords*. London, Fontana.

Williams, R. (1977) *Marxism and Literature*. Oxford, Oxford University Press.

Williamson, J. (1986) *Consuming Passions: The Dynamics of Popular Culture*. London, Marion Boyars.

Index